The Evolving Global Economy

The Harvard Business Review Book Series

The Evolving Global Economy

Making Sense of the New World Order

Edited with a Preface by
Kenichi Ohmae

A Harvard Business Review Book

Editor's Note: Some articles in this book have been written before authors and editors began to take into consideration the role of women in management. We hope the archaic usage representing all managers as male does not detract from the usefulness of the collection.

The *Harvard Business Review* articles in this collection are available as individual reprints. Discounts apply to quantity purchases. For information and ordering contact Customer Service, Harvard Business School Publishing, Boston, MA 02163. Telephone: (617) 495-6192, 9 a.m. to 5 p.m. Eastern Time, Monday through Friday. Fax: (617) 495-6985, 24 hours a day.

The paper used in this publication meets the requirements of the American National Standard for Permanence of Paper for Printed Library Materials Z39.48-1984

Library of Congress Cataloging-in-Publication Data

The evolving global economy : making sense of the new world order /
    edited with a preface by Kenichi Ohmae.
        p.   cm.—(The Harvard business review book series)
    Includes index.
    ISBN 0-87584-640-8
    1. International economic relations.   2. Capitalism.
3. International trade.   4. International business
enterprises—Management.   I. Ōmae, Ken'ichi, 1943–
II. Series.
HF1359.E95   1995
337—dc20   95-2910
                                                                CIP

Contents

Singapore, Hong Kong, the People's Republic of
China, the United States, and beyond. Based on his
research study of more than 150 Chinese
entrepreneurs, Kao explores why many Chinese
businesses have failed in the recent past and contends
that a new ideology of economic self-interest will
eventually lead to even greater integration of the
commonwealth.

The American system of allocating investment capital
is failing, placing American companies at a great
disadvantage and threatening the long-term growth of
the nation's economy. Michael Porter traces the
problem to the external capital allocation system by
which capital is provided to companies, as well as the
system by which companies allocate capital internally,
and presents five recommendations for reform.

Singapore is one of the most technologically advanced
countries in the world and is further evolving into
what will be the first networked society, in which all
homes, schools, businesses, and government agencies
will be interconnected electronically. Rajendra Sisodia
outlines the government investment strategy behind
Singapore's rapid rise and questions how the
government of this "nation-corporation" will manage
the democratization of information.

Three internationally recognized management experts
react to the *Harvard Business Review*'s 1990 World

Leadership Survey, in which 12,000 managers worldwide commented on "transcending business boundaries." Charles Hampden-Turner addresses the cultural bias of the survey, Tom Peters confronts the meaning of global partnerships, and Jay Jaikumar discusses why some companies are hesitant to embrace the "logic of technology."

workers, *not* in decreased living standards for the First World.

The nation-state is giving way to the emerging region-state, which is defined by economic activity rather than political borders. Kenichi Ohmae explores the key factors behind this shift and suggests that political leaders can no longer resist acknowledging the demise of the nation-state. Only those leaders who accept and promote region-states within and across their borders—"putting global logic first"—will be able to enlarge their economies and provide the best quality of life for their people.

Part III   The New Realities of Trade

With the growing emphasis in the United States on revitalizing and securing national competitiveness, Robert Reich raises the question of exactly who is "us." The answer, he explains, is the American work force, though not particularly the American-owned corporation. The United States should not assume that its corporations will lead in the race for a competitive edge. Instead, government policy should open the door to foreign investment, while promoting human capital at home.

In a follow up to his definition of who is "us," Robert Reich now addresses the identity of "them," contending that "they" are global managers with no allegiance to any one nation: the global manager aims to improve economic performance and achieve market leadership and higher profits. Reich argues that local workers must bargain with global managers—"them"—to attract investment on terms that are favorable to "us."

While industrial performance is America's chief concern in the global competitiveness debate, David Hale believes that the debate will soon turn to the more fundamental issue of money. With the rise of Japanese financial power and recent evidence of U.S. policy flaws, it is critical that America reverse this competitive slide. Consequently, the United States will likely forgo its traditional commitment to free trade and instead embrace a global financial system based on "managed trade"—a results-oriented process that will set new political rules for financial competition among the United States, Europe, and Japan.

America's economic strength stems from its exceptional ability to assimilate foreign products, people, and ideas, while Japan's notable resistance to outside influence is a source of cultural isolation and international economic conflict. Kazuo Nukazawa however, has faith in the Japan-U.S. relationship and believes that Japan will even use the United States as an economic model in the future. Noting that Japan and the United States are the two strongest promoters of the General Agreement on Tariffs and Trade, Nukazawa foresees a day when an integrated world community will evolve from the give-and-take of Japan-U.S. relations.

Part IV   The Management Agenda

response to the Japanese challenge was shortsighted, with companies miscalculating the timing and practicality of their strategies. Through a detailed study of the television and tire markets, Hamel and Prahalad suggest that U.S. companies must think more analytically about strategy if they want to overtake their competitors.

Today's borderless economy requires that managers see and think globally. Kenichi Ohmae believes, however, that too often managerial reflexes in this borderless world do not maintain an equidistant view of all customers. Managers need to learn that a borderless world does not necessarily lead to global products that are uniform. They should look past their own entrenched systems and behaviors to clearly evaluate the distinctive needs of each of their national markets. Only then can they manage—and compete—in a borderless world.

Preface

Kenichi Ohmae

It used to be much simpler. A manager could know, with confidence, where the borders ran between one nation state and the next, between one industry and the next, between one company and the next, between one market segment and the next, between one product and the next, and between one technology and the next. It was a straightforward matter to add up flows of economic activity at any of these levels into a meaningful—and actionable—aggregation. At base, it was easy to answer the question posed by the titles of Robert Reich's articles in this collection—"Who Is Us?" and "Who Is Them?"—and to know how to act on the answers.

It is simple no longer. Information and capital now migrate around the globe in the blink of an eye. The collapse of the Mexican peso, for instance, has immediate effects on currencies and capital markets around the world. Once-separate industries—those that now comprise multimedia being only the most dramatic example—now blend and overlap in countless new permutations. Individual companies now rarely provide all the services or produce all the components that ultimately deliver value to their customers. The convergence—what I have elsewhere called the "California-ization"—of consumer taste now blurs the familiar boundaries between markets and products. And perhaps most unsettling, traditional nation states, those artifacts of the eighteenth and nineteenth centuries, are now either coming apart at the seams (for example, the former Soviet Union or Czechoslovakia) or showing themselves to be relatively meaningless as units in which to think about economic activity.

In a sense, this fluidity of economic environment is nothing new.

Industrial economies have never been static. Their history has always been marked by great, unsettling changes: in the nineteenth century, the migration of previously unimaginable numbers of people from Europe to America; in the early and mid-twentieth century, the migration of corporations toward a multinational presence from their original domestic base in a home country; in the years leading up to the twenty-first century, the migration of disaggregated business activities—through the digital network—to various points around the globe.

As private sector managers and government policymakers are discovering, it makes no practical sense in so borderless a world to think, say, of countries like "Italy" or "China" as discrete economic entities. Their internal variations are too great and their external linkages too extensive for such slipshod generalizations to be useful as guides to action. Equally important, the sheer speed of business-related migration through the digital network now vastly outpaces the ability of governments—both leaders and institutions—to adapt and respond. Left to their own devices, governments simply cannot move quickly enough to build prosperity for their people. Instead, they must find ways to tap into—to forge linkages with—the global economy. Only by inviting that economy in can they harness twenty-first-century-speed migrations to improve their people's quality of life.

Indeed, the global economy in which both managers and policymakers must now operate is not the neat, easily divisible sum of separate national economies. It has its own reality, its own rules, and its own logic. The leaders of most nation states have a difficult time accepting that reality, following those rules, or accommodating that logic. This is perfectly understandable: the demands imposed on them by the entrenched constituencies to which they are responsible and beholden cannot help but push them in a different direction. But the situation does not change the facts. All it does is render their nation states even less relevant and less effective as ports of entry to the global economy. It also leaves them less equipped to harness its resources to improve the quality of life of their people. And it makes them less able to cope with the rapid "hollowing out" not just of their traditional manufacturing, but also of their newer service, industries. In their earlier, mercantilist phase, nation states may have been powerful engines of wealth creation. Today, they have all too often become equally powerful engines of wealth destruction.

The secret is out. In both the developed and the developing worlds, citizens and consumers have noticed and, quite naturally, are far from pleased. These days, few government leaders and even fewer administrative bureaucracies enjoy broad popular confidence or support. The reason is clear. Unlike their leaders, most people do accept the new facts of global economic life. They do want the information needed to make their own choices. They do want the improved quality of life to which such choices can lead, unimpeded access to the best and cheapest products (wherever they may come from), and the entrepreneurial freedom to participate in wealth-creating activities. In a word, they want to be able to vote with their energies and talents and pocketbooks. And the evidence shows that, when they have the chance, they do.

This rush to the polls is most visible in the activities not of nation states, but of what I have elsewhere called "region states," those geographic areas—such as Hong Kong and the adjacent coastline of China, Dalian in the northeast of China, Bangalore in India, San Diego/Tijuana, or even greater Tokyo—that represent discrete, coherent participants in the global economy. Unlike nation states, with their inevitably protectionist impulses, these region states have given entrée to economy and have tried to harness its information and choice and access and freedom to improve the lot of their citizenry.

In nation states, by contrast, most people fear the implications of such things, if poorly managed, for established industries, jobs, and networks of social support. Unhappily, they have little reason to believe that these things will be intelligently managed. Worse, as history shows, such fear and disbelief, if cleverly manipulated, can provide excellent tinder for the powerful who would protect their own turf by igniting a wall of flame as a defense against any change that might threaten it. As daily headlines attest, it is already being so manipulated. To be sure, these angry, reactionary flailings will eventually die away. They always do. In the interim, however, they can do—and are doing—significant damage.

Historical periods of transition are, inevitably, stressful. The bigger the transition, the greater the stress. And by any reasonable standard, the development of a genuinely global economy is a "big" transition. It is rapidly making obsolete not only a complex web of long-standing institutional arrangements, but also the whole universe of assumptions—the commonsense knowledge of what is unarguably "true"—on which those arrangements are based. Vested interests aside, people rarely give up comfortable certainties without a fight. Indeed, that is precisely why fear of the unknown, especially when coupled with a lack of confidence in leaders, makes such excellent tinder for the flames of reaction.

Against such fear of the economic future, there can be no guaranteed remedy. But there is a fairly effective over-the-counter medicine: timely, accurate, and insightful commentary about the scope, shape, and likely consequences of the emerging new economic order. Providing such commentary is exactly what this four-part collection of articles from *Harvard Business Review* attempts to do. Part I challenges the notion that, with the defeat of communism as a viable ideology, there remains only one legitimate, workable model for economic activity in a borderless world: democratic capitalism as practiced in the United States. Part II sketches the contours of this borderless world and finds, in its rapidly expanding interdependencies, none of the signs that some claim to observe of an inescapable zero-sum game. Part III examines how these interdependencies affect the core—and extremely sensitive—issues of trade and trade policy. Finally, Part IV assesses their implications for the responsibilities, tasks, and practices of professional managers.

During more than 20 years of consulting to leading international companies, I have consistently tried to help senior managers wrap their minds—and arms—around the practical challenges of steering their companies through the unfamiliar landscape of an increasingly global economy. For many, the foremost question about dealing with this borderless world was how to choose among possible organizational, as well as strategic, emphases on product, function, and geography. That is, these managers saw themselves as having access to three major levers or axes of response and, therefore, as needing to strike the right balance among them. Should they focus primarily on global products, on local geographies, or on functional expertise? Which of these considerations should be uppermost in the way they designed their organizations and prioritized their strategic aims?

In a global economy, the fundamental questions may not change, but the answers do—and, more than that, so do the metrics against which such answers need to be judged. In the past, for example, if a company opted for a geographical focus, it would dedicate its energies to building country-specific operations in each national environment—the United Kingdom, say, and France and Germany—in which it participated. It would then typically aggregate these operations under the umbrella of a regional headquarters—in this case, of course, a European headquarters—to encourage and facilitate cross-border synergies, where possible, as well as shorten top management's span of control.

But does this United Nations–style, country-based aggregation make sense when it involves bundling under the same umbrella the advanced economies of Germany and France with those of the former Eastern Bloc? Does it make sense when it involves bundling China with its US$ 300 per capita GNP, and Japan ,with a per capita GNP of US$ 30,000? In fact, does it make sense to treat China itself or India or Indonesia as a coherent economic entity, subject to a single, consistent level of so-called country risk, given the enormous differences between their various internal regions? Moreover, what about the tightly linked overseas Chinese community, which is so influential throughout the whole of Southeast Asia? Is it really best divided up by country—Thailand, Indonesia, Singapore, and so on? On paper, of course, the exercise is appealing in its neatness: Europe here, Asia there, China there. But in managerial terms, such aggregations simply cannot provide the materials management needs to build concrete, actionable understanding of the real clusters of economic activity in a borderless world.

For top managers, relying instead on the functional axis to assert control and filter information does not help. True, the functions—finance, R&D, personnel—once belonged largely to headquarters and, thus, provided the means by which those at the center could monitor as well as influence decisions of those at the periphery. In a borderless world, however, it is increasingly difficult to manage functional activities across so wide a spectrum of operating environments from a single, central point. Moreover, advances in digital networks and information technology allow those activities to be disaggregated on a global basis and outsourced, creating, in effect, a virtual functional network spanning the globe. Seen in this light, companies are no longer standalone institutions but, rather, oddly and often asymmetrically shaped parts of transnational "webs" of functional activity. And in a world defined by such webs, traditional notions of centralized control rapidly lose their meaning.

Much the same holds true along the product axis as well. Companies once built, in each of their geographic markets, more or less complete, end-to-end business systems to develop, make, market, and distribute each of their separate products. Throughout today's global economy, however, long-established channel structures are breaking down. (Even in Japan, for example, direct marketers and discounters are rudely shaking up the traditional, multi-tiered distribution system.) So, too, are the lines separating competitors, customers, and suppliers, as well as between product categories—fax machines, cameras, and personal computers, for example.

In so complex an environment, what it means to organize around product is neither simple nor obvious. Old road maps do not help; old rules of thumb mislead more than direct; good students make poor teachers. What used to be "knowledge" has to be unlearned, and the confidence that mastery of such knowledge once brought must inevitably give way to the uncertainty that comes with first-cut empirical observation. Managers need to learn how to "see" all over again.

This, perhaps, is the most important lesson of the articles collected here. A genuinely global economy really *is* something new under the sun. It observes laws and follows a logic all its own. Moreover, both its logic and its laws are still evolving, still in process. Analogies can help increase awareness—but only to a point. Beyond that, the only sure guide is the experience built up along the way. There are no safe or certain solutions. Searching for them is useless. Much better to make a judgment about general direction, to experiment, to build on what works, and to abandon what does not. In a global economy, both managers and policymakers will have to construct the roads they travel as they go.

The Evolving Global Economy

PART

I

Alternative Capitalisms

1
The New Era of Eurocapitalism

Herbert A. Henzler

Capitalism was born in Europe. But for nearly half a century, its most vigorous offshoots have flourished in the United States and Japan, while our economic performance has been lackluster. Or so the familiar litany goes. Despite our venerable commercial achievements—and the great European thinkers who defined the very institutions of capitalism—the continent that dominated world events for thousands of years seems to have fallen irretrievably behind.

First came the devastation of World War II and the enormous work of reconstruction in Europe, work that only government had the resources to undertake. Then in later years, as the United States and Japan prospered, we grappled with stagnant economies, high unemployment and social welfare costs, and an exaggerated fear of invasion by American business interests. Now, with the drive toward 1992 and the single market gaining momentum, other difficulties have arisen: we are lagging badly in critical sectors like electronics; a new regulatory bureaucracy has emerged in Brussels; and once again we face the threat of economic invasion—this time from the Japanese.

All in all, the verdict seems inescapable. Try as we might, politicians and media pundits say, we simply cannot manage as well as our American and Far Eastern competitors. "Eurocapitalism" has lost its historic edge.

My own view, however, is that this conventional verdict is wrong. Many European businesses are doing far better than anyone would have predicted ten years ago, and their future looks brighter still. Indeed, I believe that our capitalist system is, in many ways, better suited than its U.S. or Japanese counterparts to meet the economic, social, and environmental challenges of the years ahead.

The conventional wisdom, with its handwringing conclusions, seriously misreads both the likely prospects of European business in the 1990s and the nature of the worldwide contest in which we are engaged. The competitive battle senior managers now face is not some kind of factory-to-factory combat with mirror-image rivals in other parts of the world. Rather, it is a deeper struggle among different capitalist systems, each with its own distinctive set of values, priorities, institutions, and goals.

In this contest of competing systems, the measure of success should not be limited to trade flows, exchange rates, or productivity improvements, significant as those measures are. Instead, the most important question is: Which of the three capitalist systems can give its people the best standard of living and most fully prepare them for the future?

Consider some of the challenges global competition presents, especially with this question in mind. Managers from every country are now required to deal effectively with employees of many nationalities and to maintain cohesiveness not just in the workplace but also in the rest of society. They must structure and oversee alliance-like relationships with other organizations. They are expected to balance the need for corporate economic growth with the health of the physical environment and with the broader social welfare of the countries in which they operate.

On each of these dimensions, Europe's accumulated skill and experience give its managers a distinct advantage. European forays abroad are not a recent add-on to a history of domestic enterprise. As traders, we roamed the world for centuries, and, as industrialists, we have been similarly adventuresome: given the limited size of Europe's national markets, we have always had to think internationally. Nor has our pattern been to set up shop in a country and then pull out as soon as current earnings decline. Since its arrival in 1894, Siemens has outlived several revolutions in Mexico, and the Brazilian and Argentinean subsidiaries of what is now ABB are also nearly a century old.

The ability to maintain a genuinely international outlook and to balance economic performance with social inclusiveness is what Eurocapitalism does best. More to the point, it is what every economic system will have to do in order to compete successfully in a global economy. And that gives Europe's managers a historic opportunity to recapture lost ground, an opportunity they are well equipped to grasp.

In fact, a new generation of industrialists has taken command at many of Europe's leading corporations. More than their immediate predecessors, these "Europreneurs" are fired by the kind of entrepreneurial energy and vision that animated the late nineteenth- and early twentieth-century founders of European enterprises such as Siemens and Daimler-Benz. But unlike those founders, today's leaders are dedicated to reenergizing large, well-established organizations.

Obviously, their course will be neither easy nor smooth. Upheaval in eastern Europe, the loss of competitiveness in a range of technology-intensive industries, the long arm of Brussels, and the bad habit of central planning—all pose serious threats to our successful renewal. But the odds now favor a different direction. For the first time in many decades, Eurocapitalism has the chance to regain its position of global leadership.

The basic tenets of capitalism—free markets, private ownership of assets, private direction of investment, the "law" of comparative advantage—are the same throughout the world. But the constraints under which companies and their senior managers operate, the degree of legitimacy they enjoy, the goals their actions must serve, and the standards by which they are judged vary markedly from region to region.

For example, managers in the United States are most deeply committed to free markets and the effectiveness of individual action. U.S. capitalism typically does not favor collective solutions to social problems, nor does it expect institutions such as employers' associations, unions, and government bodies to play an important role in the management of private enterprise. Basically, so long as shareholder value grows, managers can follow their own unrestricted course. The fruits of capitalism are commonly expected to benefit investors, and the most widely accepted measure for evaluating corporate performance is increasing shareholder wealth.

Capitalism in Japan is far less individualistic than its U.S. counterpart. But it is also focused largely on private gain, although it is the company or *keiretsu* that benefits from current earnings rather than dividend-receiving individual investors. Japanese managers are expected to use profits to fund high and sustained levels of corporate investment, not to distribute them to shareholders (who have traditionally made money on share-price appreciation) or to company employees. Indeed, one of the really interesting questions for Japan is whether employees will continue to accept the comparatively poor quality of the country's services now that their performance has made it a world-class competitor.

For example, in the 1992 *World Competitiveness Report* (issued jointly by IMD and the World Economic Forum in Switzerland), Japanese survey respondents rated their quality of life below that of every European country except Portugal. And that response came from people in large, international companies, not from workers in suppliers or small businesses, where low wages and insecure employment are a routine consequence of Japan's intensely competitive domestic markets.

Whether Japan's citizens will rebel against this economic and social disparity remains to be seen. Signs of class struggle are few—more than 90% of all Japanese fervently declare themselves to be members of the middle class—and thus far the country's homogeneity has largely relieved its economic system of the need to balance competing interests. Europe, however, has enjoyed no such freedom. Our form of capitalism has necessarily been shaped by an extraordinary mix of social and ethnic groups, political factions, religious influences, historical divisions, and economic classes. As businesspeople, we Europeans have had neither a unified culture like Japan's to draw on nor a uniform ideology like America's cult of individualism that would permit us to concentrate solely on economic affairs.

Eurocapitalism itself does not, of course, exist in a single common form. Wage levels vary markedly from country to country. So do labor legislation, social security provisions, and the degree of unionization. And so do many of the challenges facing management. Scandinavian companies, for example, tend to be much smaller in scale and less globally oriented than companies in France or Germany. In France, the government owns a majority share of many large industrial groups. By contrast, the financial markets of the United Kingdom are closer to those of New York City than they are to the markets of Frankfurt, Paris, or Milan. Yet even the United Kingdom shares the deeply held European belief that the fruits of capitalist enterprise should be distributed across society. Thus Eurocapitalism supports a social compact to which the great majority of our people subscribe.

Although an actual written compact obviously does not exist, we Europeans explicitly accept our roles as members of society who must act responsibly within the bounds of that society. In return, we also assume that society is, in the broadest sense, responsible for everyone in it. In this civic polity, jointly engaged in economic affairs, all sorts of people are bound together and responsible to one another.

Consider, for example, management's characteristic attitude toward the work force. Laws on codetermination, combined with a tradition of patriarchal concern, have made European CEOs deeply committed to their employees, treating them more like partners in a long-term enterprise than anonymous "factors of production." To a great extent, this special relationship reflects the long-standing commitment in much of Europe to the general education of both blue- and white-collar employees. Such a work force cannot be ordered about nor considered disposable or interchangeable. Its workers must be taken seriously, kept informed, and included in the decision-making process. Yet a work force that strongly identifies with the interests of the company also provides a critical source of competitive advantage.

As participants in an implicit social compact, European managers have sought to build and sustain a vibrant economic system that embraces diversity and, at the same time, keeps the gap between rich and poor from growing too wide. Thus "socially healthy" top pay at European companies is generally set at no more than 12 to 15 times the average paycheck—a far cry from the 100 to 1 relationship that exists between the pay of CEOs and shop-floor workers in many U.S. companies. One result is that ours is largely a middle-class work force: even the line workers at Daimler-Benz often have a Mercedes in their driveways.

To achieve this social inclusiveness, we accept that government will play a greater direct role in the economy than it does in the United States or Japan and that managerial activities will be more tightly restricted. Government's share of GNP in most European countries still hovers between 45% and 55%, while in Japan and the United States it is roughly half that level. Moreover, every phase of economic activity carries a large burden of social overhead. In the leading countries, wages are high. Employment and plant closure laws are strict. Pension rights are well-established. Social welfare benefits—health care, for example, and education or training in technical skills—are substantial and widely available to the whole population.

The costs of this social overhead are considerable, and there is growing concern about our continued ability to absorb them in the face of ever greater demands from needy constituencies and ever stronger challenges from foreign competitors. The number of effective working hours is smaller than it is elsewhere in the "Triad" of capitalist systems: in 1970, average working hours in Europe were down 15% when compared with Japan, and by 1989 this difference had widened to 22%. In general, labor costs are also higher: a weighted average of $17.50 per hour in manufacturing industries during 1990 compared with $15.00 in the United States and $16.00 in Japan. More to the point, expenses associated with supplementary, personnel-related items such as paid vacations, pensions, and medical benefits make up a larger portion of these labor costs.

In return, however, these social costs lay the groundwork for stable, long-term alliances among economic constituencies—workers and managers, suppliers and distributors, private industry and government—as well as a heightened degree of social cohesion. For years, some European business leaders have included social "accounts" in the annual reports for their companies. Since 1977, for example, the creation of such accounts has been mandated by law in France. Elsewhere, especially in Germany, these social balance sheets, which are produced on a voluntary basis, provide detailed information on issues like employment, wages, fringe benefits, social security expenditures, working conditions, job training, environmental programs, and community-related activities. Because European senior managers tend to balance company growth with benefits for employees and the public at large, they can maintain good relationships with unions and works councils rather than acting as natural adversaries.

Europe's social balancing act, as we know it today, has no place in the anonymous, atomistic market envisioned by Adam Smith. Rather, it is the linchpin of a civic universe that also functions in economic terms. We have long understood that homelessness, illiteracy, and other social ills are not only morally unacceptable but also economically harmful. Unlike people in the United States, most Europeans think of themselves as riding in the same boat. In addition, and here we differ from Japan, we are accustomed to sailing along with quite a diverse and various crew. Given its homogeneity and insularity, Japan has yet to confront the difficult questions of inclusiveness that an aging population, more women and minorities in the work force, foreign operations, and economic success inevitably will raise.

Day to day, of course, Europe's community of interest does not ensure the absence of tension among different constituencies, just a relatively more effective balance among them. Take business-government relations. Thanks, in part, to our mercantilist tradition, Europeans know that the interests of private companies and the state can run together in comfortable harness. As historian Alfred Chandler points out in his essay "Government Versus Business: An American Phenomenon," government in Europe achieved maturity well before big business did. Hence the rise of industrial organizations posed no threat to government bureaucrats charged with administering the public welfare. In the United States, however, where big business appeared before big government, relations between the two estates have been marked by uneasy suspicion at best and outright hostility at worst.

Yet the stability of these arrangements comes at a price, which is ultimately borne by individual Europeans, both as consumers and as taxpayers. For years, we've railed against the inefficiency, excessive cost, sluggish innovation, and poor service generated by the cozy relations between government and industry. Getting a properly itemized bill from a national telephone service is still an experience Kafka would have understood; while the high price of train tickets in Germany reflects the fact that the railways' supervisory boards are packed with suppliers. Indeed, removing artificial distortions like these is one of the primary economic goals of moving toward a single market in 1992 and beyond.

Nevertheless, it is a mistake to compare the performance of competing capitalist systems in terms of economic efficiency alone. Given a choice between better profits and higher dividends on the one hand, and the social stability represented by high employment rolls on the other, Europeans have usually chosen stability. Up to now, we have been willing to accept the overhead burden this choice imposes by paying higher prices and accepting lower returns on equity and smaller compound annual growth rates from our companies. Economic outcomes, for both companies and individuals, are more tightly "bunched" than they are in the United States and Japan. And most Europeans would sacrifice the possibility of an unrestricted business environment that rewards a few with extreme wealth for the reality of many more people with comfortable incomes.

Still, the question remains: Why does Europe place such an emphasis on stability? In part, the answer lies in our history. The French and Russian Revolutions, the English Industrial Revolution, Germany in the 1920s and 1930s, uprisings in a Polish shipyard: we have learned over and over that social dislocation cannot be contained easily. That helps explain why the Federal Republic of Germany has been so ready to absorb the costs of unification and why Europeans have been relatively quick to acknowledge the need for aid to the Commonwealth of Independent States. To avoid the long-term costs of serious unrest, almost any short-term price is usually worth paying.

In addition, however, Europeans place a high value on quality of life. American and Japanese observers routinely comment on the pleasures of life in Europe, from affordable concerts to longer vacations to shorter working days. But achieving a decent quality of life for the largest number of people is a conscious social choice. For example, theaters in Germany are heavily subsidized: ticket prices cover only about 30% of the cost; government picks up the rest. No one is eager for this largesse to disappear. That applies even more strongly to Germany's completely free university system and its generous health-care system.

If it is possible to supply these benefits and run the country's economic engine more productively at the same time, well and good. If products can be made even more competitive around the world, even better. But if the choice appears to lie between maintaining economic performance or quality of life, public opinion will tilt toward the latter. Higher return on equity is abstract. Reasonably priced theater tickets and affordable health care are tangible. And social cohesiveness is priceless.

A decade or so ago, these choices and the overhead burden they imply began to raise fundamental questions about Europe's long-term prospects. Remember where our economies stood at the beginning of the 1980s: world market shares had tumbled in industry after industry; unemployment hovered between 10% and 15%; inflation was soaring; England's slump looked incurable; Italy was fumbling inconclusively with yet another government; France was busy sealing its markets against Japanese products and its companies against acquisition from abroad. Eurocapitalism is rooted in a noble vision, the common argument ran. But it is hopelessly unrealistic as the basis for a modern industrial system.

The remarkable thing, of course, is how quickly this concern over Europe's economic paralysis, or "Eurosclerosis" as it was called, has been stood on its head. With the real, if slightly belated, approach of a genuine single market and with the practical inclusion of European Free Trade Area countries in a unified, continent-wide zone, Europe no longer looks even remotely like an economic backwater.

What lay behind this reversal was renewed vigor in the private sector, which in many European countries had taken a backseat to government ever since 1945. Back then, we had no choice. With Europe in ruins, only government could restart the economy because only government had the resources. In sector after sector, the task was not to explore the frontiers of industrial strategy but to produce enough goods and services to meet the basic needs of a continent in turmoil. Food had to be produced and distributed, energy supplied, buildings and transportation rebuilt, clothing returned to the store shelves.

No wonder government's share of GNP often jumped as high as 50% or 60%. When government wasn't doing the rebuilding itself, it was often the only stable customer and client for those who were. In the 1950s and 1960s, given a choice between private citizens and the government as customers, wise companies chose government.

Moreover, business leaders themselves were self-effacing. For the most part, the postwar industrialists were engineers and production men, functional specialists without any formal business or managerial training. They joined their companies when young, then slowly and steadily worked their way up through the ranks. They were not visible public figures, nor were they statesmen on some broader stage.

Everyone knows about the German "miracle," for instance. But almost no one knows who led the companies that produced the miracle. During the early 1960s, I worked for the Shell Oil Company in Germany. Neither then nor later could I have told you the names of the men running the company. While postwar leaders of industry were well respected for what they accomplished, they themselves were largely invisible.

Then, toward the end of the 1960s, a deep shift in social attitudes led to troubling questions about business and its managers. People who no longer remembered or had never experienced the deprivations of the postwar years began to challenge the materialism evident in Germany, France, and other western European nations. As individuals, industrial leaders were no more visible than before. But now they were deprived of public respect as well.

By the mid-1970s, the weather vane of public opinion had shifted again. As the effects of the OPEC oil shocks rippled through European economies, people looked to the private sector to support the standard of living that politicians still kept promising. Like a milk cow, business obliged, until the drag on long-term performance became so great that even industry's critics could not fail to see the costs to society overall. Margaret Thatcher's election as Britain's prime minister in 1979 confirmed the reversal. Italy, remembering at last that it was broke, discovered that the only institutions creating value and paying taxes were corporations. France backed away from its ill-fated experiment with wholesale nationalization. Germany voted the Social Democrats out of office and the more conservative Christian Democrats in.

At the heart of a reinvigorated private sector stand the new Europreneurs. Percy Barnevik of ABB, Edzard Reuter of Daimler-Benz, Jérôme Monod of Société Lyonnaise des Eaux, Helmut Maucher of Nestlé, Floris Maljers of Unilever, Mark Woessner of Bertelsmann, Karlheinz Kaske of Siemens, Carl Hahn of Volkswagen—these managers and others like them represent a turning point in European industry. Faced, in many cases, with the need to revive companies grown sluggish and bureaucratic, they have responded by breaking with the world of management in which their own careers were shaped. In particular, they are more entrepreneurial, more cosmopolitan, and more publicly outspoken than the generation who preceded them.

A brief biographical comparison may help to bring this generational divide into focus. Consider and contrast Edzard Reuter and Werner Breitschwerdt. Reuter has been chairman of the board of Daimler-Benz since 1987 and is the architect of its move into aerospace and electronics; Breitschwerdt served as chairman from 1983 to 1987, just before Reuter took charge. Werner Breitschwerdt's father was an engineer, and he himself studied electrical engineering. He spent his entire career at Daimler-Benz, primarily in the department responsible for constructing car bodies, and his appointment challenged none of the company's long-held traditions.

Edzard Reuter's father, on the other hand, was the first postwar mayor of Berlin. The young Reuter grew up in Turkey, where his family had moved in 1933. His academic studies were in mathematics, physics, and law, and his early career included stints with two other companies. Reuter's promotion to CEO after serving as chief financial officer represented a radical departure on the part of Daimler-Benz's board.

In contrast with the venture-capital-driven entrepreneurs or the stock-option-endowed executives of the United States, Reuter and the other Europreneurs are managers, not owners. Most, in fact, serve under multiyear contracts from their supervisory boards. Nevertheless, they are all entrepreneurs in the best Schumpeterian sense of the word: aggressive, risk-taking shapers of a future they themselves have imagined rather than consolidators of a heritage that others have already defined.

Thus the Europreneurs are closer in spirit and accomplishment to late nineteenth-century visionaries such as Robert Bosch, Anton Philips, Gottlieb Daimler, and Werner von Siemens—who founded enterprises based on new technology and innovative products—than they are to the men who rebuilt postwar Europe. Unlike that earlier generation of visionaries, however, the Europreneurs have not had the opportunity to build from scratch. Their hallmark has been revitalization of the huge, globe-circling organizations in their care.

Part of what makes this new generation so effective is their distinctive approach to managerial tasks. Responsible for companies that have become "mini states" in their own right, with networks of affiliates and embassies around the world, the Europreneurs have had to act as industrial statesmen, not tacit agents of mercantilist home governments. And that, in turn, has meant coming to see government not as a dominant partner but as a potential source of managerial ideas and approaches.

Not so long ago, for example, the functional heads in major European corporations would officially announce new policies to their colleagues only after the fact or if they needed help with implementation. Managers would rarely seek out a wide range of views while immersed in the planning process itself. Far more typical was the head engineer's approach at Daimler-Benz: after lunch he would announce the design of a new car by inviting fellow board members to visit his shop, where they could view the completed model.

Today's top managers have no such option. To lead global organizations, they must manage the claims of competing constituencies, whether these come from external parties like customers, regulators, and shareholders or from the internal factions in every large company. Managers have looked to government for lessons in how to build the necessary coalitions. And they are keenly aware of how easily expanding the range of interested parties can bog down a company in red tape and infuriating delays.

Just think of the endless contention between country or division managers with turf to protect, on the one hand, and product managers or powerful staff specialists on the other. Yet European managers are well schooled in adapting to local laws and customs, adjusting to local customer needs and preferences, and training and developing local workers. It is characteristic of our experience that Gessy Lever, the Unilever affiliate in Brazil, is thought of as a Brazilian company, not a European adjunct.

The Europreneurs have learned how to create and draw on a network of outposts around the world, as well as what to do when those outposts become lightning rods for local animosity. Sometimes this anger is directed against the company, such as when airline ticket offices or bank branches are attacked. But far more often its true target is the company's home government.

To address such complicated issues, European business leaders have mastered problem-solving techniques that are more familiar to government officials than private-sector managers: convening task forces or special commissions; lobbying for bipartisan support of major investment decisions; circulating "confidential" discussion drafts on crucial policy issues to test the waters; holding unofficial talks to sound out positions and opposition; speaking publicly on important issues as a way of sending messages to their own organizations. No one should be surprised by this similarity in technique. In business as in government, today's problems can be solved only through an iterative, consensus-building process.

A distinctively European managerial style also characterizes the way Europreneurs deal with subsidiaries, especially foreign ones. From a distance, European industry looks hopelessly jumbled—an organizational crazy-quilt of minority shareholdings, limited liability companies, joint-stock companies, and the like. This is true even at the company level, where over one hundred different units may report to a Nestlé or a Daimler-Benz. But looks can be deceiving. There is a clear logic that runs through all of these organizational arrangements, a logic premised on local autonomy.

In contrast to their counterparts in the United States and Japan, European CEOs often give the heads of their operating companies an exceptionally long managerial leash. Written guidelines and objectives are few, and reporting lines often seem ambiguous. Yet the performance of these subsidiaries has been impressively strong, despite the difficulties involved in turning local operations into worldwide product headquarters, centers for global production, or companywide centers of competence.

European managers are willing to trust subsidiaries abroad with a great deal of freedom because they know they can rely on their organization's deeply embedded culture—its almost tangible sense of "the way we do things around here"—to ensure that quality is maintained. Precise reporting lines, tight organizational boundaries, minutely detailed policy handbooks and performance numbers—all of these are largely beside the point for Europeans. What truly matters is the set of broad and encompassing principles that keep independent managers aligned with one another and with the company's overall goals.

Consider the relations between Siemens and what used to be GTE's Transmission Systems Division. Siemens's top managers have not imposed their planning or control systems on the division, nor have they placed very detailed expectations on its senior management. They have acknowledged that it will take three to five years before the new organization is operating as it should; and interfering during that period would be just that—interference. In much the same way,

Bertelsmann made an explicit decision at the outset not to graft its German management culture onto Bantam or Doubleday. So, for example, while Bertelsmann follows a team-at-the-top leadership model at home, its U.S. operations remain under the control of a strong, "presidential" CEO.

The organizational structure this approach fosters is more organic than mechanistic. And it is more apt to grow through incremental expansion and the inculcation of shared values than through major acquisitions hard-wired by rigid reporting relationships. In fact, we Europeans tried playing with structure in the 1960s and 1970s, when many of our leading companies engaged in extensive, division-focused reorganizations based on American models. These efforts did much to close the perceived efficiency gap between U.S. and European levels of performance. But in a number of cases, they also created great organizational discomfort. As a result, the major reorganizations of the past five years—Siemens, Daimler-Benz, Hoechst, and BASF among them—have followed a path that has been much less wrenching though equally far-reaching in effect.

Rather than make huge new structural adjustments, the Europreneurs have chosen to ensure that the right areas of responsibility are attached to the right people. Rarely has this led to larger management teams. Instead, existing members have taken on additional responsibilities, such as heading the supervisory boards of newly acquired companies or newly created businesses. Siemens, for example, now has 15 independent product groups instead of 6, while at Hoechst, every member of the management board now oversees a complete business-based unit rather than a product sector.

And the net result: a top-management cadre with functional, product, and geographic responsibilities. This "triple grouping," in the words of Alfred Herrhausen, the late chairman of Deutsche Bank, re-creates the conditions of classic entrepreneurship while forfeiting none of the advantages of membership in a large and complex organization.

Ultimately, of course, Europe will stand or fall on its ability to deliver on the promise of a continually rising standard of living for everyone. But so will the United States and Japan. In a global economy, every nation faces the challenge of incorporating diverse populations, subcultures, and interest groups under one roof and improving the quality of life for all. To compete, companies—and societies—must have well-educated workers who can think for themselves, solve problems creatively, and make decisions wisely. Because of the social overhead Europe has been willing to carry, we have been able to provide benefits like affordable health care and quality education, which help create such a work force, as well as a sense of stability overall.

But this willingness may not last forever, and stability can be its own worst enemy. The greatest threat to Europe's economic health is not our social burden but our limited ability to move quickly enough into new value-added businesses. Certain balancing acts are so much a part of the European mind-set—individualism and collectivism, government and business, social order and entrepreneurialism—that the tendency of the whole is toward continuity and stable development, not rejuvenation or radical change.

Where the essence of a business is project management, solid engineering, product quality, or systems management, Europe's unique mix of skills, educated workers, and sophisticated customers stands it in good stead. But when it comes to moving out of old industries and into new ones, we have a habit of falling behind.

Semiconductors are a prime example. Europe lags in the race to develop this new technology because we attempted to develop semiconductors in the same way that for generations we had produced mechanical parts. Then, as it became clear the old ways no longer worked—that quality and performance were not enough, for example—our high-tech companies couldn't adjust fast enough. We worried too much about quality, not enough about cost, and hardly at all about time-to-market.

We face other potentially explosive problems as well. If millions of refugees pour into western Europe from the east or from northern Africa, it will surely upset the delicate balance we have struck between local citizens and foreign nationals. If our loss of competitiveness in electronics seriously injures other industries like machine tools and automobiles, it could eventually put millions of people out of work. Last but hardly least, if the same protectionist impulse that has led us to devote 70% of the European Community's budget to agricultural support programs is invoked with respect to cars, shipbuilding, textiles, chemicals, and other industries, the long-term competitive effects could be disastrous.

Daunting as the challenge of economic renewal is, however, it looks less formidable when viewed in perspective. Eurocapitalism has long had to negotiate between competing pressures that the United States and Japan have yet to experience in full force. That it has done so at all, let alone in a fashion that seems appropriate to the vast majority of its people, is no small accomplishment.

On balance, therefore, I am optimistic about Europe's future, especially given our renewed confidence in ourselves. We have once again taken a leading position in international affairs, and we are quickly regaining our self-assurance in producing new technologies in chemicals, environmentally friendly products, fiber optics, and many other areas. Moreover, we have discovered that U.S. management models are no panacea and that Japanese management models don't automatically apply outside Japan. Thus our greatest strengths remain the ones we have long drawn on: our people and our tradition of inclusiveness.

That we can rely on well-trained and well-educated employees at every level of our companies is a distinct source of competitive advantage. And our tradition of inclusiveness helps us put that advantage to work. Over time it has taught us that there is no one right way to manage either a single company or an entire economy. Rather, a variety of acceptable ways—of different capitalist systems—exist, each of which may work best under a given set of circumstances. In a rapidly changing world, where the importance of accommodating diverse cultures and corporate styles will only increase, Europe's tradition has much to offer both competitors and friends.

2
The Worldwide Web of Chinese Business

John Kao

Most discussion of today's global economy centers on three power-houses: North America, Europe, and Japan. In turn, economists usually divide Asia into Japan, a People's Republic of China that is rapidly changing and on the rise, and the industrialized "dragons" of South Korea, Taiwan, Hong Kong, and Singapore. Yet this standard economic definition doesn't match Pacific Rim realities. In fact, Chinese businesses—many of which are located outside the People's Republic itself—make up the world's fourth economic power.

The very definition of "China" is up for grabs. What we think of as Chinese now encompasses an array of political and economic systems that are bound together by a shared tradition, not geography. For many generations, emigrant Chinese entrepreneurs have been operating comfortably in a network of family and clan, laying the foundations for stronger links among businesses across national borders. And Chinese-owned businesses in East Asia, the United States, Canada, and even farther afield are increasingly becoming part of what I call the *Chinese commonwealth*.

Not based in any one country or continent, this commonwealth is primarily a network of entrepreneurial relationships. From restaurants to real estate to plastic-sandal makers to semiconductor manufacturing—from a staff of five or six family members to a plant floor of thousands—the Chinese commonwealth consists of many individual enterprises that nonetheless share a common culture.

It's the kind of global network many Western multinationals have tried to create in their own organizations. Now these same Western companies are casting about for Asian joint venture partners, looking for ways to tap into the increasingly powerful Chinese network. For most multinationals, Asian-based or not, it's time to take the commonwealth seriously.

To begin with, countries with Chinese-based economies have astonishingly large capital surpluses. Taiwan, one of the smallest countries in the world, has the largest foreign exchange reserves. Singapore, a country of 2.7 million people, has foreign exchange reserves exceeding $34 billion. Then there are the private and informal capital markets of Chinese family and clan associations, in which financial resources are deployed for new venture activities without the intervention of commercial banks, professional venture capital companies, or government investment agencies.

In addition, the Chinese entrepreneurial network and Japan represent two very different integrating forces in Asia. Unlike the Japanese, the Chinese commonwealth has, in computer terms, an "open architecture." It represents access to local resources like information, business connections, raw materials, low labor costs, and different business practices in a variety of environments. In contrast to the Japanese *keiretsu*, the emerging Chinese commonwealth is an interconnected yet potentially open system—and in many respects, provides a new market mechanism for conducting global business.

Thus it's now possible to reach markets in the People's Republic of China through Chinese entrepreneurs in Taiwan. Outsiders may be able to access Southeast Asian markets through the Hong Kong and Singaporean business communities. And ultimately, both Chinese and non-Chinese entrepreneurs may come to take advantage of opportunities in North America and Europe through the Chinese network in those regions.

Many of these Chinese entrepreneurial connections, of course, still involve few outsiders. The traditional small size and family orientation of Chinese businesses certainly have hampered their growth. The Beijing Stone Group, whose stated goal was to become "China's IBM" (until cofounder Wan Runnan fled the People's Republic in 1989), offers one example of how Chinese business practices have evolved in the past 20 years—and the difficulties these companies still face. Other companies like the Acer Group in Taiwan and the Pico Group in Singapore have successfully blended the old with the new.

The new Chinese management model, like the commonwealth that underpins it, is grounded in both traditional Chinese values and Western practices that encourage flexibility, innovation, and the assimilation of outsiders. Such a shift in values has meant not only a transformation in how Chinese businesspeople view themselves and their work but also the expansion of the emerging network. And over time, a new ideology of economic self-interest, one that truly does transcend politics and the clannish constraints on traditional Chinese business, may lead to even greater integration of the commonwealth.

The Shaping Power of Confucian Tradition

For more than 2,000 years, Chinese culture has stressed the importance of social order. From the sixth to fifth century B.C., Confucius codified the ties of individual, family, and society that define a person's proper place and position. Given China's long history of political upheaval, natural disasters, waves of emigration, and, above all, economic scarcity, these well-defined relationships have often helped keep social chaos at bay.

Based on a study of Chinese entrepreneurship I've conducted over the past two years, in which my research team has surveyed or interviewed more than 150 entrepreneurs both inside and outside of China, it is clear that the Confucian tradition is remarkably persistent. For most Chinese entrepreneurs, Westernized as they may be, the enterprise is still a means for exerting control—and for achieving security in a disordered world.

My research interviews reveal a consistent pattern of personal disruption and hardship, including loss of country, wealth, home, or a family member. In my survey, 90% of the entrepreneurs who were first-generation emigrants had experienced war; 40% had gone through a political disaster like the Cultural Revolution; 32% had lost a home; and 28% had weathered economic disasters that resulted in significant loss of wealth. (See Exhibit I.)

In ancient China, farmers in a largely agrarian economy focused on surviving storms, droughts, and locusts. More recently, business has become a key to survival for Chinese emigrants, especially during the Chinese diaspora of the past century. Enterprising entrepreneurs work long hours and save wherever they can, accumulating capital in a world they still consider unsafe.

This survivor mentality and the Confucian tradition of patriarchal authority inform the values of the typical Chinese entrepreneur—one who seeks to control his own small dynasty. In fact, China's history of political and social turmoil has led to a relentless practicality, which can be summarized in the following "life-raft" values:

Thrift ensures survival.

A high, even irrational, level of savings is desirable, regardless of immediate need.

Hard work to the point of exhaustion is necessary to ward off the many hazards present in an unpredictable world.

The only people you can trust are family—and a business enterprise is created as a familial life raft.

The judgment of an incompetent relative in the family business is more reliable than that of a competent stranger.

Obedience to patriarchal authority is essential to maintaining coherence and direction for the enterprise.

Investment must be based on kinship or clan affiliations, not abstract principles.

Tangible goods like real estate, natural resources, and gold bars are preferable to intangibles like illiquid securities or intellectual property.

Keep your bags packed at all times, day or night.

These underlying values probably account for certain archetypal business choices of first-generation Chinese: real estate, shipping, and import-export companies. Such industries generally require a limited span of control and can be managed effectively by a small group of insiders who can be members of the same family. Even Chinese en-

Exhibit I.

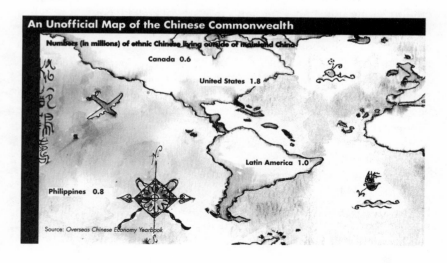

An Unofficial Map of the Chinese Commonwealth

Numbers (in millions) of ethnic Chinese living outside of mainland China

Canada 0.6

United States 1.8

Latin America 1.0

Philippines 0.8

Source: *Overseas Chinese Economy Yearbook*

terprises that have grown quite large tend to maintain immature organizational patterns—for example, management "spokes" around a powerful founder "hub" or a management structure with only two layers. Of the entrepreneurs I surveyed, 70% noted that they still operated around one of these two simple structures.

In such imperial organizations, Chinese entrepreneurs manage traditional enterprises much as a Chinese emperor would his empire. Not surprisingly, the assets of the business usually are passed on only to family members. My research interviews indicate that many Chinese entrepreneurs still consider imperial organizations crucial to their success, regardless of the entrepreneurs' age or generational identity. As one old Chinese saying puts it, "Better to be the head of a chicken than the tail of a large cow."

The founder of Formosa Plastics in Taiwan, Y.C. Wang, still controls this successful chemicals and plastics company, which now employs more than 30,000 people. Wang directs the company through an inner circle of fewer than 10 professional managers who are not family members. These executives, in turn, work with an administrative group of about 200 other managers.

The purpose of this administrative group is to channel and distill information into a series of daily reports, which reach Wang either in person or by fax. And Wang's son, an operations manager, occupies a

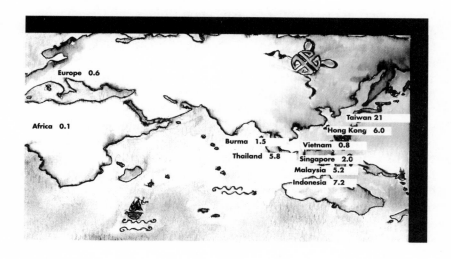

plush office at corporate headquarters—much as the princes in an imperial bureaucracy lived in different wings of the palace.

There are plenty of other recent examples of dynastic "succession"—from former prime minister Lee Kuan Yew, whose son, Lee Hsien Loong, became Singapore's Minister of Trade and Industry to Wee Cho Yaw, the founder of Singapore's United Overseas Bank, who installed his son, Wee Te Cheong, as deputy president not long ago. As original founders like Hong Kong's Li Ka Shing of Cheung Kong Holdings, Malaysia's Robert Kuok of the Shangri-La Hotel and other ventures, and Indonesia's Liem Sioe Liong of the Salim Group approach the end of their careers, control of these global companies will probably remain in family hands as well.

But dynastic aspirations may explain why companies that appear as cosmopolitan as Wang Laboratories in Lowell, Massachusetts still maintain an imperial model at their core—and often fall apart. Fred Wang, whom his father An Wang finally called an inadequate manager, seemed quite capable when he was promoted to president of Wang. Still, the American management group that surrounded Fred Wang didn't fully accept his inherent right to run the company.

In Asia, the executives in a professional management group would have accepted unquestioningly a family member as leader. They might have wondered if it was too early for that person to achieve power, but they would not have contested the basic promotion. At Wang Laboratories, such East-West value differences led to many additional conflicts and contributed to the company's eventual decline.

By its very nature, the life raft of a familial business is unstable for key outsiders. Based on my research, a non-Chinese professional manager can't expect the same level of trust he or she would have as a family member in the company. Outsiders can never know family insiders as well as they know each other. And non-Chinese professionals often have to work doubly hard to understand the reasons underlying certain decisions.

Anyone who routinely deals with successful Chinese businesspeople soon realizes that while 90% of a given entrepreneur's decisions may be brilliant, the other 10% often make no business sense. The typical Chinese entrepreneur may keep a poor manager on because "he's family"; sit on decisions that involve outsiders; conceal information because "she's not family"; avoid necessary confrontations; and in many respects, behave toward subordinates like a guilt-provoking parent.

Most telling, however, is how quickly traditional organizations hit snags when they expand beyond the limits of family control. In a 1990

Fortune survey of Pacific Rim businesses, only one Chinese enterprise made the list of the top 150 based on size. As these companies start to grow, the conventions of traditional Chinese business, especially caution toward outsiders, become a clear competitive disadvantage.

In the classic story of a Chinese dynasty's fall, a weak emperor, along with a weak group of imperial managers, can no longer satisfy the people and loses the "mandate of heaven." In today's global economy, the need for continual innovation may provide a new earthly mandate for organizational change.

Breaking with Tradition

"In Chinese culture, you have to respect your father and mother," notes James Yen, the president of Advanced Microelectronic Products in Taiwan. "This respect kills creativity. If you have to respect what your father says, then you tend to kill your own thinking."

Along with the adherence to traditional Chinese values across generations, my research also reveals that the "life raft" has expanded. The emergence of an economically powerful commonwealth is due to a number of changes over the past three decades, including a break with traditional life-raft values.

The sons, daughters, and grandchildren of first-generation entrepreneurs have assimilated to a far greater extent. People of Chinese descent are now born all over the world; they are multicultural and have lived and been educated in a manner different from their parents. While second- and third-generation Chinese still respect the family enterprise, these younger entrepreneurs have absorbed other values as well, particularly if they live in Western countries like the United States.

D.Y. Yang of Winbond in Taiwan, who considers his computer chip company to be Chinese, says, "A Chinese company depends less on data and more on intuition, feelings, and people." At the same time, he notes that no blood relatives, including his children, are part of Winbond. "You have to depend on the system to work. Of course you have to respect the family business structure, but since this is a high-tech company, individual contributions are important."

The commonwealth's new breed of entrepreneurs have shifted from a survivor mentality to a focus on self-actualization, a goal that reflects Western philosophies and practices. In my research, respondents cited these "soft" factors most often as crucial for improving their businesses in the future: managing growth, nurturing creativity, developing more open communication and confrontation skills, and encouraging professionalization of the organization and smooth assimilation of outsiders.

For example, the Acer Group in Taiwan markets its own brand of computer clones in more than 70 countries and is one of the largest personal computer companies in the world. Acer's employees are encouraged to own shares of company stock; the company's emphasis on decentralization, doing its own R&D, and creating its own brand name have become highly praised models for other enterprises in Taiwan. Yet CEO and cofounder Stan Shih attributes many of the company's greatest strengths—especially the stability of its senior managers—to traditional Chinese culture.

The Pico Group in Singapore is another amalgam of traditional and Western management styles. Pico includes 300 operating companies in 25 countries, which focus on everything from design and fabrication of exhibits to marketing services to leisure businesses like game centers and Broadway shows. Pico's 2,500 employees receive bonuses and stock options and can participate in profit-sharing plans. Managers can direct the investment of any surplus from their operating units.

Yet Pico was founded by three brothers; and three of its four main business groups still are run by family members. The executive director of the fourth group, which focuses on the new business area of entertainment, is a long-time family friend. In fact, all of Pico's top managers, half of whom were educated abroad, started out as family friends rather than raw hires.

In contrast, the Beijing Stone Group introduced what cofounder Wan Runnan called a "modern Western concept" of business from the very beginning. Stone, which in 1984 started in a two-room office that was formerly a collective's vegetable shop, grew much larger than any enterprise in the People's Republic of China during the 1980s. It included more than 40 companies, from computer equipment manufacturers to CAD product designers to technical typesetters—with subsidiaries in various parts of the People's Republic, as well as in Hong Kong, Australia, Japan, and the United States.

By 1989, just before Wan fled the country for his open espousal of democratic principles, Beijing Stone had developed the sophisticated matrix organizational structure favored by many Western multinationals. Wan's charismatic leadership style alone made Stone look like a Western company. He and the other founders established a strong corporate culture and compensation policies keyed to performance—

with salaries much higher than those offered by other companies in the People's Republic but with fewer automatic benefits like free housing.

While Wan Runnan paid the price for moving too fast in the People's Republic of China, Chinese entrepreneurs are now on the cutting edge when it comes to establishing new democratic processes. China itself has yet to evolve a true model of Chinese democracy; its traditional institutions always have been based on the imperial mode, be they the government, business enterprises, or the family. Yet new business practices often lead to new ways of thinking about political and social organization. Witness the rejuvenating effects of the most recent spate of economic reforms in the People's Republic of China.

Capital as the Springboard

The explosion of high-technology industries in Asia and the political opening of China in the 1980s have reinforced and will continue to expand today's Chinese commonwealth. But perhaps the most important development that has consolidated the commonwealth is how rich many Chinese communities have become.

In Indonesia, one individual of Chinese descent, Liem Sioe Liong, is reputed to generate 5% of the country's gross domestic product through the Salim Group. And *Institutional Investor* has estimated that the private wealth of Southeast Asia's 40 million ethnic Chinese exceeds $200 billion.

Because of the unprecedented availability of capital, a sophisticated Chinese plutocracy has emerged on the world scene. In effect, these plutocrats are the guardians of large-scale entrepreneurship within the Chinese commonwealth, whether it has to do with building a highway or creating a satellite broadcasting service from virtually a standing start.

Billionaire Li Ka Shing's Star TV in Hong Kong broadcasts entertainment and information services to an Asian market of 2.7 billion. Gordon Wu's Hopewell Holdings, oversees construction of the highway, which runs from Hong Kong to Guangzhou through the province of Guangdong in southern China.

Since the 1970s, the growing wealth of Chinese communities clearly has fueled significant levels of investment across national borders. In fact, cross-border investments alone are responsible for turning the de facto network of loose family relationships into today's Chinese commonwealth. While the invisible or unofficial capital market of family, friends, and clan affiliations is on the rise, the opportunities provided by official banking and government sources also have increased.

For example, Thailand's Charoen Pokphand Group, an agribusiness conglomerate headed by ethnic Chinese, was one of the first companies to make large investments in the People's Republic of China. Or take the development funds provided by the Taiwanese government or the Monte Jade Association, which help finance joint ventures and encourage the flow of market information between expatriate high-tech entrepreneurs and their homeland.

Chinese entrepreneurs have become the first or second most prominent source of foreign investment in countries such as Thailand, the Philippines, and Vietnam. These entrepreneurial links are forged through extensive networks of ethnic Chinese: Taiwanese to Thai-Chinese, Hong Kong Chinese to mainland Chinese; American Chinese to Vietnamese Chinese.

Of the entrepreneurs I surveyed, 52% noted that more than half of their domestic working relationships were with Chinese principals—and 39% of their international working relationships were with other Chinese, a percentage that's much higher than one would expect in a multinational. In general, foreign direct investment in the People's Republic reportedly has reached more than $30 billion, most of which has come from Chinese businesspeople in Hong Kong and Taiwan.

But most significant for the emergence of the commonwealth, these investment patterns across borders, forged through cultural links, have become more visible. For example, Western media recently have paid much more attention to Vancouver's expatriate Hong Kong Chinese, who have invested significantly in Canadian real estate and business in preparation for Hong Kong's return to China in 1997.

Of course, the entrepreneurial network that I have been calling the Chinese commonwealth is not a unified interest group or unofficial "nation." According to an old saying, "The Chinese are like a bowl of loose sand." The sudden wealth of expatriate Chinese communities and the new possibilities for business afforded by them still come down to a global patchwork of many small enterprises that, in some cases, have little or no respect or love for one another.

Yet entrepreneurs who are motivated primarily by economic self-interest generally don't let personal animosity get in the way of shrewd business decisions. And with new large-scale business opportunities bankrolled by Chinese money come a range of new financial intermediaries. While these outside deal brokers, bankers, and lawyers are not exactly welcome in the traditional entrepreneur's orbit, they are nevertheless part and parcel of dealing on a broader financial canvas.

"Knowledge Arbitrage" in a New Economy

Inevitably, capital abundance leads to greater business flexibility and mobility. The ability to transfer funds is equivalent to the ability to transfer corporate flags across national boundaries. And making such transfers is much easier when the enterprise is not tied to immovable assets. Thus the Chinese entrepreneur—who may still believe in the importance of tangible goods and a closed circle of family to manage them—now finds himself or herself in an expanding social network, trafficking the most intangible of assets.

Many of today's Chinese businesspeople have successfully made the shift from the role of trader in a relatively small market to that of international arbitrageur. In other words, they've moved from the perspective of individuals clinging to a life raft to a view from above that takes in the whole ocean.

According to the usual definition of arbitrage, Chinese entrepreneurs have been quick to exploit fully the financial anomalies in Chinese markets. Obviously, the Chinese commonwealth encompasses a wide array of disparate growth rates, investor psychologies, and approaches to valuation. The significant capital markets within the network include Hong Kong, Singapore, Taiwan, the United States—and, most recently, the People's Republic of China—yet each of these markets often value assets in completely different ways.

For example, at its height in 1989, the average price/earnings ratio of a share on the Taiwan Stock Exchange was more than seven times greater than the average p/e ratio on the New York Stock Exchange. That meant a U.S. company with an established marketing and sales arm in Taiwan could, after satisfying residency and regulatory requirements, go public in Taiwan, thereby raising "cheap capital." Companies like Wang and Qume were among those attempting such strategies.

But when it comes to the new opportunities available to entrepreneurs in the Chinese commonwealth, I would like to expand the strict definition of arbitrage. Given the strength of the entrepreneurial network, Chinese businesspeople are well positioned to take advantage of other market differences—a process I call *knowledge arbitrage*.

Precisely because of its scale and diversity, the Chinese common-

wealth now includes fundamental differences in labor costs and product markets. Given varying levels of technology development and
resources in different countries, an engineer from Taiwan can start a
company in Silicon Valley, which then carries out low-cost manufacturing on an Indonesian island—with Chinese financing organized by
the government of Singapore.

Labor-cost differences, in fact, offer some of the most dramatic opportunities for knowledge arbitrageurs. For example, making shoes in
Taiwan started in the 1950s as a low-cost commodity manufacturing
industry that took advantage of the country's low labor costs and
Confucian work ethic to produce cheap shoes like plastic sandals for
export. Gradually, manufacturers developed higher priced running shoes
and other products, and labor costs began to skyrocket in Taiwan.

At the same time, business links were forged between Taiwan and
the People's Republic of China, not through official channels but through
gray-market mechanisms. Typically, a cash-rich Taiwanese entrepreneur would create at low cost a "paper" company in Hong Kong, using
it as a trans-shipment point for goods and services between Taiwan
and the cash-starved mainland.

Then, in 1987, Taiwan's shoe companies suddenly began to relocate
their operations to the People's Republic. Manufacturing equipment
was transferred through Hong Kong to the mainland, and key personnel from Taiwan moved as well. The Taiwanese Shoe Association
estimates that up to 80% of Taiwan's shoe companies have moved to
the People's Republic of China in search of labor cost advantages.

Another form of knowledge arbitrage involves differing consumer
trends in the Chinese commonwealth. Knowledge arbitrageurs who
bridge Chinese communities in diverse countries can link products
with markets in innovative ways. For example, the Quanta Group in
Taiwan, a leader in the consumer business, established itself by representing Western companies in Chinese markets. Under David and
John Sun, two brothers who were educated in the United States, the
company brought McDonald's and Disney merchandise outlets to Taiwan in the early 1980s.

In many respects, of course, the political opening of the People's
Republic of China now represents the ultimate arbitrage for entrepreneurs in the commonwealth. China offers a huge pool of low-cost
labor and untapped natural resources to countries like Singapore, in
which labor costs have steadily risen and resources have always been
restricted.

And China's 1.1 billion population of new consumers, who have had little access to outside products for decades, are hungry to buy. The recent run on Avon cosmetic packs and Bausch & Lomb optical products in the People's Republic are just two examples of a wildly shifting consumer focus.

Of course, whether social change can keep pace with China's rapid economic change remains to be seen. The Chinese Communist Party still controls the country's social machinery and numbers its membership at some 50 million people. Yet the People's Republic, where gunfire echoed in the streets a scant four years ago, is also a country where its citizens now can watch MTV and count their stock certificates while munching on Big Macs. Such contradictions—and opportunities—abound for today's Chinese commonwealth and all who can tap into it.

The Future of the Fourth Power

There's an old Chinese saying that goes "the shrewd rabbit has three holes." Taiwanese entrepreneur Steve Tsai has interpreted this to mean having one business base in the People's Republic to represent the future, one in Taiwan to capitalize on the present, and another "hole" in the United States to serve as insurance. By his account, Chinese entrepreneurs want to be where the action is but where the risks are not—and show little inherent loyalty to home.

Steve Tsai's "shrewd rabbit" metaphor is a good representation of how Chinese entrepreneurs view the world today, their position in it, and how they still may need to change. "Doing business is like driving a car," says P.T. De of San Sun Hats. "In the United States, everything has rules and regulations, and you just follow the rules, and it's easy. In Taiwan, even if the light is red, somebody can get through it. If it's green, there still aren't rules to tell you how to go."

Obviously, what I've been calling the Chinese commonwealth contains no official clearinghouse for coordinating joint ventures or operating as a united economic community. Singapore with its sophisticated technological infrastructure, Hong Kong with its capital markets and trading infrastructure, and Taiwan with its incredible foreign exchange reserves are all major power centers. Yet to the extent that Chinese communities remain apolitical, they can't act on their own behalf in most host countries, including the United States.

Still, Chinese-owned trade shows, electronic databases, consulting firms, periodicals on entrepreneurship, investment banks, business schools, and other institutions will expand the reach of the commonwealth in the future. In 1991, Singapore held the First World Chinese Entrepreneurs Convention, which brought together 800 Chinese businesspeople from some 35 countries. The entrepreneurs themselves have begun to recognize the commonwealth for what it is: a new global power base.

At the same time, the Chinese commonwealth is no longer exclusively Chinese. By participating in such a pervasive economic network, potential partners of Chinese entrepreneurs can obtain not only greater access to Chinese-based markets at much lower costs but also access to world markets in general.

Such East-West connections will be particularly important to small and midsize companies looking for ever-more efficient ways of internationalizing at an earlier stage in their development. Chinese entrepreneurs also have a great deal to gain from outside joint-venture partners, especially large ones: for example, new brand names, market information, and professional management structures.

Yet paradoxically, the continued evolution of the commonwealth depends on most of its entrepreneurs continuing to opt for a small-business management model. Through a global network, many small units can come up with a variety of solutions at an acceptable level of risk. While Chinese entrepreneurs are moving clearly toward a new management model, one that encourages growth and an openness to outsiders when a business is ready to take off, most Chinese companies have incentives to remain small, familial organizations. Such a trend is based partly on Chinese cultural biases and partly on what now appears to pay off in the world at large.

In other words, the Confucian tradition of hard work, thrift, and respect for one's social network may provide continuity with the right twist for today's fast-changing markets. And the central strategic question for all current multinationals—be they Chinese, Japanese, or Western—is how to gather and integrate power through many small units. The evolution of a worldwide web of relatively small Chinese businesses, bound by undeniably strong cultural links, offers a working model for the future.

3
Capital Disadvantage: America's Failing Capital Investment System

Michael E. Porter

To compete effectively in international markets, a nation's businesses must continuously innovate and upgrade their competitive advantages. Innovation and upgrading come from sustained investment in physical as well as intangible assets—things like employee skills and supplier relationships. Today the changing nature of competition and the increasing pressure of globalization make investment the most critical determinant of competitive advantage.

Yet the U.S. system of allocating investment capital both within and across companies is failing. This puts American companies in a range of industries at a serious disadvantage in global competition and ultimately threatens the long-term growth of the U.S. economy.

These are the principal findings of a two-year research project sponsored by the Harvard Business School and the Council on Competitiveness, a project that included 18 research papers by 25 academic experts. This article draws on those papers and my research to offer a

Author's note: This article draws heavily on the research and commentary of my colleagues on the project on Capital Choices, cosponsored by the Harvard Business School and the Council on Competitiveness. Rebecca Wayland's research assistance and insights have contributed importantly to this study.

The issues discussed in this article are the subject of a large body of literature, which is extensively referenced in the project papers. Among the more broadly based studies is Michael T. Jacobs, *Short-Term America* (Harvard Business School Press, 1991). Other valuable contributions include the report of the Institutional Investor Project at the Columbia University Center for Law and Economic Studies, *Institutional Investors and Capital Markets: 1991 Update,* and the Symposium on the Structure and Governance of Enterprise, *Journal of Financial Economics,* September 1990.

comprehensive analysis of the causes and recommended cures for the U.S. investment problem.

Critics of U.S. business frequently blame recent competitive short-comings on various issues: a short time horizon, ineffective corporate governance, or a high cost of capital. In fact, these issues are symptoms of a larger problem: the operation of the entire capital investment system. The system includes shareholders, lenders, investment managers, corporate directors, managers, and employees, all of whom make investment choices in a context determined by government regulations and prevailing management practices. The American system creates a divergence of interests among shareholders, corporations, and their managers that impedes the flow of capital to those corporate investments that offer the greatest payoffs. Just as significant, it fails to align the interests of individual investors and corporations with those of the economy and the nation as a whole.

The U.S. system for allocating investment capital has many strengths: efficiency, flexibility, responsiveness, and high rates of corporate profitability. It does not, however, direct capital effectively within the economy to those companies that can deploy it most productively and within companies to the most productive investment projects. As a result, many American companies invest too little, particularly in those intangible assets and capabilities required for competitiveness—R&D, employee training and skills development, information systems, organizational development, and supplier relations. At the same time, many other companies waste capital on investments that have limited financial or social rewards—for example unrelated acquisitions.

The problems in the U.S. system are largely self-created. Through a long series of regulatory and other choices with unintended consequences, changes have occurred in areas such as the pattern of corporate ownership, the way investment choices are made, and the nature of internal capital allocation processes within companies. At the same time, the nature of competition has changed, placing a premium on investment in increasingly complex and intangible forms—the kinds of investment most penalized by the U.S. system.

Finally, the American economy has become far more exposed to global competition, making investment even more important and bringing a cross-section of U.S. companies into contact with companies based in nations with significantly different capital allocation systems. It is this comparison between the U.S. system and other nations' systems that points up the real danger of continuing current practices.

The U.S. system first and foremost advances the goals of shareholders interested in near-term appreciation of their shares—even at the expense of the long-term performance of American companies. It is flexible, capable of rapidly shifting resources among sectors—even if this is not the path to innovation, dynamism, and improved productivity. It helps the United States prosper in some industries because of the high rewards it offers—even as it pressures others toward under- or overinvestment in differing ways.

The systemic nature of the problem also suggests the need to question much of what constitutes the American system of management: its emphasis on autonomy and decentralization, its process of financial control and investment decision making, its heavy use of incentive compensation systems. Failure to change the system will simply ensure the continued competitive decline of key sectors in the U.S. economy.

Yet our analysis of the U.S. investment capital allocation system also reveals how much potential for competitive strength exists in the United States. The United States possesses an enormous pool of investment capital. The problem lies in how this capital is allocated—at what rates and into what kinds of investments. One consideration is whether there is over- or underinvestment. A second is whether an investment is complemented by associated investments—that is, whether there are linkages among different forms of investments. For example, a physical asset such as a new factory may not reach its potential level of productivity unless the company makes parallel investments in intangible assets such as employee training and product redesign. A third consideration is whether private investments also create benefits for society through spillovers or externalities. For example, a company that invests in upgrading its employees and suppliers not only enhances its own competitiveness but also creates better trained workers and stronger suppliers that may allow it to pursue entirely new strategies in the future. Nations that encourage appropriate investment across a wide variety of forms and create these social benefits can leverage their pool of capital to build a strong and competitive national economy.

Meaningful change will be difficult because the American investment problem is far more complex than the conventional wisdom suggests. Many proposals to solve America's investment problem focus on only one aspect of the system, and they ignore the critical connections that tie the system together. To work, reform must address all aspects of the American system, and address them all at once. Policy-makers, institutional investors, and corporate managers must all play a role in creating systemwide change.

Evidence of an American Investment Problem

For more than a decade, anecdotal evidence from managers and academics has suggested that American companies have invested at a lower rate and with a shorter time horizon than German or Japanese competitors. There are a variety of measures of the comparative rates, patterns, and outcomes of U.S. investments and the behavior of U.S. investors that support and expand that earlier view. Among them are the following:

The competitive position of important U.S. industries has declined relative to those of other nations, notably Japan and Germany.

Aggregate investment in property, plant and equipment, and intangible assets, such as civilian R&D and corporate training, is lower in the United States than in Japan and Germany.

Leading American companies in many manufacturing industries such as construction equipment, computers, and tires are outinvested by their Japanese counterparts.

American companies appear to invest at a lower rate than both Japanese and German companies in nontraditional forms such as human resource development, relationships with suppliers, and start-up losses to enter foreign markets.

R&D portfolios of American companies include a smaller share of long-term projects than those of European and Japanese companies.

Hurdle rates used by U.S. companies to evaluate investment projects appear to be higher than estimates of the cost of capital.

U.S. CEOs believe their companies have shorter investment horizons than their international competitors and that market pressures have reduced long-term investment. Foreign CEOs agree.

The average holding period of stocks has declined from more than seven years in 1960 to about two years today.

Long-term growth has declined as an influence on U.S. stock prices.

Many recent U.S. policy proposals such as government funding of specific industries, R&D consortia, and joint production ventures implicitly reflect a private investment problem.

These findings present a broadly consistent picture of lagging American investment. But interestingly, the research has turned up some important complexities that derail simplistic explanations of America's reduced investment levels and shorter time horizon. For example:

The American investment problem varies by industry and even by company. A convincing explanation—and worthwhile remedies—must address these differences.

The United States does well in funding emerging industries and high-risk startup companies that require investments of five years or more. How does a low-investing, short-horizon nation achieve such a performance?

The average profitability of U.S. industry is higher than that in Japan and Germany, yet American shareholders have consistently achieved no better or lower returns than Japanese (and recently German) shareholders. There is thus no simple connection between average corporate returns on investment and long-term shareholder returns, as much conventional wisdom about shareholder value seems to suggest.

U.S. industry has overinvested in some forms, such as acquisitions. How does this overinvestment square with lower average rates of investment and underinvestment in crucial forms such as intangible assets?

There is persuasive evidence that some American companies systematically overinvest—this is documented by studies of the gains achieved from takeovers. Why is it that some companies underinvest while other companies apparently invest too much?

The United States has the most efficient capital markets of any nation and highly sophisticated investors. How can such efficient capital markets be guilty of producing apparently suboptimal investment behavior?

The investment problem seems to be more significant today than it was several decades ago. What accounts for this worsening situation?

Explaining these paradoxes and the differences in investment behavior across industries, companies, and forms of investment is essential to gaining a complete understanding of the American investment problem.

The Determinants of Investment

The determinants of investment can be grouped into three broad categories: the macroeconomic environment; the allocation mecha-

Exhibit I.

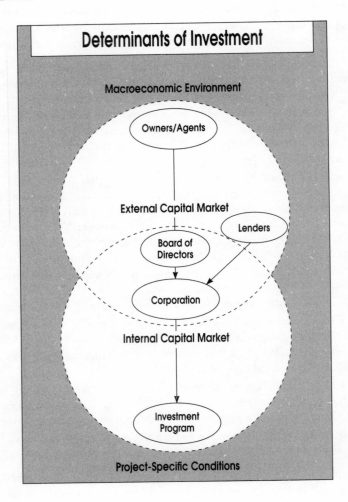

nisms by which capital moves from its holders to investment projects; and the conditions surrounding specific investment projects themselves (see Exhibit I).

The macroeconomic environment establishes the context in which investment by all companies in a nation takes place. A stable and growing economy tends to encourage investment, reassuring investors that returns will persist over the long term. In the United States, high federal budget deficits, low national savings rates, sporadic and unpredictable changes in tax policy, and a consumption-oriented tax code have dampened public and private investment over the past two decades.

Capital allocation mechanisms determine how the available pool of capital in a nation is distributed among industries, companies, and forms of investment. They operate through two distinct but related markets: the external capital market through which holders of equity and debt provide capital to particular companies; and the internal capital market in which companies allocate the internally and externally generated funds at their disposal to particular investment programs. The Harvard Business School Council on Competitiveness research has focused on the operation and linkages between these dual markets and their effects on investment behavior.

Finally, some projects will yield greater payoffs than others, depending on the nature of the industry, the competitive position of the company, and the nation or region in which the investment is made. As my previous research in *The Competitive Advantage of Nations* has indicated, the capacity to invest and innovate depends on the presence of specialized skills, technology, and infrastructure; sophisticated and demanding local customers; capable local suppliers; competitive local companies in closely related industries; and a local environment that encourages vigorous competition.

The External Capital Market

Investment behavior in the external capital market is shaped by four attributes (see Exhibit II). First is the pattern of share ownership and agency relationships—the identity of the owners, the extent of their representation by agents such as pension funds and money managers, and the size of the stakes they hold in companies. Second are owners' and agents' goals, which define the outcomes they seek to achieve through their investment choices. Goals are affected by a number of factors, including whether owners can hold debt and equity jointly and whether there is a principal-agent relationship. Third are the approaches and types of information used by owners and agents to measure and value companies. Fourth are the ways in which owners and agents can influence management behavior in the companies whose shares they own. These four attributes of the external capital market are all interrelated, and over time they will become mutually consistent.

Although exceptions may exist, each nation is characterized by a

Exhibit II.

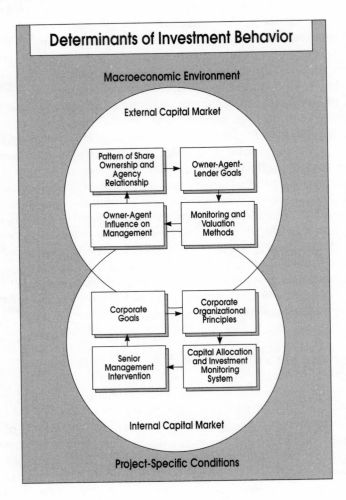

consistent system of influences that affect the majority of investors and corporations. The predominant configuration of the external capital market in the United States is strikingly different from that in Japan and Germany.

In the case of the United States, the attributes combine to create a system distinguished by fluid capital: funds supplied by external capital providers move rapidly from company to company, usually based on perceptions of opportunities for near-term appreciation. In the United

States, publicly traded companies increasingly rely on a transient ownership base comprised of institutional investors, such as pension funds, mutual funds, or other money managers, who act as agents for individual investors. In 1950, such owners accounted for 8% of total equity; by 1990, the figure had reached 60%.

These institutional agents hold highly diversified portfolios with small stakes in many—perhaps hundreds—of companies. For example, in 1990 the California Public Employees Retirement System (CalPERS) reportedly held stock in more than 2,000 U.S. companies; its single largest holding was 0.71% of a company's equity. This fragmented pattern of share ownership is due in part to legal constraints on concentrated ownership, fiduciary requirements that encourage extensive diversification, and investors' strong desire for liquidity.

The goals of American institutional investors are purely financial and are focused on quarterly or annual appreciation of their investment portfolio compared with stock indices. Because managers are measured on their short-term performance, their investment goals understandably focus on the near-term appreciation of shares. Mutual funds and actively managed pension funds—which represent 80% of pension assets—hold their shares, on average, for only 1.9 years.

Because of their fragmented stakes in so many companies, short holding periods, and lack of access to proprietary information through disclosure or board membership, institutional investors tend to base their investment choices on limited information that is oriented toward predicting near-term stock price movements. The system drives them to focus on easily measurable company attributes, such as current earnings or patent approvals, as proxies of a company's value on which to base market timing choices. The value proxies used vary among different classes of companies and can lead to underinvestment in some industries or forms of investment while allowing overinvestment in others. Given the difficulty of outperforming the market with this approach, some institutions have moved to invest as much as 70% to 80% of their equity holdings in index funds. This method of investing capital involves no company-specific information at all.

Finally, in the American system, institutional agents do not sit on corporate boards, despite their large aggregate holdings. As a consequence, they have virtually no direct influence on management behavior. Indeed, with small stakes in the company and an average holding period of two years or less, institutional agents are not viewed by management as having a legitimate right to serious attention.

The Japanese and German systems are markedly different (see Ex-

Exhibit III.

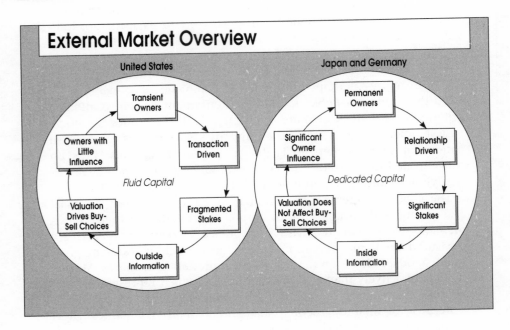

hibit III). Overall, Japan and Germany have systems defined by dedicated capital. The dominant owners are principals rather than agents; they hold significant stakes, rather than small, fragmented positions. These owners are virtually permanent; they seek long-term appreciation of their shares, which they hold in perpetuity. Unlike the U.S. system, in which the goals are driven solely by the financial transaction, the goals in these systems are driven by relationships. Suppliers and customers own stakes in each other, not to profit from the share ownership itself but to cement their business relationship.

The pattern of ownership and the goals of owners directly affect monitoring and valuation approaches. Since owners hold significant shares for long periods of time, they have both the incentive and the ability to engage in extensive and ongoing information gathering about the companies they own. And unlike the American system, principal Japanese and German owners are driven not by the need to make quick decisions on buying or selling stock for profit-taking but by the desire to assess the ongoing prospects of the company. They therefore command the respect of management, have access to inside information concerning the company, and, particularly in Germany, can exert considerable influence on management behavior.

Interestingly, while the permanent Japanese and German owners hold their company shares for long periods of time, the nonpermanent owners in these countries are prone to high-velocity stock churning, turning their shares over more frequently than owners do in the United States, and basing their investment decisions on even less information. While roughly 70% of Japanese stock is held for the long term, the remaining 30% is traded at such a rapid frequency that the average rate of trading in Japan is similar to the rate of trading in the United States. Yet in both Japan and Germany, share prices and pressure from nonpermanent owners and agents have virtually no direct or indirect influence on management decisions.

The Internal Capital Market

The internal capital market, the system by which corporations allocate available capital from both internal and external sources to investment projects within and across business units, mirrors the external capital market. The four attributes that shape investment behavior in the internal capital market parallel those that shape the external market (see Exhibit II). These four attributes are the particular goals that corporations set; the organizational principles that govern the relationship between senior management and units; the information and methods used to value and monitor internal investment options; and the nature of interventions by senior managers into investment projects.

An important aspect is highly imperfect information about future prospects and information asymmetries between capital holders—top managers—and those overseeing specific investment opportunities— business unit or functional managers. How a company organizes and manages its operations will affect the information that is available and the investments made by the company.

The U.S. internal market system is structured to maximize measurable investment returns. It is organized to stress financial returns, to motivate managers to achieve financial targets, to raise accountability for unit financial, and to base decision making and investment allocation heavily on financial criteria.

In the U.S. system, corporate goals center on earning high returns on investment and maximizing current stock prices. Management exercises the dominant influence on corporate goals, interpreting signals about desired behavior from the external capital market, influenced by compensation based on current accounting profits or unrestricted stock options that heighten stock price sensitivity.

Boards, which have come to be dominated by outside directors with no other links to the company, exert only limited influence on corporate goals. The presence of knowledgeable major owners, bankers, customers, and suppliers on corporate boards has diminished. An estimated 74% of the directors of the largest U.S. corporations are now outsiders, and 80% are CEOs of other companies. The move to outside directors arose out of calls for greater board objectivity. But the cost of objectivity has been directors who lack ties to the company and whose own companies are in unrelated businesses. As a consequence, they often lack the time or ability to absorb the vast amounts of information required to understand a company's internal operations. Moreover, most directors have limited stakes in the companies they oversee. While the median aggregate holdings of the board account for an estimated 3.6% of equity, many directors have no shares at all or only nominal holdings.

In terms of the organizational principles, the structure of American companies has undergone a significant change over the past two decades, with a profound impact on the internal capital market. Many American companies have embraced a form of decentralization that involves highly autonomous business units and limited information flows both vertically and horizontally. As a consequence, top management has become more distanced from the details of the business. Senior managers have little knowledge or experience in many of the company's businesses and often lack the technical background and experience to understand the substance of products or processes— partly because such knowledge is unnecessary in the typical decision-making process. Understandably, decision making in this system involves comparatively limited dialogue among functions or business units. Extensive diversification by American companies into unrelated areas has accentuated these tendencies and has further impeded the flow of information throughout the organization.

Both as a cause and an effect, capital budgeting in the U.S. system takes place largely through "by the numbers" exercises that require unit or functional managers to justify investment projects quantitatively. The system rarely treats investments such as R&D, advertising, or market entry as investments; rather they are negotiated as part of the annual budgeting process, which is primarily driven by a concern

Exhibit IV.

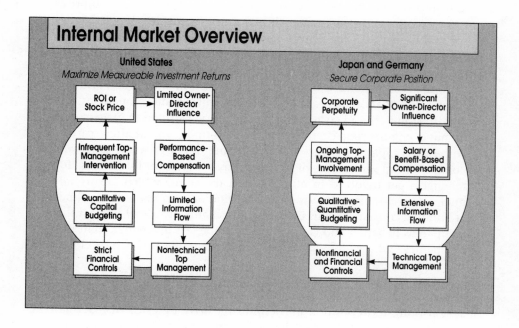

Internal Market Overview

United States
Maximize Measureable Investment Returns

Japan and Germany
Secure Corporate Position

for current profitability. Intangible investments such as cross-functional training for workers may not even be tracked in the financial system—and thus may be sacrificed in the name of profitability.

Senior managers intervene infrequently, exerting central control through strict financial budgeting and control systems that focus on the unit's performance. Investment projects are placed on accelerated schedules under tight budgets, and senior managers step in only when financial measures indicate that a project is failing.

Both the Japanese and German systems are profoundly different from the American system (see Exhibit IV). For both, the predominant aim is to secure the position of the corporation and ensure the company's continuity. Information flow is far more extensive, and financial criteria play less of a determining role in investment decisions than in the United States.

In both systems, the perpetuation of the enterprise is the dominant goal. In Japan, this goal is reinforced by the fact that most directors are members of management; moreover, lifetime or permanent employment is the norm in significant-sized companies. In Germany, the

supervisory board consists of representatives of banks and other significant owners, and in large companies, 50% of the board comprises
representatives of employees. All major constituencies thus influence
corporate goals. As far as top managers' performance incentives are
concerned, in both Germany and Japan, current earnings or share
prices play only a modest role in promotion or compensation.

Companies practice a form of decentralization that involves much
greater information flow among multiple units in the company as well
as with suppliers and customers. Japanese and German managers tend
to have engineering or technical backgrounds, spend their careers
with one company, advance through tenure in one or a few units, and
possess a deep knowledge of the company's important businesses. Top
managers get involved in all important decisions, which are usually
made after extensive face-to-face consultation and discussions aimed
at building consensus. This is both an effect and a cause of the fact that
companies in Japan and Germany tend to be less diversified than U.S.
companies; where diversification occurs, it tends to be into closely
related businesses.

Financial control and capital budgeting are part of the management
process—but technical considerations and a company's desire to ensure its long-term position in the industry drive investments. German
companies are particularly oriented to attaining technical leadership;
Japanese companies especially value market share, new product development, technological position, and participation in businesses and
technologies that will be critical in the next decade.

In comparing the U.S., Japanese, and German systems, important
differences in management practices emerge. For example, American
managerial innovations have resulted in less face-to-face consultation,
information flow, and direct management involvement in investment
choices—all in the name of responsiveness and efficiency. Many of
these innovations were the American solution to the problems of size
and diversity that arose in the diversification boom of the 1960s and
preceded the major changes that have occurred in the external capital
market.

In contrast, Japanese innovations in management, such as just-in-
time manufacturing, total quality management, and greater cross-
functional coordination, have resulted in more vertical and horizontal
information flow and involvement by management in decisions. This
comes at the expense of efficiency in the short run—but often results
in greater effectiveness and efficiency over time, as knowledge and
capabilities accumulate.

The extensive flow of information is perhaps the most potent strength of the Japanese and German systems. Ironically, the U.S. system, designed to boost management responsiveness to the marketplace, actually limits and constrains managers in responding effectively by limiting the information used in decisions, working against crucial forms of investment, and all but blocking the achievement of cross-unit synergies.

Comparative Systems of Capital Allocation

The external and internal capital allocation markets are linked; together they combine to form a self-reinforcing national system for allocating investment capital. The way companies allocate capital internally is influenced by their perceptions of how equity holders and lenders value companies. Conversely, the perceptions of owners and agents about how companies are managed and how they allocate their funds internally will influence the way in which investors value companies and the way in which they attempt to affect management behavior. The use of stock options in management compensation creates a direct link between stock market valuation and management behavior.

Overall, the nature of the American system of capital allocation creates tendencies and biases in investment behavior that differ greatly from those in Japan and Germany (see Exhibit V). The American system:

Is less supportive of investment overall because of its sensitivity to current returns for many established companies combined with corporate goals that stress current stock price over long-term corporate value. This explains why the average level of investment in American industry lags that in both Japan and Germany.

Favors those forms of investment for which returns are most readily measurable—reflecting the importance of financial returns and the valuation methods used by investors and managers. This explains why the United States underinvests, on average, in intangible assets, where returns are more difficult to measure.

Is prone to underinvest in some forms and, simultaneously, to overinvest in others. The U.S. system favors acquisitions, which involve assets that can be easily valued, over internal development projects that are more difficult to value and constitute a drag on current earnings. The greater overall rate of acquisitions in the United States is consistent with these differences.

Exhibit V.

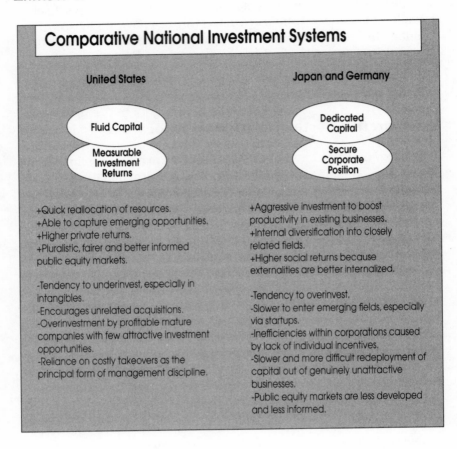

Encourages investment in some sectors while limiting it in others. It is at its best with companies in obviously high-technology or emerging industries, especially those with rapid growth and high perceived upside potential. The American system also supports investment in turnarounds or other situations of clear discontinuity. In these cases, investors recognize that current earnings are irrelevant and seek other value proxies such as patents, new product announcements, research pipelines, and growth of new service locations that are more supportive of investment. This explains why the United States invests more than its competitors in some industries but less in others, why it performs well in funding emerging companies, and why it often awards high stock prices to turnarounds with current losses.

Allows some types of companies to overinvest. For example, case studies of takeovers demonstrate a tendency by managers to continue investing (and to continue accumulating cash) as long as current earnings are satisfactory or until the company's situation so clearly deteriorates that it changes hands. This explains why some companies waste resources while American industry as a whole lags in investment.

It is important to note that there are companies and owners in the United States who operate differently from the predominant national system—who have overcome the disadvantages of the American system and achieve superior results. Examples of these are companies that have permanent and active family ownership, such as Cargill, Hallmark, Hewlett-Packard, Motorola, and others, which seem to enjoy competitive advantages in investing.

For example, two of Motorola's most important businesses, semiconductors and cellular telephones, were almost canceled in their early stages because they did not generate clearly measurable financial returns. Robert Galvin, a member of the founding family of Motorola and the company's chief executive officer, intervened in both cases and continued the investments. In the semiconductor situation, Galvin overrode the decision of his board of directors. Today semiconductors and cellular telephones form the foundation for a large part of Motorola's business, generating substantial financial returns for its shareholders.

Investors such as Warren Buffett's Berkshire Hathaway have succeeded by, in effect, becoming permanent owners of acquired companies, supporting capable managements and concentrating on building the company. Overall, however, the U.S. system as it applies to the great majority of American owners, investors, managers, directors, and employees works at cross-purposes to investment decisions that will produce competitive companies and a strong national economy.

Trade-Offs Among Systems

While the U.S. system has significant disadvantages, it would be incorrect to conclude that it lacks any advantages or that the systems of Japan and Germany are ideal. Each national system necessarily involves trade-offs; thus while the U.S. system needs reform, it also embodies important strengths that should be preserved.

The U.S. system, for example, is good at reallocating capital among sectors, funding emerging fields, and achieving high private returns each period. These benefits, of course, come at a price. The responsiveness and flexibility of the system are achieved at the expense of failing to invest enough to secure competitive positions in existing businesses, investing in the wrong forms, and overinvesting in some circumstances.

The Japanese and German systems also have strengths and weaknesses. These systems encourage continued, aggressive investment to upgrade capabilities and increase productivity in existing businesses. They also encourage internal diversification into related fields, building upon and extending corporate capabilities. These qualities, however, also exact a cost in Japan and Germany. For example, these systems create their own tendency to overinvest in capacity, to proliferate products, and to maintain unprofitable businesses indefinitely in the name of corporate perpetuity. They also exhibit a slower tendency to redeploy capital out of genuinely weak businesses and an inability to enter emerging fields rapidly, particularly through start-ups. Managers generally have fewer performance incentives, and companies have a harder time dismissing poor performers.

In general, the U.S. system is geared to optimize short-term private returns; the Japanese and German systems optimize long-term private and social returns. By focusing on long-term corporate position and creating an ownership structure and governance process that incorporate the interests of employees, suppliers, customers, and the local community, the Japanese and German systems better capture the social benefits that private investment can create.

There is some evidence that the national systems are converging—that Japan and Germany are moving toward a more American-like system. Japanese banks may be forced to liquidate some of their equity holdings to maintain adequate cash balances; in Germany, there are proposals to limit bank ownership of equity. Yet these changes are modest—if Japanese or German owners are forced to sell some of their equity holdings, they will first sell their nonpermanent shares that are actively traded and have little influence on corporate behavior. Any major change in Japan and Germany would represent a substantial threat to those nations' economies due to their relatively uninformed traded capital markets.

Changes are also occurring in the United States, as institutional investors have discussions with management and some boards take a more active role in corporations. As in Japan and Germany, these changes appear isolated and sporadic, and the underlying causes of the U.S. investment problem remain the same. Neither small improvements in the United States nor hopes that Japan and Germany will change are substitutes for meaningful reform of the U.S. system.

The Case of Cummins Engine

Cummins Engine Company, a $3.4 billion industrial corporation illustrates how a creative management team can structure a "privately owned, publicly traded" American company, approximating some of the advantages in the Japanese and German systems. In 1990, Cummins chairman and chief executive officer, Henry Schacht, concluded a deal that resulted in 40% of the company's stock being in the hands of patient investors, including three of its important business partners, company employees, and the founding Miller family. While it is still too early to evaluate the arrangement definitively, recent results indicate that Cummins' strategy may be paying off.

The Cummins story begins in 1919, when the company was founded in Columbus, Indiana. After World War II, Cummins enjoyed rapid growth into the 1970s. By 1979, Cummins Engine was the world leader in large, heavy diesel engines, with a 46% share of the market for over-the-road trucks. Following a succession of financings, the family stake in the company diminished; by 1980, 75% of the company's shares on the New York Stock Exchange were held by fragmented public investors.

In the 1980s, three factors combined to change the diesel engine market. First, the market's overall growth slowed significantly. Second, the emergence of energy efficiency and clean air as important policy issues put increased pressure on Cummins to invest in R&D—an expenditure that had already mushroomed from $22 million in 1971 to $68 million in 1980. Third, foreign competition intensified as Japanese producers prepared to enter the U.S. market armed with an estimated 30% cost advantages.

To respond to these challenges, Cummins embarked on a three-part strategy supported by an ambitious investment program. Cummins broadened its traditional product line within the heavy-duty markets and expanded into smaller diesel engines; entered the non-truck engine markets and developed its international operations; and initiated a full-scale restructuring program designed to reduce its costs by 30%, with prices scheduled to come down with costs. Cummins estimated the three measures would cost $1 billion; the company's total market value was $250 million.

By 1985, Cummins' strategy had yielded a new product line and a 5% reduction in costs. That year, however, Japanese producers entered the U.S. diesel market with products priced 30% below Cummins'. Faced with this challenge, Cummins chose to cut its prices to match the Japanese competitors, even though its costs had not yet fallen to that level—thereby sacrificing profits rather than market share. As a consequence, Cummins suffered losses for the next three years, while reaching cost parity with the Japanese by the late 1980s.

In 1989, Cummins faced a different kind of challenge. After Hanson PLC, known for buying companies and dramatically cutting costs and investment, acquired a 9.8% stake in the company, Cummins' customers became alarmed at the threat of future cuts in Cummins' investment program. In July 1989, the Miller family took the unprecedented step of buying back the Hanson shares, ending the uncertainty. However, almost immediately, Hong Kong investor Industrial Equity Pacific began acquiring a large position in Cummins and demanded a seat on the board. Cummins initiated a lawsuit against IEP, which ultimately sold its stake at a loss in 1991.

These two threats convinced Schacht and other top Cummins managers that the interests of the current shareholders and the interests of customers, employees, the community, and managers were in danger of diverging—and that Cummins' strategy was potentially in jeopardy. To address this issue, Schacht sought to revise Cummins' ownership structure.

In 1990, Schacht concluded a deal with three important business partners. Ford, which bought a 10% stake, Tenneco-J.I. Case, a 10% stake, and Kubota, a 5% stake. In addition, Ford took an option for an additional 10% of Cummins' shares. Each owner paid a 25% premium above Cummins' then-current stock price of $52 per share and agreed not to sell the stock for six years. The two largest shareholders, Ford and Tenneco, each received a seat on the Cummins board of directors. Financially, the deal targeted a 15% return on equity over a seven-year business cycle.

The Miller family retained a 4% stake in the company; employees held 10%. Together, these stable, long-term shareholders held 40% of the company's equity. Interestingly, other Cummins' customers applauded the move, even though it involved their competitors, citing the advantages of stable ownership and better products for all customers.

Under the new ownership structure, representatives of Ford and Tenneco participated on the board and actively supported the investment program. Senior managers worked without employment contracts, preventing management entrenchment and allowing strong board intervention. Accompanying the shift in ownership at Cummins were several reorganizations designed to streamline operations.

In 1990, Cummins continued to suffer reversals, this time a result of the recession and the onset of competition from a revitalized Detroit Diesel Corporation. In January 1991, Cummins stock hit a low of $32.50 per share.

Recent indications, however, suggest that Cummins' nine-year effort is beginning to pay off. New product introductions have been successful; in the traditional heavy duty truck market, Cummins' market share appears to have stabilized and begun a recovery. The company's international off-highway business has continued to grow. The Japanese challengers have exited the major U.S. markets. During 1991, Cummins reached breakeven and showed a profit for the first quarter of 1992. Finally, Cummins' stock rose to $76 per share in June 1992, a 100% increase over its $32.50 price of January 1991.

—Rebecca Wayland

Proposals for Reform

Overall, the American system for capital allocation is not serving the American economy well. None of the participants in the system is satisfied, and each one blames the other for the problem. American managers complain that owners and agents do not have the company's long-term interests at heart and are seeking only high, short-term profits. Institutional investors see managers as self-serving, over-paid, and underperforming when it comes to shareholder value. Owners are dismayed that many institutional investors underperform market averages. Small shareholders feel vulnerable and powerless. Employees fear a system that may cost them their jobs. Communities and their elected representatives worry about takeovers that threaten people's jobs, income, and the stability of the whole community.

Each group is behaving rationally—given the current circumstances. All are trapped in a system that ultimately serves the interests of no one. Each is pursuing its own narrow goals within the system—but the goals operate at cross-purposes.

Not surprisingly, there are calls for reform and regulation from all sides. Also, not surprisingly, many of the current proposals for reform would actually prove counterproductive, treating either symptoms or only a fragment of the problem and, in the process, further skewing the operation of the larger system.

One set of proposals, for example, seeks to slow down securities trading by taxing securities transactions or increasing margin requirements. These proposals, however, merely increase the inefficiency of the equity markets without addressing the underlying problem—the lack of alignment between investors' and managers' goals. Another set of proposals seeks to reduce the rate of trading by limiting corporate disclosures—for example, doing away with quarterly financial reports. The most likely result of this reform, however, would probably be to make investors even less informed.

A third group of proposals seeks to rebalance the relative power of owners and managers, for instance, by strengthening the proxy system or increasing the number of outside directors. These proposals also fail to address the systemic nature of the problem. "Objective" outside directors, for example, are closely aligned with management, they are not as expert in the business, and they lack the detailed knowledge of the company needed for a truly objective evaluation of a business's prospects. Moreover, if the goals of owners, managers, and shareholders remain unaligned, strengthening one player at the expense of another will only tip the system in one particular direction.

A fourth set of proposals would increase the use of stock options in management compensation. Yet unless restrictions were placed on managers' ability to exercise those options, this step would only heighten current pressures toward maximizing current stock price.

Finally, there are proposals that address the investment problem indirectly while seeking to improve overall U.S. competitiveness; for example, calls for providing government subsidies to particular sectors, creating joint production ventures, and relaxing U.S. antitrust laws. These measures may allow companies to economize on investment—but they run the risk of blunting innovation and undermining competitiveness. They do not address the reasons why companies seem unable to make the investments needed for competitiveness. The only real solution to the failure of the U.S. capital allocation system is to address the system as a "system."

Directions For Systemic Reform

The aim of reform should be to create a system in which managers will make investments that maximize the long-term value of their companies. The interests of capital providers must be aligned with those of the corporation so that investors seek out high-quality information that fosters more appropriate investment choices. CEOs and top managers must organize and manage their companies in ways that encourage investment in the forms that build competitiveness. And public policymakers must craft laws and regulations designed to align private returns and the public good. Policymakers should not create protective measures to shield companies from these pressures but can exert constructive pressures on companies and managers, provided they have appropriate goals and information.

In all of this, it is essential to remember that the United States is an internally consistent system with many component parts. Reform should therefore come through a series of changes, ideally all at once. In addition, appropriate reform will require that each important constituency in the system give up some of its perceived benefits. For example, institutions should not expect to gain greater influence over management without giving up some of their current trading flexibility; management should not expect informed and committed owners without giving them a real voice in decisions.

Reform is needed in five broad areas:

1. Improve the macroeconomic environment; enlarging the pool of capital and increasing the stability of the environment will reduce risk premiums and lower the cost of capital. Public and private sector saving should be increased and a more stable macroeconomic environment created to encourage a stronger foundation for investment.

2. Expand true ownership throughout the system; the current concept of ownership in the U.S. system is too limited, involving just capital, and ownership is largely restricted to outside shareholders. Outside owners should be encouraged to hold larger stakes and to take a more active and constructive role in companies. Directors, managers, employees, and even customers and suppliers should all hold positions as important corporate owners.

3. Align the goals of capital providers, corporations, directors, managers, employees, customers, suppliers, and society. It is possible to create a system of incentives and to alter the rules in a way that helps align the goals of all these constituencies, which share an inherent long-term commonality of interest.

4. Improve the information used in decision making; even if goals are better aligned, the quality of information used to allocate capital throughout the system will affect investment choices. This means greater access to information that better reflects true corporate performance and more use of qualitative assessments of a company's performance and capabilities.

5. Foster more productive modes of interaction and influence among capital providers, corporations, and business units.

Accomplishing these reforms will require changes on the part of government, institutional investors, directors, and managers.

Implications for Public Policy

Government, through policies, laws, and regulations, plays a decisive role in creating a nation's system for allocating investment capital. The current U.S. system reflects explicit regulatory choices, most of which emerged in the 1930s to deal with abuses in the financial markets at that time. Yet the cumulative effects of regulation have had unintended consequences for U.S. corporations; these consequences have never been carefully examined.

The following reforms rest on principles that differ markedly from those that have defined the regulatory framework of the traditional U.S. system. It is possible to modify incentives and eliminate unneeded regulatory guidelines to encourage more competitive investment behavior and, at the same time, avoid abuses. For example, current regulations limit the size of ownership stakes to prevent abuses by large owners. A better approach would be to broaden corporate ownership and align the goals of capital providers, corporations, managers, employees, and society. Through this approach, capital providers would become knowledgeable and constructive participants rather than adversaries.

Remove restrictions on investor share ownership; encourage long-term employee ownership; lower tax barriers to holding significant private ownership stakes. It is essential to modify the structure of corporate ownership. The regulations and tax policies that artificially restrict the ability of investors to hold significant corporate stakes should be reexamined. Ownership by employees is desirable, provided that employee owners are long term rather than transient. Under this provision, the market would continue to have the strength of a wide investor base, while gaining the benefit of owners with larger stakes in particular companies. The large number of substantial U.S. institutional investors will prevent any undue concentration of economic power.

Create a long-term equity investment incentive. The single most powerful tool for modifying the goals of owners and agents is a significant incentive for making long-term investments in corporate equity. This proposal aims to change the concept of ownership and the approach to valuing companies and, at the same time, to encourage the broad form of investment where the social benefits are the greatest.

Such an incentive would be carefully designed and narrowly drawn. It would apply only to investments in corporate equity of operating companies, and it would not apply to capital gains from investments in nonoperating companies holding real estate or other financial assets. Capital gains from bond appreciation, real estate appreciation, collectibles, and other sources would also be excluded. The incentive would require a minimum five-year holding period, with greater incentives provided for even longer holdings. It would be applied prospectively, limited to new investments and new gains.

The enactment of such an incentive would lead to changes throughout the entire system by changing the goals of owners and agents. Owners would begin to favor agents who deliver a greater proportion of income in the form of long-term equity gains and to penalize those who realize only short-term gains from rapid trading. Institutional investors, in turn, would modify their monitoring and valuation approaches, seeking out companies with attractive prospects five or more years in the future. A further consequence would be the development and distribution of better information, detailing the investment programs of companies and their long-term prospects, including physical and intangible assets.

If the long-term equity incentive is to have its full impact, it should be extended to currently untaxed investors, such as pension funds that account for a substantial fraction of equity capital and trading. The most practical way to do this is to pass through an equity investment incentive to pension or annuity beneficiaries. Beneficiaries would pay a rate of tax that varied depending on the source of their pension income. The effect of instituting such an incentive would be to create pressures from pension beneficiaries and trustees on their investment managers to deliver a higher and higher proportion of income from long-term equity gains. It should also be noted that extending the long-term equity incentive to pension beneficiaries extends the tax benefit to the U.S. work force, not just to Americans with high incomes.

Eliminate restrictions on joint ownership of debt and equity. Financial institutions should be allowed to hold equity for investment purposes in companies to which they have provided debt financing. Debt holders who also hold equity have greater incentive to invest in information and monitoring and to provide new debt financing for worthy projects.

Reduce the extent of subsidies for investment in real estate. U.S. tax policy has led to a disproportionate investment in real estate compared with other forms of investment that create greater social returns. Future investment incentives should redress this imbalance, favoring R&D, corporate equity, and training, rather than real estate.

Modify accounting rules so that earnings better reflect corporate performance. Because many of the most important forms of investment must be expensed under current accounting standards, accounting earnings are a flawed measure of true earnings. The accounting profession should create new standards for accounting for intangible assets such as R&D.

Expand public disclosure to reduce the cost of assessing true corporate value. Disclosure should be extended to include areas such as a company's expenditures on training, its stock of patents, or the share of sales contributed by new products, information that provides important measures of long-term corporate value.

Allow disclosure of "insider" information to significant long-term owners, under rules that bar trading on it. A small group of institutions and other owners who have held a significant ownership stake for a qualifying period—1% or more for one year or more—should have access to more complete information about company prospects than is required to be disclosed publicly, provided they do not disclose the information to third parties. Greater disclosure would open up an avenue for significant long-term owners to have a more informed dialogue with management, and it would support more informed valuation based on long-term prospects.

Loosen restrictions on institutional board membership. A direct role for significant owners on boards of directors will make boards more representative of long-term owner interest—provided, that is, that the goals of owners and managers have been realigned.

Encourage board representation by significant customers, suppliers, financial advisers, employees, and community representatives. The current trend in board membership has created boards populated by busy, underinformed CEOs. A far better approach would be to create a role on boards of directors for significant customers, suppliers, investment bankers, employees, and others linked closely to the company and with a direct interest in its long-term prosperity.

Codify long-term shareholder value rather than current stock price as the appropriate corporate goal. Existing corporate law identifies long-term shareholder value as the appropriate corporate goal. In practice, however, short-term stock price may take precedence as managers or directors who clearly compromise short-term shareholder returns are often subject to lawsuits. To remedy this situation, long-term shareholder value should be identified as the explicit corporate goal. The burden of proof should shift so that managers must explain any decision that is not consistent with long-term shareholder value.

Extend tax preferences only to those stock options and stock purchase plans with restrictions on selling. The use of unrestricted stock options and employee stock purchase plans fails to make managers and employees true owners because managers are prone to sell shares based on short-term stock price movements. To qualify for tax benefits, such plans should be restricted in terms of holding period and percentage of shares sold at any one time.

Provide investment incentives for R&D and training. Making the existing R&D tax credit permanent and creating a parallel tax credit for training investments would help stimulate private investments that become valuable national assets.

Implications for Institutional Investors

The American system of capital allocation creates perverse outcomes for institutional investors, especially for pension funds. These institutions should be the ideal long-term investors. Instead, the American system produces the paradoxical situation in which many institutions are entrusted with funds for extremely long periods, yet they trade actively. Transaction costs mean that many institutions underperform the market. Institutions are at odds with management, whom they see as misapplying corporate resources, yet they feel powerless to do anything about it. And worst of all, institutions are trapped as crucial actors in a system that undermines the long-term earning power of the American companies on which they have ultimately to depend.

Even without public policy changes, action by institutions can change this system. First and foremost, institutions must understand why managements view them as adversaries. They must understand the subtle consequences of their monitoring and valuation practices on corporate investment behavior. And they must recognize that greater influence over management will require less flexibility, slower trading, and greater knowledge of and concern for company fundamentals. Here are some specific changes institutional investors can pursue:

Increase the size of stakes. Increasing the size of stakes will help align the goals of investors and companies, improve the ability of investors to conduct in-depth research on the companies whose shares they hold, and send signals that institutions are serious owners who are interested in the long-term performance of the company.

Reduce turnover and transaction costs. Institutional investors underperform the market largely because of the transaction costs associated with the high turnover of investments. Reducing stock turnover will improve the return that institutions provide to their clients.

Select companies more carefully based on fundamental earning power. Companies with sustained growth potential and earning power will ultimately be rewarded with higher stock prices, even in the current system. The focus of valuation models should shift in this direction. To address information costs, institutions might also form syndicates in which one institution acts as the lead owner in the relationship.

Encourage changes in agent measurement and evaluation systems to reflect long-term investment performance. A new bargain between owners and institutional agents should shift the measurement and reward system toward fees tied to annual or multiyear results and ongoing reporting of fully loaded transaction costs from trading.

Transform interactions with management to productive, advisory discussions. Current interactions between institutional investors and managements are too often cat-and-mouse games played around guessing next period's earnings. What is needed instead are substantive discussions about the long-run competitive position of the company.

Create special funds to test these new approaches. Institutions should create special funds earmarked for long-term investing in significant corporate stakes in exchange for greater influence over management. If necessary, new agreements with owners would be drafted, modifying the funds' fiduciary responsibilities.

Support systemic public policy changes. By supporting the public policy reforms outlined above, institutional investors can help balance and integrate the American system.

Some institutions will resist these changes; they involve new skills, a new definition of investment success, and reductions in liquidity and flexibility. But institutional investors will realize big direct benefits—and benefit further by the creation of stronger, more competitive U.S. companies, on which their portfolios ultimately depend.

The Case of Thermo Electron Corporation

Thermo Electron Corporation, a $676 million company with products in a variety of high-technology fields, illustrates how a large company can structure itself within the U.S. capital allocation system to overcome the market's pressure toward underinvestment and to create opportunities for smaller, riskier, high-growth divisions.

Since its founding by George Hatsopoulos in 1959, Thermo Electron has grown from a startup focusing on high-technology capital equipment to a *Fortune* "500" company with products and research operations in the environmental, energy, metals processing, and biomedical fields. As Thermo Electron increased its portfolio of high-technology activities, its image in the capital markets became that of a large, mature company rather than an entrepreneurial venture. The startup losses required to develop and commercialize new technologies drained corporate earnings while the growth consolidated financial results. Hatsopoulos, deeply concerned about the high effective cost of equity capital in the United States, set out to devise a way to finance the expansion of Thermo Electron that minimized the cost of funds and motivated employees. In 1983, he began the practice of issuing minority stakes in promising high-technology divisions to the public.

One example of how the practice works—and why it is important—is the spin-off Thermo Cardiosystems, Inc. (TCI), which is currently commercializing its research on HeartMate, implantable cardiac-assist devices (called "ventricular assist devices" or VADs) that could ultimately offer an alternative to heart transplants. The initial research on HeartMate lasted 22 years and cost a total of $50 million, with grants from the National Institutes of Health providing the funding. The research was conducted at Thermo Electron and later at Thermedics, a division that was one of Hatsopoulos's early partial spin-offs. When the product reached the commercialization stage in 1988, the grant began to diminish substantially. Initial product tests for HeartMate had been promising. However, it would take at least another seven years of investment to complete the regulatory process, build manufacturing facilities, and develop the market. This need for continued investment threatened to drag down the earnings of the parent.

In 1988, the company created Thermo Cardiosystems, Inc. and sold a 40% stake on the American Stock Exchange. The partial spin-off shifted TCI's ownership structure from a fragmented group of Thermo Electron and Thermedics investors to a structure in which Thermedics-Thermo Electron owned 60%, and a number of other investors, who were specifically interested in the long-term development of the heart technology, owned the balance. The partial spin-off also allowed TCI to raise $14.5 million in new equity at a far lower cost than its parent. TCI managers and employees received options in TCI stock, undiluted by the performance of the larger corporation.

As the controlling investor in TCI, Thermo Electron remained actively involved in its operations. Thermo Electron top managers were active members of TCI's board of directors (7 of whom were insiders), reviewed its five-year plan and quarterly financial results (often benchmarking them against other divisions), met with managers each month, and engaged in frequent brainstorming sessions to resolve divisional problems. Employees from the parent corporation's research department and from other divisions shared specialized expertise in medical-related areas, and in the process of making the transition from research to manufacturing and sales. Top managers' compensation plans included options in the stock of other Thermo Electron companies to encourage this cooperation. The parent also provided cost-effective and sophisticated administrative services that TCI could not support independently.

Since 1989, TCI has continued its investment in HeartMate, receiving Food and Drug Administration approval for clinical trials, implanting the VAD in over 80 patients worldwide, and establishing 16 FDA-approved test centers in the United States and four sites overseas. In the marketplace, TCI has benefited from the credibility with hospitals and customers in the medical field established by other Thermo Electron products. Although the commercialization process is still underway, TCI managers believe that the partial sale strategy created by George Hatsopoulos has already been instrumental in supporting the investment and other activities needed to bring HeartMate to the medical market.

—Rebecca Wayland

Implications for Corporations

Managers are not simply victims of the American system; they have helped create it. Managers have not only shaped the internal market through organizational and managerial practices, but they have also defined their relationship with the external market through such things as board composition, disclosure practices, and the nature of discussions with investors. American managers can play the leadership role in redefining the U.S. capital allocation system; they are the group best positioned to make changes in the current system and to benefit most from reform.

They also may have the most to change. Stated boldly, our research suggests the need to reexamine much of what constitutes the U.S. system of management, with its extreme approach to managing decentralization, its limited flow of information, its heavy use of certain types of incentive compensation systems, and its reliance on financial control and quantitative capital budgeting processes. This system, a post-World War II innovation, carries subtle costs for investment behavior, particularly investments in intangible and nontraditional forms. Some of the most significant changes that management can initiate are the following:

Seek long-term owners and give them a direct voice in governance. The most basic weakness in the American system is transient ownership. However, managers seem to underestimate their ability to do anything about this fundamental problem. As a remedy, managers should seek to have a smaller number of long-term or nearly permanent owners, thus creating a hybrid structure of a "privately held" and publicly traded company. Having fewer long-term owners would alter virtually every facet of the owner-management relationship—including governance, information sharing, measurement, and valuation.

Refrain from erecting artificial antitakeover defenses that insulate management. In the absence of pressure from owners and directors on managers for long-term performance, takeovers are a necessary form of oversight. There have been, however, some inappropriate takeovers, and most takeovers occur only after a prolonged period of corporate decline. The solution is not to erect antitakeover provisions. Rather, it is to reshape the American system so that takeovers are limited to those situations where they are an appropriate response to management's failure to build a long-term competitive position for the company.

See management buyouts as a second-best solution. Management buyouts are only a second-best solution to the problems of the American system. Invariably, the controlling owner in management buyouts is a transaction-driven, financial owner who seeks to realize returns on the investment over a short period of time in order to distribute them to investors.

Nominate significant owners, customers, suppliers, employees, and community representatives to the board of directors. Directors from these categories are likely to have the company's long-term interests at heart and to encourage management to make investments that will improve long-term competitive position.

Link incentive compensation to competitive position. The incentive compensation systems now used in much of American business are counterproductive. The incentives are simply based on the wrong things. Bonuses based on current profits obviously undermine investment, and stock options increase managers' attention to short-term share prices, particularly if there are no restrictions on selling shares. Compensation systems need to move in the direction of linking pay more closely to long-term company prosperity and to actions that improve the company's competitive position.

Move away from unrelated diversification. Unrelated or loosely related diversification only wastes capital and exacerbates the current management biases against long-term investment. The only way to build competitive companies is to concentrate on a few core fields and invest heavily in them to achieve a unique position.

Shift from fragmented to integrated organizational structures. The decentralized, profit center-based management structure in many American companies must be overhauled. What is needed is a system that recognizes strategically distinct businesses as the proper unit of management but manages them differently. Senior managers at the corporate level must have a substantive understanding of the core technology and the industry. Top management must be involved directly and personally in all significant decisions, particularly investment decisions. There must be extensive consultation and coordination among related business units, with opportunities for the units to share functions and expertise. Such a system would shift measurement and control away from solely financial results, raise senior management confidence in understanding complex investment choices, and better capture complementarities among discrete investment options.

Transform financial control systems into position-based control systems. A new philosophy of management control must be instituted, based as much on the company's extended balance sheet as on its income statement. A company's extended balance sheet measures the assets that constitute its competitive position. Included in such a measurement would be: a broader definition of assets, such as market share, customer satisfaction, and technological capabilities; a measurement of asset quality and productivity in addition to asset quantity; and relative instead of absolute measures, tracking the company performance against significant competitors.

Move to universal investment budgeting. Conventional approaches to capital budgeting were never ideal for evaluating investment choices; they fail to deal with the changing nature of investment. A new system is needed to evaluate investment programs instead of just discrete projects; to treat all forms of investment in a unified manner; and to evaluate investments in two stages—first, determining the asset positions needed for competitiveness and second, evaluating exactly how to achieve those positions.

Toward a Superior American System

The recommendations outlined above are designed to attack the weaknesses of the American system systematically, while preserving the system's considerable strengths. These changes will align the goals of American shareholders, their agents, and American corporations; improve the information used in investment decisions; better capture the externalities in investment choices; evaluate management decisions on criteria more suitable for competitive performance; and make internal management processes more consistent with the true sources of competitive advantage.

If America can make progress on these fronts, it will not only reduce the disadvantages of the U.S. system but also produce a system that is superior to Japan's or Germany's. A reformed U.S. system would be characterized by long-term rather than permanent owners, well-informed rather than speculative traders, and flexible rather than life-time employees. A reformed U.S. system would produce more careful monitoring of management and more pressure on poor performers than what exists in Japan or Germany. The result would be less wasted investment and less internal inefficiency. Finally, a reformed U.S. system, with its higher levels of disclosure and transparency, promises to be fairer to all shareholders than the Japanese or German systems.

But altering the American system will not be easy. There is a natural tendency to limit change to tinkering at the margins, yet systemic change will be necessary to make a real difference. All of the major constituencies will have to sacrifice some of their narrow self-interests in pursuit of a system that is better overall.

Nevertheless, today there is widespread dissatisfaction with the system as it exists and concern over the direction and performance of American companies in global competition. This suggests that systemic change may be possible. If real change were to occur, the benefits would certainly accrue to investors and companies. But what is more important, the benefits would yield improved long-term productivity growth in the United States, and thus greater prosperity for the entire American economy.

4

Singapore Invests in the Nation-Corporation

Rajendra S. Sisodia

A small island-city located at the tip of the Malay peninsula is the site of an astonishing economic and technological achievement. Singapore not only embodies what is already perhaps the most technologically advanced environment in the world but is also poised to become the world's first fully networked society—one in which all homes, schools, businesses, and government agencies will be interconnected in an electronic grid.

Success in that endeavor would go a long way toward ensuring both a continually higher standard of living for Singapore's citizens and the position it needs to prosper in the global marketplace of the future. Singapore's leaders have long believed that their country should make itself extraordinarily convenient for multinational companies to do business with and in. In that, Singapore has succeeded famously. But achieving its avowed objective of becoming a "developed nation" will require an even greater measure of home-grown commerce and technology—and a more open society—than the country has displayed in the past.

Singapore's story demonstrates the capacity of a country with almost no natural resources to create economic advantages with influence far beyond its region. It represents one scenario for what can happen when a government assumes an instrumental position in shaping and managing the economic environment. And it underscores the importance of identifying and investing in certain key capabilities. The Singaporean government, though widely criticized for its repressive politics, determined that if it invested enormously in technological and human capabilities, it could create an economy where both individuals and organizations would be more likely to flourish.

This strategy holds lessons not only for other small nations but also for large countries and companies of all sizes. Technology management and the effective use of information technology have become the central managerial concerns of our time; Singapore is a significant world presence precisely *because* of its prowess in these two factors.

There are very few inherent advantages that nations and corporations can count on. Advantages have to be created and continuously renewed. In this vein, Singapore has many imitators but few peers.

Planning for an Information Future

Reduced to its essentials, Singapore's recent economic strategy has been straightforward: it has leveraged its single natural advantage of strategic location by establishing world-class transportation and materials handling facilities; extended such "hubbing" into the financial and other service domains by establishing a sophisticated communications and information technology infrastructure; continuously upgraded the skills of its work force to keep up with the more challenging demands placed upon it; and closely monitored relevant global technological developments, absorbing them as quickly as possible. In manufacturing, historically the island's main attraction to multinationals, Singapore now also encourages companies that want to establish highly sophisticated, automated, and flexible manufacturing centers.

Singapore's information technology strategy has been the centerpiece of its overall economic planning. A comprehensive National Information Technology Plan (NITP) was issued in 1986 by the National Computer Board (NCB), which was established in 1980 to set and implement Singapore's information technology policies. The plan included specific objectives and deadlines for training people; creating an IT culture; enhancing the communications infrastructure; generating and supporting IT applications; fostering a world-class indigenous IT industry that includes software, hardware, and computer services; and pioneering new information technology applications through R&D. In most of these objectives, the National Computer Board has either achieved or surpassed its goals.

The NCB has been largely responsible for ensuring that all the elements of NITP work together. And the elaborately orchestrated crusade has paid off. (See "Singapore's Firsts.") The next phase of

Singapore's strategy is aimed at transforming commerce and society on the tiny island nation to create what everybody there now calls an "intelligent island." The government has dubbed this new plan "IT2000." There are no existing models for what Singapore is attempting to do with IT2000. Painted in broad strokes, the objective is to pull disparate functions such as videoconferencing, artificial intelligence, robotics, and networking into a unified whole.

Singapore's Firsts

Despite its diminutive size (244 square miles, 2.7 million people) and diverse population (77% Chinese, 15% Malay, 7% Indian), Singapore has already achieved a disproportionate number of "firsts."

In the 1991 *World Competitiveness Report* issued jointly by IMD (a non-profit foundation with its headquarters in Lausanne, Switzerland) and the World Economic Forum of Geneva, the overall quality of Singapore's telecommunications infrastructure received a score of 96.67 out of 100, followed by the United States and Japan. In addition, according to Singapore Telecom, 12 out of every 100 Singaporean citizens have pagers, the highest percentage in the world.

The country's work force has been rated by the Business Environment Risk Information service in the United States as the best in the world in each of the last ten years. And its profit opportunity and operations risk ratings only slightly trail those of Switzerland, Japan, and Germany.

Moreover, the worldwide recession has barely caused a ripple here: Singapore's stock market led all others in the first half of 1991 and the economy was projected to grow a robust 8% for the year.

The country boasts the world's highest savings rate (45%), achieved largely through mandatory contributions to the government-operated Central Provident Fund. The island-city of Singapore also has the busiest and most efficient port in the world, the highest rated airport, the highest proportion of technologists, the most preferred airline (and by far the most profitable), and the lowest telecommunications costs.

In large part, these achievements are the result of governmental vision, a partnership with multinationals, and an orientation toward the future. Singapore's government structure comes into play here, as does the nation's size: a single level of government that manages a relatively small arena presents an opportunity for control and progress not afforded by larger, more diverse systems.

These components, which clearly work well together, may also achieve a larger objective: the evolution of Singapore into what many have started calling a "nation-corporation."

Much of the groundwork for IT2000 is already in place. In 1989, Singapore became the first country to achieve 100% ISDN (integrated services digital network) availability. Compare this with the United States, in which the percentage of phone lines that can provide ISDN service today ranges from 0.1% for Bell Atlantic and Pacific Bell customers to 1.9% for Bell South customers.

Fiber optics deployment and ISDN availability, which the government-run telephone company Singapore Telecom has set as top priorities at the urging of the NCB, represent the backbone of Singapore's ability to connect all businesses and homes. Singapore Network Services (SNS), a "private," for-profit company set up by the government, already has in place systems such as AutoNet (for manufacturing automation), RealNet (for real estate), LawNet, PortNet, MediNet, BizNet, OrderLink (for purchasing departments), InfoLink (for government, private, and international databases), $Link (for electronic payments), and SchoolLink (for linking all schools with the Ministry of Education).

Consider, for example, the impact of TradeNet, a project that saves Singaporean traders approximately one billion U.S. dollars a year. Initiated by the government and run by SNS, TradeNet has been an unqualified success in helping to manage Singapore's huge external trade of $115 billion a year—3.3 times the GNP. International trade has traditionally involved an enormous amount of paperwork. With TradeNet, traders simply fill out one electronic form, which can be submitted by modem to the Trade Development Board's main computer 24 hours a day. Information is then routed, again electronically, to the appropriate government agencies from among the 18 involved in issuing trade documents. Approvals, often generated with the help of expert systems, are deposited in the electronic mailbox of the trader, typically within 15 minutes. Application fees and customs duties are automatically debited from the trader's bank through electronic funds transfers. TradeNet also automatically routes approved permits to the Port and Civil Aviation authorities to facilitate the physical clearance of goods.

Singapore Telecom also offers the most advanced videotext system anywhere. In fact, Teleview is the only photovideotext system currently available and the only interactive system that comes close to realizing the multimedia potential of the personal computer. By using broadcast technology for the transmission of high-resolution photographs, Teleview is able to bypass one of the major drawbacks of other videotext systems, which must compromise the quality of graphics to increase transmission time or vice versa. Teleview also provides sound so that users can hear musical notes or phonetically learn new languages. This feature will prove extremely valuable for the large number of students who struggle with the complicated Mandarin dialect of Chinese, Singapore's second language after English.

Singapore all along has invested heavily in the computerization of its civil service. As a result, its service is the most automated in the world. The time needed to register a private company, for example, has dropped from 50 days to 8, a sole proprietorship from 30 days to 1. At the airport, passports are checked in 15 seconds (machine-readable passports will soon speed this procedure even further). And admission to government hospitals takes about 1 minute.

Civil service personnel are highly trained. The top 3% of college graduates each year are targeted for intensive recruitment efforts by the civil service, and all government employees receive annual bonuses based on the performance of the Singaporean economy. The projected 6% to 8% growth in 1991 and 1992 will result in a bonus equivalent of up to three months' salary.

Despite its apparently pervasive influence, however, the public sector has been pruned from 8.9% of the work force four years ago to 6% now. These reductions have been achieved through the privatization of government-owned "statutory boards" such as Singapore Airlines, the extensive use of information technology, and constant streamlining to make the government more efficient. Singapore Telecom is the next government-owned company to be privatized.

The networks and their efficient operation are only part of the technological crusade. This year all public phones are supposed to use stored-value phone cards, making coin-operated phones obsolete. And Singapore Telecom recently launched a new service called CT/2, a system that offers a bridge between today's cellular technology and the personal communication networks of the future. PCNs are radio frequency-based telecommunications systems consisting of very small, lightweight handsets. Phone numbers become linked to persons rather than locations.

The phone company and myriad private enterprises on the island are bringing many other new products on-line in Singapore as well. Among them: ISDN-based Group 4 fax machines (high-speed, high-resolution systems that are mostly being used to connect Japanese companies with their corporate headquarters), digital phones, multimedia terminals, and infrared communications devices. And in 1991, Singapore Telecom introduced the world's first public videophone booth. Available for transmitting to ten cities in Japan, the service costs about $20 for the first five minutes of each outgoing call. The videophone sends and receives full-color, full-motion (if somewhat choppy) video and is quite popular with Japanese expatriates.

An ingenious new Fujitsu product called the "Howdyphone" integrates a telephone with an attached electronic sketchpad. Using ordinary phone lines, the Howdyphone can simultaneously transmit a conversation as well as freehand sketches to another Howdyphone at the other end—thus achieving one of ISDN's promises without requiring an ISDN line or expensive ISDN equipment.

The greater promise of ISDN lies in its availability to individuals at affordable rates. The Information Technology Institute, an applied research arm of the NCB, has developed an ISDN card for personal computers that allows users to bypass much of the expensive equipment otherwise needed for ISDN. It is also close to releasing a PC-based ISDN visual communication system, which will enable a personal computer to operate as a videoconferencing terminal at a much lower cost than stand-alone videoconferencing systems.

The telephone company has spent over one billion dollars in the past five years on capital improvements. It boasts direct undersea cable links, four INTELSAT satellites, two earth stations covering two-thirds of the globe, optical fiber linking all exchanges, packet switching data exchange since 1982, mobile telephones capable of underground use, and radio paging. Singapore Telecom plans to spend another $1.5 billion in the next five years. Yet its rates range from low (international direct-dial rates are the lowest in the world, about 50% lower than Hong Kong's and 200% lower than Japan's) to almost giveaway: a tone pager costs $2.50 a month, a pager that displays messages on a screen $7.50 a month.

However, for all its capital spending and low prices, Singapore Telecom is highly profitable. It generated a net surplus of over $500 million in fiscal 1989–1990 on revenues of $1.2 billion. Productivity gains have been dramatic: the ratio of operating income to employee costs has gone up by 51% in five years, and value added per employee has doubled. The company's performance is doubly impressive when one considers its globally competitive rates and that it is owned by the government. Government ownership in most countries is tantamount to bureaucratic and unprofitable operations.

Leveraging Location

Singapore's only natural assets remain its strategic location and deep-water harbor (see "From Trading Outpost to Strategic Hub"); it imports the bulk of its food and even its water from Malaysia (characteristically, it sells some treated water back to Malaysia at a profit), and all of its energy comes from oil imported from Brunei and Indonesia. Recognizing this, the Singaporean government has concentrated on developing an infrastructure that more than compensates for the country's lack of natural resources and small size.

From Trading Outpost to Strategic Hub

Singapore's modern history began in 1819, when Thomas Stamford Raffles, a representative of the British East India Company, established a trading post in the southern part of the Malay Peninsula—a location that had become particularly strategic with the opening of China to foreign trade and the development of shipping routes to Europe around the Cape of Good Hope. With the opening of the Suez Canal in 1869, Singapore—a British colony—became the West's "Gateway to the East," and its importance as a trading hub grew enormously. Singapore continued to prosper into the twentieth century, its population evolving into a mix of maritime voyagers and middle-class traders.

Singapore remained relatively untouched by World War I, but the brutal four-year Japanese occupation during World War II brought an abrupt halt to Singapore's growth and destroyed forever the colonia-era illusion of British invincibility. Most of Singapore's post-war leaders, including Lee Kuan Yew, prime minister from 1959 to 1990, came of age during this traumatic period; the experience shaped their world views and intensified their insecurities about their city-state.

Singapore became a sovereign nation in 1965, following a brief, ill-fated union with Malaysia. At that time, Lee Kuan Yew sought to create an export-led economy and attracted a large number of labor-intensive manufacturing industries. The government gradually shifted investment incentives toward more sophisticated, capital-intensive industries, and by the mid-1970s, Singapore had virtual full employment. Service industries started to become more important, and annual growth rates of close to 10% were the norm.

In the 1980s, the government decided to focus on "brain intensive" industries. This led to the current emphasis on information technology,

aerospace technology, pharmaceutical products, and computer-aided manufacturing. The National Computer Board was founded then, and Singapore's on-line development went into high gear.

The port, for example, handles cargo at more competitive rates than
any other international port. Hundreds of shipping lines squeeze their
way through Singapore Strait on their way to and from Europe, the
Americas, the Middle East, Japan, and Southeast Asia. Most ships stop
in Singapore for refueling, repair, and trade, and more than 200 information technology applications have been implemented at the port to
streamline such processes. These applications include expert systems
for container planning, a system called PortNet for the electronic declaration of vessel calls, electronic data interchange links with other
ports for processing arriving ships, and artificial-intelligence-based pattern recognition systems that automatically encode container numbers. So well managed and attractive are Singapore's port services that
ships often go days out of their way to use them. As a result, Singapore
takes in nearly a billion dollars a year in ship repair and maintenance,
a fivefold increase since 1985.

The airport is also a well-oiled operation. Supported in part by the
extraordinary worldwide success of Singapore Airlines, Changi Airport
is widely acclaimed for its aesthetics and efficiency. Singapore has a
special advantage in the symbiotic relationship between its seaport and
airport; it can complete sea-to-air shipments in a matter of hours, at
a better rate than any other country.

The Singaporean subway, built in the mid-1980s, reflects the government's pragmatic approach to solving problems. The government
asked for bids to build the system at a time of global recession, and
the subway was completed under budget and two years ahead of
schedule. The government reclaimed several large parcels of land from
the sea, and used the profits derived from selling leases on the newly
formed land to pay for the entire subway system. In one stroke, the
island developed an important infrastructural element and expanded
prime real estate and the ability to accommodate more overseas investors.

Singapore, even more so than its neighbors such as Thailand, has
much to fear from the runaway congestion and pollution that headlong development normally brings. With no room to expand (except
into the sea), the prospect of urban gridlock and severe air pollution,
Bangkok-style, has caused the government to take steps that would
be unthinkable in many countries.

The government first levied duties of approximately 200% on cars to discourage ownership. When this failed to curb new car purchases adequately, the government added a quota system, offering to the highest bidder each month a limited number of "Certificates of Eligibility" for each category of automobile—which has brought in bids as high as $15,000. A lower priced certificate for "weekend cars" allows them to be driven only on weekends and after 7:00 P.M. on weekdays; the penalty for driving a weekend car Monday through Friday during the day can run into thousands of dollars. To offset these restrictions, the government keeps taxi fares extremely low. And as a result of such policies, Singapore can claim traffic that flows and a comparatively unpolluted environment.

Singapore's financial system is very sound as well. The government routinely accumulates a budget surplus, though there is no sales tax, no capital gains tax, and the top income tax rate is 31%. By the end of 1990, it had amassed foreign reserves of $27.5 billion. Singapore has an extensive international banking system, low interest rates (between 4% and 5% for most transactions), no restrictions on the flow of foreign exchange, and a strong currency, which has risen 18% against the U.S. dollar since 1987.

The Singaporean stock exchange is technologically sophisticated though still undercapitalized. The exchange is unusual in that it lacks a trading floor; buy and sell orders are keyed into an advanced computer and communications system and there matched by a system called CLOB (Central Limit Order Book). In January 1990, the month CLOB was installed, turnover on the exchange increased 80%. It now handles greater volumes at lower cost than before and has plenty of spare capacity for future growth.

The exchange will probably play a greater international role in the future, perhaps as a distribution center for ASEAN (Association of Southeast Asian Nations) stocks. Already a number of Malaysian issues have been floated in Singapore, and a direct communications link with the National Association of Securities Dealers' NASDAQ system allows for real-time investment in those stocks.

Promoting Knowledge Work

In its current drive to add knowledge work, Singapore consistently (and materially with incentives and tax rebates) favors design and development activities over rudimentary manufacturing and automated, overly labor-intensive processes. The Economic Development Board refers companies in search of low-cost labor to neighboring Malaysia or Indonesia; Singapore's own companies have invested more than $1 billion in Indonesia. The Singaporean government urges the creation of local research and training facilities and attempts to ensure that the island will quickly become self-sustaining in most new technologies, thus easing an excessive dependence on multinationals.

A prime example of this orientation is the GINTIC Institute of Computer Integrated Manufacturing. Director Ho Nai Choon outlines the Institute's ambitious mission: to propel Singapore into the forefront of integrated, flexible, and intelligent design and manufacturing activities.

Originally established with the assistance of Grumman Corporation of the United States, using offsetting credits from Singapore's purchase of Hawkeye fighter jets, GINTIC is now an independent institute with world-class equipment, facilities, and research programs. For instance, a stereolithography machine from 3D Systems in California is used to produce physical prototypes within hours of a design's completion. The machine is state-of-the-art technology; nonetheless, GINTIC closely monitors development efforts in Israel and by Sony in Japan that may soon provide an advantage over the 3D Systems machine.

The Institute is also pioneering several innovative CAD/CAM applications, such as a new knee-joint prosthesis uniquely suited to Asians (who do a great deal of kneeling and squatting in accordance with traditional customs and rituals), and a computer-aided design and fabrication process for Singapore's rapidly growing jewelry industry. GINTIC has also helped design a new lightweight, diskless laptop computer. The Institute's industrial collaborators span three continents and include Apple Computer, AT&T, Black & Decker, Digital Equipment Corporation, Deutsche Bank, Grumman Data Systems, Hewlett-Packard, IBM, Matsushita, NEC, and Philips.

Singapore has benefited from the growing recognition of how important it is to locate R&D work and manufacturing in close physical proximity. For example, Motorola recently launched in Asia a credit-card-sized pager, which was both designed and manufactured in Singapore.

Companies that were attracted to Singapore a generation ago by cheap, pliant labor and a highly solicitous government continue their manufacturing endeavors on the island even as they create and expand research and design centers. Over 650 multinational corporations have manufacturing facilities on the island. Singapore is the disk-drive capital of the world, accounting for over 60% of global production, much of it on fully robotized lines developed in Singapore.

The world's largest VCR factory (a joint venture between Thomson SA and Toshiba) is on the island, as is the largest compressor factory (Matsushita's, which recently produced its one-hundred-millionth compressor). Philips's Singapore tuner factory is that company's largest automated facility in the world. Apple Computer's flexible computer assembly lines in Singapore produce one computer every 20 seconds: the company finds it 40% to 50% cheaper to automate manufacturing in Singapore than in the United States. AT&T's extensive telephone equipment manufacturing in Singapore has earned a reputation within the company and with customers for outstanding quality; returns of its Trimline phones dropped dramatically after Singapore production came on-line. One of AT&T's largest customers, Sears, has twice recognized the Singapore factory for its manufacturing quality.

Singapore now positions itself as a "value-added switching node" and a gateway. The government promotes it as the logical entry point for businesses interested in participating in the region's booming economy and an ideal place to locate a regional manufacturing, sales, and technical-assistance base.

The Price of Prosperity

The government's well-known ability to influence investment and direct development has been central to Singapore's achievements. The technocratic leaders of Singapore are as likely to quote Michael Porter on the competitive advantage of nations and Kenichi Ohmae on the globalization of economies as they are to espouse Hegelian views on the march of history. However, Singapore has paid a high price for its rapid economic strides. Simply put, the government exercises a degree of power rarely seen in democratic countries and uses it in no uncertain terms.

Singapore's current character has been dominated and shaped by one man—Lee Kuan Yew. Henry Kissinger called him the "smartest man in the Western world"; others have called him arrogant, authoritarian, and puritanical. In 1959, when he came to power, Lee inherited a parliamentary system of government from the British but over the years altered it significantly, in order, some say, to perpetuate his own rule. A believer in democracy—up to a point—Lee said in his most telling quote: "We decide what is right. Never mind what the people think."[1]

The Singaporean government historically has had a low tolerance for dissent. In fact, it has consistently denied its citizens some rather fundamental civil liberties, such as a free press and the right to a speedy trial. The circulations of the *Asian Wall Street Journal* and the *Far Eastern Economic Review* were cut severely after disputes with the government over coverage of various political developments in Singapore. Lee Hsien Loong, Lee Kuan Yew's son and the deputy prime minister—and the man many believe will be Singapore's next prime minister—has said, "We recognize no first amendment right to freedom of the press. We do not aim to approximate U.S. practice as an ideal."[2]

One government opponent, Chia Thye Poh, was jailed for 23 years under the country's draconian Internal Security Act without ever being tried or formally charged. And other opposition politicians have also been targeted by the government for criminal or tax investigations. The *New York Times Magazine* ran a cover story in 1988 titled "City of Fear," referring not to Beirut or Bucharest but to Singapore.

Citizens of Singapore cannot own satellite dishes, since they are not supposed to receive unauthorized broadcasts. They are also not allowed to bring in unapproved magazines from abroad. The government has repeatedly justified these restrictions for the sake of "maintaining harmony" and preventing the breakdown of societal order.

By and large, however, the people accepted Lee's actions and his government system when he was in power. Singaporeans apparently have been willing to give up a degree of personal freedom in exchange for the government's continued success at increasing their material well-being.

Per capita income (in U.S. dollars) has grown between 15% and 18% for each of the past three years, while inflation has averaged only 2%; its 1990 per capita income of $12,650 puts Singapore, on paper, behind only Japan in Asia. And some Japanese expatriates in Singapore suggest that the island-city's public amenities, lower prices, and green spaces make for a higher quality of life than in Japan.

Some 87% of Singaporean citizens live in high-rise apartment buildings built by the Housing and Development Board; the majority of people own their units. Singapore has minimal public assistance and no unemployment benefits, yet only 0.3% of its families live in poverty. Moreover, citizens have affordable access to a health-care system that has become a magnet to immigrants in the region.

All of which serves to encourage the citizens' continued approval of their leaders. Most Singaporeans appear apolitical, at least publicly.

And despite all of its limitations on the free exchange of information and other curbs on citizens, Singapore remains a democratic society, with open and honest elections.

There are even signs that the government may be ready to relax its repressive policies. For example, it has allowed Dow Jones once again to circulate up to 2,500 copies daily of the *Asian Wall Street Journal* (although 5,000 copies were distributed before the restrictions). The *International Herald Tribune* is still printed in Singapore, and CNN is now broadcast live for two hours a day.

These changes are significant because they foreshadow a problem that the Singaporean government will have to address in the near future. Singapore's drive to create an information-enabled, networked society has a built-in irony: there is an inherent conflict between the democratization of information creation and access and the government's long-standing determination to control closely the information its citizens receive.

The revolutions in Eastern Europe and the former Soviet Union—and the near revolution in China—were helped along by the extensive use of various information technologies such as faxes and international computer networks. So, given its past focus on centralized control, why is the Singaporean government in a headlong rush to create what will likely be the world's most fully realized information society? It is hard to imagine that a government known for its planning and attention to the minutest detail has not explicitly considered the possibility that, in a wired information society, centralized control of information flow and exchange will be virtually impossible. One ominous sign is the relative lack of attention given to privacy issues in Singapore's technological crusade. The government's ultimate control over the information society could give it the power to exercise "Big Brother" surveillance over numerous aspects of its citizens' lives.

However, the emigration of substantial numbers of skilled professionals because of Singapore's high-pressure society—and what many have perceived as the government's "idiot child" treatment—has speeded the liberalizing trend now underway. Current prime minister Goh Chok Tong, who was elected in 1990, has brought a more informal, open style to the government, and the sense of released tension after Lee's strict rule is almost palpable. The government has pledged never again to use the Internal Security Act against political opponents. Singapore now may be headed toward a more comfortable balance between its sustained economic miracle and emerging political maturity.

The Shape of Things to Come

Singapore has become a symbol of economic and technological possibilities for small countries with large ambitions. Malaysia, Taiwan, Turkey, and Cyprus have created their own versions of national information technology plans following Singapore's lead. Other countries have sent delegations to study Singapore's computerization of its civil service. Malaysia's politicians frequently ask their citizens to look south at the tiny island and try to emulate its achievements. They have adopted many of the island-city's farsighted planning and implementation methods; indeed, Malaysia's new economic plan lays down certain Singapore-like objectives for the year 2050.

Singapore is very well armed but dwarfed by its large neighbors; it appears to live with a constant sense of geopolitical insecurity. Its prosperity, like that of Kuwait's, could conceivably prove irresistible to its relatively impoverished neighbors. Unlike Kuwait, however, Singapore's resources are mostly intangible and thus quite perishable. The Singaporean government is now using these resources to create its own version of a "co-prosperity sphere" (Japan's current term for the Asia-Pacific region) to ward off any acquisitive tendencies. Just as Hong Kong has long prospered because of its Chinese hinterland (where 80% of its manufacturing is conducted), Singapore is now attempting to establish areas such as southern Malaysia and portions of the Indonesian archipelago as its own manufacturing hinterland.

An ambitious plan to create a "growth triangle" comprising Singapore, Johor Bahru in Malaysia to the north (connected with Singapore by a causeway, with a second link planned,) and the Indonesian Island of Batam to the southwest (30 minutes by ferry) is well underway. By fueling such an undertaking with direct investments and technical assistance, the Singaporean government hopes to catalyze the economic development of its huge neighbors and also reduce any future security threats. The resources of the three complement one another: Singapore provides the technology, telecommunications, and transportation, while Batam and Johor provide much-needed land, low-cost labor, water, and electric power.

The pace of development so far has been startling. Batam was a jungle in January 1990, but today several companies have already commenced operations there, and 35 more have signed up to occupy its fledgling industrial park. Bintan, a second Indonesian island that is twice the size of Singapore, is likely to be added to the plan.

This tiny tail at the southern tip of Malaysia has succeeded in wagging the entire region in search of answers to their developmental challenges. When Singapore was a part of the Malaysian federation, Lee Kuan Yew had visions of it becoming the "New York of Malaysia." Since 1965, what Singapore is in the process of achieving as a sovereign state may transcend even that lofty goal; it is making itself indispensable to any major undertaking in a huge and rapidly growing region.

Given its small size, Singapore must frame most of its aspirations in terms of quality rather than quantity. Although it cannot be the largest in many things, it can still seek to be the most efficient, technologically advanced, and best-managed nation on its own terms. If it cannot be the final destination of goods, it can still be a place to send them on their way. If it cannot absorb much more large industry within its own borders, it can facilitate and help manage industrial operations in a nearby location.

Singapore today can no longer be regarded as merely an astute follower of technological trends initiated elsewhere. It is very much an innovator in its successful use of information technology across the spectrum of administrative, commercial, and social life. And the "intelligent island" is only now beginning to achieve the critical mass that will allow it to make even more rapid progress in the coming decade. Every trend indicates that by the end of the 1990s Singapore will be a fully enabled information society.

Notes

1. Brian Kelly and Mark London, *The Four Little Dragons*, (New York: Touchstone/Simon & Schuster, 1990), p. 382.
2. *The Four Little Dragons*, p. 364.

5

The Boundaries of Business: Commentaries from the Experts

The World Leadership Survey in the November-December 1990 HBR began a worldwide dialogue on the important issues facing managers in the 1990s. The survey results were published in "Transcending Business Boundaries: 12,000 World Managers View Change" (HBR May-June 1991). What follows is another installment of the discussion among internationally recognized management experts who draw on their own experiences and expertise to examine the boundaries of business identified in the survey.

The Boundaries of Business: The Cross-Cultural Quagmire

Charles Hampden-Turner

Despite its title, the HBR World Leadership Survey tells us more about American views on management than about the views of managers around the world. The methodology of the survey, the questions it asks, and the findings it reports all reflect distinctly American presuppositions and perspectives. As a result, the survey tells us almost nothing about the most important boundaries in the business world today: the often subtle but all-pervasive differences in cultural perspective that shape how managers from different societies conceive of their roles and their work.

This observation isn't intended as a criticism, so much as an example of the many traps that waylay the cross-cultural researcher and the cross-cultural manager. At a time when more and more corporate leaders are preoccupied with bridging the differences in corporate and national cultures, exploring the cultural limitations of the World Leadership Survey is one way to highlight the special difficulties of cross-cultural management.

Culture is prior to research. The very questions we ask are already shaped by our cultural assumptions and cast in our cultural categories. We pull our respondents' answers into our own mind-sets—and in the process, often lose the distinctive ways they think. To some degree, this is unavoidable. No one can cast off his or her culture. But we can show greater awareness of our presuppositions. If we do not, then some of the competitive advantages achieved by other cultures will continue to elude us.

The distinguishing characteristic of the American cultural paradigm is "universalism"—the conviction that principles of general validity can be discovered that apply to all people everywhere. You have to believe this *before* you start to look for the principles or you will never find them. Universalism colors the American approach to everything from politics to sports to business. After all, the Declaration of Independence says that "all men are created equal," not just Americans. And however strange and disquieting it may seem to a foreigner, it is no mere coincidence that the championship of the American "national pastime" is known as the World Series.

So too in business. Americans tend to assume that their own techniques have universal applicability and appeal. Americans invented scientific management in the confidence that wide ranges of human behavior could be subsumed under the principles of engineering and the logic of mass production. And the very idea of a "business school," based on the assumption that general principles of good management exist and can be taught, is a thoroughly American invention.

In research I have conducted with Alfons Trompenaars at the Centre for International Business Studies in Amsterdam, we present managers with hypothetical dilemmas that pit universal principles against particular exceptions to those rules. We have found that American managers are by far the most universalist of all our subjects from some 36 countries. Americans, it would seem, search ceaselessly for generalities capable of knitting together a very large, multiethnic society.

There was a time when the strength of the U.S. economy made American managerial universalism exportable around the world. More recently, however, American principles of management have come into question. Certainly, managers in some of the most successful national economies—countries such as Germany, Japan, Sweden, Italy, and Korea come to mind—do not act as if they believe that management is a profession with its own generalizable codes.

Managers from these countries seem curiously uninterested in teaching the world to emulate their practices. One reason is that these managers are usually more interested in emphasizing their uniqueness than in claiming the universality of their cultural perspective. To take just one example, so many books are published every year about the uniqueness of Japanese culture that there is a special name for the genre—*nihonjinron*. Perhaps the Japanese exaggerate the incomparable nature of a culture isolated for centuries from the rest of the world, but perhaps Americans exaggerate the value of their own psychological yardsticks in taking the measure of foreigners.

The World Leadership Survey is a good example. The methodological equivalent of universalism is empiricism. The assumption is that you should start with "the data"—in this case, many isolated fragments of individual opinion—and gradually construct the larger picture from these parts.

Thus the survey asks its respondents a set of extremely general questions about their attitudes. Then it scores their responses for the most part on a linear scale, which takes for granted, incorrectly I believe, that equivalent responses actually mean the same thing in very different cultures. Finally, it assumes that psychological factors like people's opinions and attitudes are critical to understanding larger social, cultural, and economic practices.

But this is simply not the way that members of many of the world's cultures think. In particular, Asian and continental European cultures prefer to start by discerning a meaning in the larger whole that is endorsed by the group and then showing how this same pattern repeats itself in multitudes of small details. Instead of focusing on individual "facts" or "opinions," they emphasize the social meanings that organize those facts or opinions into a coherent whole.

Therefore, to understand the responses of managers from such cultures would require first considering the shared beliefs that inform their individual responses. But the survey's format makes this impossible. It forces foreign managers to put their responses into an American logic.

This bias toward universalism goes a long way toward explaining some of the more curious and contradictory findings of the survey. Consider the intriguing example of Japan. The high levels of government guidance in the Japanese economy and widespread protection of certain domestic industries are well known. And yet the Japanese respondents to the World Leadership Survey say they strongly oppose such activities. Similarly, extensive research has documented the way large Japanese companies nurture sole suppliers who deliver just-in-time. But according to the survey, Japanese managers are significantly less inclined to involve suppliers in product development or to spend money training suppliers.

What explains these contradictory findings? Is what we know about the Japanese economy wrong or are the Japanese respondents to the survey being dishonest? Neither. The real reason is the inability of the survey to capture the fundamental cultural characteristics of Japanese management.

Americans, and people from other English-speaking cultures, for that matter, tend to think in terms of sharp dichotomies: "free trade" (good) versus "protectionism" (bad), "free markets" (good) versus "government interference" (bad), "competition" (good) versus "cooperation" (bad). But surveys attempting to measure along an imagined line between these "opposed" tendencies—as does the World Leadership Survey—will most likely find little of value.

Japan's genuine competitive advantages are far more subtle than such dichotomies suggest. As long as we see the world this way, we largely miss the organizing logic of Japanese management: to protect companies, but just long enough to let them build their capability to compete worldwide; to provide government direction, but just enough to free private companies to develop; to compete fiercely but also to cooperate closely. The ultimate goal of all these activities is to create harmony, what the Japanese call *wa*. By harmonizing what Westerners see as contradictions, a Japanese manager functions much like a judo fighter who uses an opponent's momentum against him.

My own research also showed negligible differences between the attitudes of Japanese managers and those of managers from other countries—until we began to probe for the crucial differences in how Japanese managers reconcile competition and cooperation. We found that in Japanese companies, a competitive phase designed to contrast two or more ways of doing something was followed by a cooperative phase in which the more successful practitioners taught the less successful ones to integrate the superior method. And guiding both the competition and the cooperation was the desire to learn through comparison (followed by communication) or through differentiation (followed by integration). The key to effective management was the harmonization of the two phases.

Michael Porter has identified both these processes as critical for *national* economic development. Strong competition raises standards within an industry and spurs suppliers toward better cooperation with their clients, as a general improvement in effectiveness is communicated to most players.

Of course, to Western eyes, the Japanese desire for harmonization can appear excessive—a mechanism for suppressing conflicting interests rather than reconciling them. For example, most Japanese survey respondents do not see interrupting vacations for work as bad for the family. The reason: in the long term, anything that benefits the company benefits the family. This contrasts sharply with Western attitudes toward the division of time between work and family.

Whether one approves or disapproves of such attitudes, it is clear that only when such subtleties are taken into account can researchers and managers get to the really interesting question: What can we learn from the way a different culture conceives of a particular problem or issue? For example, the survey results tell us that over 90% of respondents from both the United States and Japan believe that business has either a "primary" or "active" role to play in solving their nation's environmental problems. But this masks fundamental differences in the way each culture perceives the issue. Environmental cleanup in the United States has been stalled for a decade by a sterile debate about the "costs" of government regulation to economic competitiveness. In Japan, by contrast, government intervened to encourage the development of antipollution technologies. The result: both cleaner industries and a new generation of companies internationally competitive in the emerging global market for these technologies.

The recent Global Environmental Charter, published by *Keidanren* (the Japan Federation of Economic Organizations) last April, calls on Japanese companies to "seek appropriate means for the domestic and overseas transfer of their technologies, know-how, and expertise for dealing with environmental problems." By taking environmental problems seriously, the charter argues, Japanese companies can "foster a mutually beneficial relationship between producers and consumers, thereby encouraging the healthy development of the economy."

For the most part, HBR's survey misses such cultural complexities, and the implications go far beyond the limitations of a single survey. They speak to what may be an ingrained inability on the part of American managers to learn from other cultures.

The American bias toward individualism and specificity leads to the assumption that learning takes place at the level of the individual. As a result, a premium is put on skilled individuals—the fast-track manager, the outstanding performer—which tends to bid up the price of the best. The end result: Lee Iacocca of Chrysler earns 34 times more than the head of Honda.

But suppose, as managers from Asian or continental European cultures regularly do, that real learning doesn't so much adhere in individuals but in groups. From this perspective, knowledge accumulates *within* organizations and *between* people rather than being confined in the heads of individual job-hopping employees. Specific ideas, especially "big ideas," are quickly stolen, imitated, or re-engineered. But the holistic culture of a learning organization is impossible to appropriate. It pervades the tools, techniques, and mind-sets that the organization's members share. Such a learning corporation requires longer-term commitments from employees to deepen their organizational knowledge over much of their lives.

In the end, the American penchant for universalism may turn out to be the narrowest of parochialisms. When it comes to addressing the business challenge of the current decade, this parochialism puts American managers at a distinct disadvantage compared with their Asian and European competitors. The most rigid boundaries of business may be those in our heads.

The Boundaries of Business: Partners—The Rhetoric and Reality

Tom Peters

A close business associate, who runs a several billion-dollar piece of a U.S. consumer-goods corporation, recently sent me a speech he gave on the importance of strategic alliances to future competitive success. A few months later, he invited me to address his 300 top general managers at their annual strategic-planning conference. "Would all of the company's strategic partners please raise their hands?" I asked. Silence filled the room, heads turned but no hands were raised.

There is a rhetoric of partnership in the business world today—and then there is the reality. According to the rhetoric, we are moving toward a seamless global economy, in which "borderless" companies work with an ever-shifting array of partners to take advantage of new opportunities and to achieve mutually beneficial goals. Ten years ago, the idea that a major corporation like Procter & Gamble would have a permanent office at the Wal-Mart headquarters in Bentonville, Arkansas would have been laughable. Today it constitutes conventional wisdom.

But we have many miles to go in translating slogans like "strategic alliances" and "borderless company" into competitive reality. The World Leadership Survey underscores the distance left to travel.

Respondents to the survey generally speak the language of partnership. For instance, over two-thirds say that their companies "always" or "often" have long-term relationships with suppliers. But when it comes to the specific managerial practices that make partnership real, the survey suggests a very different story.

Consider the subject of sharing strategic information, which is arguably the clearest indicator of a company's intent to open the "partnership" floodgates—both inside and outside the company—or to keep them firmly closed. Until information becomes widely available, all other aspects of partnership remain stuck at the stage of lip service or less.

Unfortunately, most respondents to the World Leadership Survey flunk this acid test. One revealing question in the section on "how companies cooperate with one another" examines the propensity of managers to share strategic information with their customers. Almost one-quarter of the respondents (23%) say they "never" share such information. Only one-quarter share "often" (26%) and just 7% "always." The remainder report sharing "sometimes."

Such findings may be worrisome, but they should not be surprising. After all, according to this survey, companies aren't even sharing with their own employees. Another question asks respondents to compare the access to company information of an organization's "top group" and "bottom group" (what an awful choice of words). Only 20% report that information sharing is the "same" or even "somewhat similar" for the two groups. On the other hand, 59% label it "very different," the most extreme category. So much for employee involvement in the 1990s.

Second only to sharing strategic information in making partnership a reality is involving suppliers and customers in product planning and design. Unfortunately, the relevant survey questions on this issue are open to broad differences of interpretation. What constitutes supplier or customer involvement in product planning? A meeting now and again with the company's product design team? Full-time membership on such teams? Something in between? In any event, the answers again suggest that rhetoric outstrips reality.

About one-third of the survey respondents "always" or "often" involve their suppliers and customers in product planning and design. An eye-catching 27% admit to "never" involving customers, and 17% report that they don't involve suppliers. This is especially troublesome because elsewhere in the survey, executives tag quality and customer service as business's top success factors for tomorrow. But how can they expect to achieve high levels of quality and customer service if they don't also have high customer and supplier involvement?

The saga is the same with strategic alliances. I would have imagined that *most* companies in 1990 would be engaged in "many" (the highest frequency category) important joint ventures, strategic alliances, or partnerships with other companies. Not so. Only 17% check that box. An astonishing 28% say "none." The remaining 55% answer "a few."

Company size explains some of this apparent reluctance to work with outsiders. Of respondents from companies with more than 10,000 employees, 39% report many alliances and only 11% report none. At the other extreme, among respondents from companies of less than 25 employees, the percentages are 7% and 48%, respectively. Still, the fact that barely more than one-third of the respondents even from the *largest* companies indicate that they have many alliances is surprising, though perhaps the modifier "important" in the question produced a conservative response bias.

A related question asks how often respondents seek outsider involvement in new business opportunities. About one-fifth (21%) look only to "internal expertise." The "not invented here" syndrome remains alive and well. Another fifth (an attractively high percentage?) look almost automatically for "external partners." The 60% majority, not unexpectedly, takes a "some of both" approach.

So the borderless company has not yet arrived, and perhaps it's not even on the way. But it's important not to read too much into the responses to the World Leadership Survey. For one thing, the lack of any meaningful trend data in the survey is a major limitation. In the absence of such data, it is impossible to identify any changes—or lack thereof—over time. Indeed, short of comparing responses with some postulated ideal (for instance, "everyone should be codesigning with customers"), it's difficult even to label a given score "high" or "low." For this reason, I hope HBR will repeat the World Leadership Survey in the future, in order to track trends in managerial practice over time.

What's more, readers should keep in mind that the "borderless" idea represents a fundamental paradigm shift in our conception of the modern organization. We are moving from a "pre-Copernican" business world, where the individual company is at the center of the universe, to a far more fluid "post-Copernican" environment, where each company is but one point in an extended network of equals. Given the enormity of this shift, the fact that today the rhetoric of partnership outstrips the reality is really no surprise. After all, not so long ago, we didn't even have the rhetoric!

Some of the most interesting findings about partnership in the survey have to do with national variations. Like survey respondents as a whole, most respondents from the three economic powerhouses—the United States, Japan, and Germany—use the rhetoric of partnership. But it is the Germans who regularly excel at the practice of partnering, with the Americans usually coming in a close second, and the Japanese a distant third.

For example, 44% of the German respondents say they "always" or "often" involve suppliers in new-product design, as compared with 38% of the Americans. But only 20% of the Japanese respondents involve their suppliers.

Involving customers in product planning produces a similar picture: some 38% of Germans do it "always" or "often," while 36% of the U.S. respondents choose these two categories. A scant 10% of Japanese managers do so—with only 1% choosing "always."

Differences of the same magnitude spill over to training suppliers and customers. Twenty percent of German respondents report providing seminars and training for suppliers, while 58% do so for customers. In the United States, it's 22% and 50%, respectively. Once again, Japan is the odd country out among the three. Only 12% of the Japanese managers responding to the survey report that their companies support suppliers through seminars and training, while 18% provide such aid to customers. In the extreme "always" category relative to customer training, 30% of Germans, 18% of Americans, and just 2% of Japanese say "yes."

The penchant for sharing strategic information is comparable: 42% of Germans, 37% of Americans, and 15% of Japanese check the "always" and "often" boxes. And executive contact with customers clinches the trend: a whopping 82% of Germans say their executives have regular contact with customers, as opposed to 65% from the United States and 42% from Japan.

American managers might be surprised by such findings. After all, we tend to think of the Japanese as masters of employee involvement and assume such relationships extend to suppliers and customers as well. And we are woefully ignorant of how the German economy works—a disturbing fact given the importance of German companies in international competition.

These consistent national differences reflect coherent national economic strategies. German companies are peerless customizers, providing highly specialized products to niche markets. By definition, customizers must follow a high-engagement strategy—thus, the relatively high German numbers on questions detailing the practice of partnership.

By contrast, Japanese companies are mass producers par excellence. For them, a high-involvement strategy is arguably not so critical, and perhaps even an obstacle. When you are working to launch quickly the latest wrinkle for the consumer, you can't get bogged down in too much back-and-forth with customers and suppliers. How else to explain the low Japanese scores?

Finally, U.S. companies are usually somewhere in between these two extremes, with a tilt in the German direction. A good example is the U.S. semiconductor industry. It has taken a beating in commodity memory chips, but its lead in so-called "design-rich" chips, the largest and fastest-growing segment of the market, remains secure. Success in that segment requires a much higher level of engagement with both customers and suppliers.

What are the implications of these national economic profiles for future global competition? It depends on which way you think the competitive wind is blowing. If trends in global markets are toward increased fragmentation and customization, then perhaps the Japanese have the longest road ahead among the three dominant economies. Japanese companies are taking clear aim at the higher-value end of markets. In the process, they are shifting production offshore and putting high value-added activities like product design close to foreign markets. But recent research has been critical of Japanese multinational management skills. The difficulty Japanese managers have dealing with the world's many cultural differences may prove a major weakness.

On the other hand, if you believe that the real wave of the future will be "mass customization," an organizational hybrid of mass production and customized production, then maybe it's the Germans who have the longest way to go. In such a competitive environment, German managers' close ties to suppliers and customers may prove too time-consuming and costly.

The United States, as befits so large and diverse an economy, confuses as always. We are the inventors of mass production and mass marketing—from Henry Ford's black Model-T to Marlboro cigarettes. Yet our current export prowess, like Germany's, tends to focus on more customized goods—for instance, Boeing's airplanes. In a mish-mash, hybrid world, our report card is mixed. We aren't standing at the back of the line, but we hardly have a lock on the future.

The bottom line is that such national differences don't translate easily into any "best" or "worst" strategies. The real value of the World Leadership Survey is to remind us that there is no "one best way" of doing business, practiced by any one nation, and worth mindless copying by all.

The Boundaries of Business:
The Impact of Technology

Jay Jaikumar

The HBR World Leadership Survey provides eloquent testimony to the fact that technology has revolutionized the work that managers do. In fact, technology has effected this transformation so thoroughly that the managers responding to the survey, typical of managers around the world, tend to react to the surface disturbances that have been created by the underlying technological shifts. Therefore, managers will tend to talk about the flatter organization or about work-force changes and miss commenting on the revolution in technology that has precipitated these changes. It is, however, this deeper revolution in technology that managers must understand, appreciate, and ultimately become a part of if they are to keep pace with the new demands of competition.

Perhaps this omission on the part of managers is understandable in light of what we know about the ways organizations adjust to technology. In the workplace, technology can precipitate revolutionary changes that have dramatic impacts on the content of work. But it usually takes time for organizations to realize how powerful technology can be. The walls set up in organizations—between managers and workers, between functions, between work and home, between company and society—constrain change, and managers are slow to dismantle them. Only when the walls begin to crumble do companies feel the full potential of technology. In my own work helping companies restructure their operations, I have found that it can take a decade or more for managers to create large enough openings in the walls for technology to change the content of work radically.

As the survey results indicate, change in the content of work is a unifying element across countries. In manufacturing, for example, companies are quick to transfer across national borders even the most revolutionary changes in production machinery, production technology, or traditional automation. But when technology is embodied in know-how and knowledge and no longer contained only in a machine, change occurs at a very slow pace. When people are the instruments of technology, organizational walls that separate functions and levels inhibit the diffusion of knowledge. That is why technological advancement often takes place at a faster pace and in a more complete way at companies with flatter, smaller organizations staffed with generalists.

While the technology should dictate these kinds of organizational shifts, companies seem slow to move. Take the fact that the survey shows managers reporting higher levels of satisfaction with their jobs but less loyalty to their companies. Company structures have changed as a result of downsizings, reorganizations, CEO changes, mergers, acquisitions, and divestitures. Yet hierarchy still rules industrial organizations and the split between the upper-level manager and the work force is as large as ever. Why? Because companies are reluctant to embrace the logic of the technology and dismantle the walls that separate levels of management.

Consider another kind of wall—the space that separates different parts of the organization—and the impact of telephones and fax machines, technologies that can break down the wall of space. With these technologies, managers can communicate with anyone around the world as easily as if he or she were down the hall. Everyone agrees that to ignore these technologies would impair a company's competitiveness. Yet the technology of the telephone, which has been around for more than a century, has not fundamentally changed management style or thinking. What could become a powerful tool to break down the walls between functions and levels in an organization, to share information and speed decision making, has instead been limited in use to enhancing the communications that already are a part of most managers' lives. Managers have used these technologies to wire the walls rather than to remove them.

In my view, the most disappointing element of the survey responses is the emphasis that managers put on the consequences of changes in the external world without examining management's role in developing those changes. This external orientation masks the fact that corporations around the world are facing the same trends regarding the content of work, although their responses may vary widely. Almost everything in the survey reinforces the notion that significant change is occurring. Managers acknowledge change in the form of apprehension about a number of things: corporate insularity, the erosion of the work ethic, government red tape and corruption, the level of investment in infrastructure, the quality of work skills. Clearly these managers are not only aware of change but also feel embattled by it.

But in the face of fundamental and rapid change, managers are simply reacting to their immediate circumstances rather than reflecting on the impact and causes of the change. The content of work, of what actually gets done on the job, has been transformed over the past decade, but the responses indicate no awareness of why that change has occurred.

Ultimately, each company will find its own solution to the technological imperatives of today—regardless of culture or nationality. For example, given components of equivalent quality and cost, cultural similarities might dispose an Italian company to do business with another Italian company instead of with one in the United States. But if the components of domestic companies are inferior or more costly, economics and competitive considerations will drive the decision. After all, exhortations to patriotism did not prevent Americans from abandoning Detroit for more economical and fuel-efficient imported cars during the 1970s. For companies in the 1990s, the same logic will hold, which is why we will see close alliances between suppliers and customers around the world, better and more rapid product development, and a world of work that emphasizes productivity, technology, and commitment.

PART

II

The Borderless Economy

1

Power and Policy: The New Economic World Order

Klaus Schwab and Claude Smadja

In the last three years, we have been told again and again that the industrialized world is undergoing a crisis—its worst one since 1945. Traditional recipes for boosting economic activity have failed to work, and every new forecast of economic growth in the Organization for Economic Cooperation and Development's *Economic Outlook* has brought a downward revision of the preceding one. (The only exception is the forecast in the July 1994 issue, which was readjusted upward). Even now, as the long-awaited recovery finally begins to gather strength and momentum, it is failing to make itself felt in the most critical domain: employment. In fact, the OECD's *Economic Outlook* has confirmed what everybody knew already: that unemployment in Europe can be expected to continue increasing, presumably until the end of 1995.

What we actually have been going through is not merely a crisis but a worldwide economic revolution, which has been making itself felt at the same time that we have been hit by a cyclical crisis. In other words, for the last three years, the industrialized world has been confronted with the cumulative impact of *two* distinct phenomena.

Let us deal first with the purely cyclical crisis. There has, of course, been an economic turnaround in the United States, and the economies of Europe are moving in the right direction as well. The recovery is gradually, if to varying degrees, taking hold in all the industrialized countries, lifting the industrialized world out of the worst recession it has faced in the last two decades. The United States is currently on a solid growth path (with a 4% growth rate expected this year), and the same can be said for Canada and the United Kingdom. Elsewhere in Europe—where Germany and France have been showing stronger than expected results since the second quarter—and in Japan, indications are that the lowest point of the downturn has already been reached.

However, the failure of the current economic recovery to translate into a significant improvement in employment is evidence that more than a mere cyclical crisis has been at work. Observers have been speaking of a "jobless recovery" or a "recovery on crutches" because neither present nor projected growth rates are sufficient for creating jobs on a large scale. The hard truth is that growth in the industrialized countries will have to be greater than the 2.6% annual average of the last two decades for these nations to achieve a substantial reduction in their unemployment levels. But because the necessary growth rates are difficult for mature economies to sustain, unemployment will remain a critical issue in the industrialized world for the next few years, and political and economic leaders will have no instant solutions to offer anxious citizens.

In fact, the weakness of the current recovery—its failure to deliver jobs—is only one of several manifestations of the worldwide economic revolution that is now under way. The many structural changes brought about by this revolution are creating new rules of the game and necessitating a new modus operandi for all the primary players in the world economy.

Perhaps the most spectacular component of the current revolution is the shift in the world economy's center of gravity to Asia. The extraordinary process of fast and steady growth in East Asia since the end of the 1960s has led to an overall redistribution of the world's economic power, the impact and implications of which are just beginning to be felt. In 1960, East Asia accounted for just 4% of world economic output. Today its share amounts to 25%. While GNP in Europe and the United States has grown at an average of 2.5% to 3% per year over the past 25 years, many East Asian countries have managed an annual average of 6.5% to 7.5%—a trend that is expected to continue beyond the turn of the century. Between 1992 and the year 2000, 40% of all the new purchasing power created in the world will be in East Asia, and the region will absorb between 35% and 40% of the global increase in imports. East Asian central banks now hold close to 45% of the world's foreign reserves, and while the United States and the major European countries keep piling up foreign debt, Japan, Taiwan, Singapore, and Hong Kong are in the remarkable position of not having any.

All those developments mean that we are already, economically speaking, in a fully tripolar world, with the three centers of power—Western Europe, North America, and East Asia—in a position of strategic economic parity. Indeed, if present trends continue (as they probably will, barring some unforeseen regional upheaval), East Asia should be poised to claim preeminence over its two counterparts before the turn of the century.

The shift of economic power in the direction of Asia has been made possible by, and in turn has helped accelerate, a number of other developments that are dramatically altering global economic arrangements. Now that national or regional barriers restricting financial flows no longer exist, and neither technology nor management and marketing techniques observe any boundaries, the key prerequisites of economic success are increasingly transferable from one country to another. At the same time, the failure of Communism and the general spread of economic liberalization have brought previously isolated countries—the most spectacular examples being China, India, and Vietnam—into the world economy. This development has resulted in fierce competition for foreign investment among countries previously hostile to it, as well as the sudden entry of 2.5 billion people into the global marketplace.

All these conditions, in the meantime, have helped bring about what is now a worldwide delocalization of industrial production. That phenomenon lies at the very core of the worldwide economic revolution and is gathering momentum. Countries that only 10 years ago were confined to low-tech, labor-intensive economic activity are now able to produce, at low cost, goods and services that were previously monopolies of the advanced industrialized nations. One especially notable example is Malaysia, which over the past 20 years has shed its dependence on commodities to become the world's leading producer of semiconductors, and which now discourages labor-intensive industry.

Not so long ago, Japan was the only major industrial power able to take full advantage of cheap production bases in its own region. Yet today, Western Europe and the United States, along with the new economic powers of East Asia, also enjoy opportunities for delocalization within their own regions. The collapse of the Soviet empire in Central and Eastern Europe now offers manufacturers within the European Union the advantage of low-cost production bases in countries such as Poland, Hungary, and the Czech Republic. Meanwhile, the North American Free Trade Agreement has provided the United States with similar opportunities in Mexico.

As these developments in Europe and North America illustrate most clearly, the whole phenomenon of delocalization has broken the linkage that previously existed among high technology, high productivity, high quality, and high wages. It was this linkage that once appeared to guarantee ever-improving standards of living in the industrialized countries. Today, however, it is possible to have high technology, high productivity, high quality, and *low* wages. Of course, as the economies of the industrializing and newly industrialized nations mature, we can expect that current wage differentials (taking skill levels and productivity into account) will eventually narrow. Yet for now, the factor of low wages in these countries will remain paramount in corporate decision making, especially for transnational corporations.

The delocalization option is one that no corporation can resist in view of the intense competition all companies are facing. In fact, it has become a matter of life and death for corporations to take advantage of such opportunities in the face of what can truly be termed megacompetition—yet another crucial aspect of the global economic revolution. Corporations and countries must now compete not only against rivals in their own league but also against a continual stream of newcomers, while at the same time playing catch-up with competitors claiming to have made the latest breakthroughs. These competitive realities are creating intense pressure to rationalize production, cut internal costs, and search for the least expensive production base.

That no country today is immune to this pressure is shown by two surprising examples: Taiwan and South Korea. These countries, which only ten years ago were themselves very low-cost production bases, must now transfer most labor-intensive activities to still cheaper production bases, such as China, Indonesia, and Vietnam. Meanwhile, the percentage of Japanese industrial production transferred to other countries in East Asia has multiplied three times since 1980. (Matsushita is planning to have a full 50% of its foreign sales come from delocalized production by March 1997—up from 38% at present.) In Europe, we now see a pattern of companies diverting investment from the former East Germany—already considered too expensive—to the Czech Republic or Hungary. (The average cost for a worker in the Volkswagen-Škoda factory in the Czech Republic is approximately ten times less than for a worker in the company's plants in Germany, but productivity in the Czech plant is 60% that of its German-based counterparts and increasing rapidly.)

The pressures created by the new megacompetition, as well as by the impact of delocalization in the industrializing and newly industrialized countries, are being compounded by a further development in the industrialized world. The burst of technological innovation in the last two decades, and the productivity gains registered as those innovations have been integrated into production processes, are severely cutting employment in industry. In this case, one example tells the whole story: between 1970 and 1993, manufacturing output doubled in the United States while industrial employment actually declined by as much as 10%, according to some estimates. The situation in Western Europe, although less striking, is much the same. Not coincidentally, we have long witnessed an opposite trend in most East Asian countries with respect to the percentage of manufacturing employees in the total labor force. From 1961 to 1991, while the share of manufacturing employment declined by one-third in the United States, one-quarter in France, and about 15% in Germany and Italy, it multiplied five times in South Korea, three times in Malaysia, and two times in Taiwan and in Singapore.

There would be nothing wrong with those opposite trends if the service sector in the industrialized countries were able to absorb the workers displaced by manufacturing, and at roughly comparable wages. But one development of the last few years has been a decrease in the rate of job creation in the service sector, compounding the problem of structural unemployment in the industrialized world. Of course, new sectors of economic activity—some of them unheard of only ten years ago—are emerging and will create new jobs, and the current recovery is boosting the creation of new jobs in the traditional service sector. Yet it remains to be seen whether that sector will be able to create the kind of high-wage jobs that manufacturing once provided to highly skilled workers. The new jobs will not necessarily pay as much as industry did in the past, and the better-paying ones will require education and training that many of the currently unemployed do not possess. (Workers caught in this gap account for a large proportion of the long-term unemployed in continental Europe.)

As the process of economic restructuring in the industrialized world continues and gathers momentum, it will take many years of effort in the area of education and training to overcome the problem of inadequately prepared workers. Meanwhile, many observers have noted that while the United States—with an ever-increasing reliance on the service sector—has fared much better than Europe in creating jobs and holding down unemployment, the other side of the coin has been a near stagnation of real living standards in the last 12 years. This fact raises the possibility of the end of another linkage, that between high employment and high wages, which has until now guaranteed ever-increasing living standards in the industrialized countries.

Much has been written about the widening gap between rich and poor in the United States during the 1980s—a phenomenon often attributed to the policies of the Reagan administration. In fact, that development seems to have had much more to do with the ongoing structural evolution of the U.S. economy in its shift from industry to services. So far, that same evolution—with its perceived consequences for wages and social welfare benefits—is meeting with strong opposition in Europe, where the welfare state is much more developed and solidly entrenched than in the United States. The broader and more generous social safety net, especially with respect to unemployment benefits, makes it easier for people to refuse lower-paying jobs when they are the only alternative to unemployment. One result is what happened in France last spring, when strong popular opposition forced the government of Prime Minister Edouard Balladur to renounce its project of scaling back the minimum wage for young people in their first jobs—a plan that had been designed to alleviate high unemployment rates among youth.

The issue must be faced directly: there is no way that the Western European nations will be able to ease their enduring unemployment problems without dealing with the structural rigidities in their labor systems, even though such an undertaking will require a kind of cultural revolution for Europeans accustomed to the notion of an ever-expanding welfare state. The European systems have so far proved more adept at caring for the unemployed than at creating employment. And European trade unions have seemed more interested in maintaining benefits for the employed than in helping the unemployed get back to work. Consequently, as the financial burden of the safety net grows to levels that may soon become unbearable, the very survival of the European systems will come into question.

Given the worldwide economic situation, the issues of job creation and job protection are sure to be paramount on the agendas of political leaders throughout the industrialized world for the next few years. As a result, we will also witness a complete modification of the international trade picture. From now on, the most important criterion in trade issues will be not the nationality of a product or a service—a notion that has, in any case, already become blurred—but rather where and to whom it provides jobs. This development was already manifest last summer when the Clinton administration broke with a long-standing U.S. tradition of protecting the interests of U.S. corporations without regard to their location. A new order of priorities set by the administration put U.S. corporations located in the United States first in line for protection, foreign corporations located in the United States second, and U.S. corporations operating outside the country a mere third. The clear emphasis on job protection for U.S. workers is being echoed in Europe with assertions of a similar order of priorities.

In this world of higher stakes, with many governments both struggling for their own survival and attempting to maintain the fundamental social and political stability of their countries, there is no risk in predicting a toughening of stances on international trade issues and an increase in international trade tensions. It is indeed quite revealing that both the European Union and the United States have adopted tougher trade postures even while assenting to the Uruguay Round Agreement. In Europe, as a price for agreeing to the deal on agricultural exports to which it had objected, France got from its partners a commitment to even tougher enforcement of antidumping regulations (measures that the Europeans have already used arbitrarily, in many cases, to penalize overly efficient competitors). Similarly, even as it was preparing to sign the Uruguay Round Agreement, the Clinton administration resuscitated Super 301, which provides for mandatory sanctions to coerce other countries into opening their markets. Moreover, in preparing to present the Uruguay Round Agreement to Congress for ratification, the Clinton administration has condoned a protectionist interpretation of the agreement's antidumping provisions—a reading that would grant the United States more leeway to act against competitors.

Of course, the Uruguay Round Agreement is, in itself, a considerable step forward, covering as it does such increasingly important domains as agricultural exports, services, investment, and intellectual property rights (none of which were previously covered by the General Agreement on Tariffs and Trade). It also creates what should become the key mechanism for policing world trade, the World Trade Organization. Yet the most immediate advantage of the agreement lies not in the $300 billion to $400 billion it should add to the current $3.6 trillion annual volume of world trade. The advantage lies, rather, in the prospect of a significant containment of trade tensions and the prevention of outright trade wars.

Taking these trade issues into account, one of the most critical challenges presented by the current worldwide economic revolution can be summarized by the following question: How will we be able to maintain and expand the multilateral trade system, integrating the many new players who want their share of the pie while also preserving the standard of living of the industrialized countries so as to prevent a possibly violent backlash? For most of its existence, the multilateral trade system has functioned with a large but homogeneous group of players. It now must operate under quite different conditions, with the number of players, for one thing, having increased dramatically in a short span of time and especially rapidly in the last few years. The field has also now become very heterogeneous, with countries operating under widely different standards of living, social traditions, and political conditions.

This situation is obviously creating severe tensions. For example, confronted with competition from low-wage countries that are attracting more and more new industrial activities while also entering fields previously dominated by the more advanced countries, Europe and the United States have launched an offensive against so-called social dumping. There has been a concerted and sometimes very vocal effort on the part of Western nations to link trade issues to workers' and human rights, social conditions, and environmental standards. Yet the newly industrialized and industrializing countries perceive those moves as a manifestation of bad faith—a case of the industrialized countries utilizing whatever pretexts lie at hand to rob the developing world of its few competitive advantages. There is, moreover, some justification for their position. If the industrialized countries freely take advantage of their technological lead and mastery of management, marketing, and financial techniques, on what grounds do they try to prevent the newcomers from taking advantage of *their* cheap labor and natural resources?

Indeed, in many quarters of Asia, there is today a lingering suspicion that behind whatever arguments North Americans or Europeans use in trade negotiations lies an unspoken reluctance to acknowledge the end of Western supremacy and to share economic power. For Europeans, however, what the competition from East Asia means above all is that the vaunted European social model is now under assault, its very essence being called into question. With so much at stake, it is not surprising that trade discussions are acquiring such an emotional tone, even more so when a cultural element is added. For example, there have been some disquieting attempts lately by Europeans, notably at the top levels of the French government, to enlist the United States in a kind of holy alliance against the East Asian countries, which the Europeans accuse of playing by different rules and flouting Western-established "universal values." As those attempts make clear, there is now a distinct risk that trade frictions will fuel cultural ones, thereby creating a dangerous spiral of tension and confrontation that would be to no one's benefit.

These emerging tensions, if well managed, could prove a passing phenomenon as the world adjusts to the shift of economic power and to the new strategic economic parity among East Asia, North America, and Western Europe. The problem is that even if most Europeans and North Americans have by now intellectually grasped the magnitude of that trend, many of them have yet to adjust to its implications. One obvious consequence of the new parity is that the West can no longer hope to dictate the rules of the game. Another is that existing international economic institutions that do not yet reflect the new realities (for example, a G7 process that includes no East Asian countries except Japan) will have to be reevaluated. The necessary adjustments will take time. And that time lag creates the danger of an escalation of tensions.

As the world economy continues both to globalize and to organize itself around the three regional centers, we are witnessing another revolutionary development that may actually help to contain interregional tensions: a desynchronizing of economic cycles in the three regions. East Asia, for example, has been booming despite the accelerating decline in the Japanese economy from 1991 to the beginning of 1994, while Europe and the United States have been stuck in one of the most severe recessions in contemporary history. And although the U.S. economy would receive an additional boost from a recovery in Europe, it has been able to climb out of the recession while Europe is still struggling to do so.

The process of regionalization and the desynchronization of regions in the world economy are, in fact, linked. Six years ago, Japan exported one-third more to the United States than it did to the rest of East Asia. Today the situation is reversed. East Asia's intraregional trade now constitutes about 43% of the region's total, compared with 33% in 1980. Meanwhile, East Asia's intraregional investment and financial flows represent the fastest growing share of the region's exchanges: from 1986 to 1992, almost 70% of all investment in East Asia came from within the region, while 10.3% came from Europe and 10.9% came from the United States.

These developments are creating a pattern in East Asia that is increasingly similar to the one that already exists in Western Europe (where intraregional trade accounts for almost 70% of the total) and that will come about in North America with the implementation of NAFTA. Under these conditions, each region is becoming less and less vulnerable to fluctuations that may occur within the others. In other words, desynchronization means that if the United States sneezes, the rest of the world will no longer automatically get the flu.

Yet for the process of regionalization to run its full course in East Asia, Japan will have to assume responsibilities to its regional neighbors more commensurate with its economic weight, particularly by opening its markets to many more East Asian exports. Doing so would be critical not only to reducing the growing trade deficit between Japan and the other East Asian countries but also to containing emerging interregional tensions created by dramatic increases in East Asian exports to Western Europe and North America. If, on the other hand, Japan continues to fail to bring its domestic consumption as a percentage of GNP to a level more in line with that in Western Europe and the United States (around 65% of GNP), then the other East Asian countries will be even more compelled to push their exports toward Western Europe and North America, if only to finance their own growing trade deficits with Japan. Thus a further opening of the Japanese market and a gradual normalization of Japan's trade and current-accounts situations are necessary for the emerging tripolar economic world order to function without frictions reaching a crisis level.

In this new context, where national and regional economies remain vitally interconnected but no one player is in a position to impose its will on the rest of the world, one crucial issue will be the management of the bilateral, regional, and multilateral dimensions of international trade so that they do not conflict with one another. The need for such management will become even more critical as the trend toward economic regionalization picks up momentum. (There are today more than one hundred regional pacts in existence.) On the bilateral front, disputes such as those still brewing between the United States and Japan, and between the United States and China, can at any moment affect the stability of the multilateral trade system because of initiatives that one or the other protagonist may feel compelled to take. For instance, when the United States periodically attempts to impose managed trade agreements on Japan and to set mandatory market shares for U.S. products or services, it contradicts the very basis of the multilateral trade framework.

The new economic world order will also increasingly result, as it has already, in variable, ad hoc alliances on the international trade scene. Europe, for example, now suffers from a huge trade deficit with Japan and voices the same complaints that the United States does about barriers to the Japanese market. Yet Europe refuses to follow Washington in its efforts to set numerical objectives, because doing so could backfire in its own disputes with the United States. However, at the same time, Europe is cooperating with the United States in its attempts to link international trade rules with issues such as social and labor rights.

In short, the revolution in the world economy—with the requirements that it puts on both countries and corporations—means that traditional trade policies are becoming more and more inadequate and may even prove harmful in their capacity to set off chain reactions that can rapidly burst out of control. Today, as countries face the challenge of establishing comprehensive economic strategies integrating fiscal, monetary, and education and training goals, they must do so in accordance with basic guidelines and rules about which the key protagonists on the world trade scene will have to reach a consensus.

Of course, the most immediate requirement for the Western industrialized nations is to take full advantage of the present recovery from the cyclical crisis so they can be in a better position to address the structural issues that confront them. Those issues include the restoration of flexibility to the European labor market in order to stimulate the creation of new jobs; an increased focus on key technologies of the future through which the industrialized countries can still hope to claim a competitive advantage; and the adjustment of education and training systems to create a supply of human resources able to generate higher and higher added value in economic activity.

As this process of restructuring evolves in Western Europe and North America, it will be complemented by three factors now at work in the industrializing and newly industrialized countries of East Asia. The first is the creation, through the process of economic growth in the region, of a widening consumer base: Singapore, Malaysia, Thailand, Indonesia, Taiwan, and South Korea can already claim spectacular increases in domestic consumption, thanks to the emergence of a middle class with both rising expectations and the rapidly increasing means of fulfilling them. Between 1992 and the end of the decade, the number of automobiles put in service in East Asia will grow from 3 million to 7 million per year, according to World Bank estimates. The nascent development of domestic consumption in southern China is another promising indication of things to come.

The second factor in East Asian economic development with important implications for Western restructuring is the exploding infrastructure and energy needs of the still emerging industrial countries of the region. This growing demand will offer unprecedented opportunities in areas such as energy, telecommunications, and transportation. (It is expected that the share of GNP devoted to infrastructure in East Asia will increase from its current 4% to 7% by the year 2000.) In the same vein, the growing concern with environmental protection and the need for clean technologies will provide new opportunities for corporations able to furnish the required technologies and services.

A third and final factor in East Asian development that holds out promise for the West is the accelerating liberalization now taking place in the region's industrializing and newly industrialized countries. South Korea and Taiwan, for example, have recently made strides in privatization, while rapid growth in regional financial markets and telecommunications will also provide new opportunities for European and U.S. corporations.

From 1980 to 1990, total imports in the industrializing and newly industrialized countries of East Asia increased by almost 250%, and the 1990s should see even more growth. Despite the increase in East Asian intraregional trade, European and U.S. corporations can hope to get their share of these markets if they adjust their strategies to the new realities of the tripolar world order, setting the right priorities and making the necessary commitments.

Uncertainty, tension, and the potential for conflict are part of any period of change, especially when the change approaches the magnitude of the one now occurring in the world economy. If the current worldwide economic revolution is to lead to a new phase of widespread and steady growth, the strongest emphasis will have to be placed on three priorities:

> The international institutions required to sustain, monitor, and supervise the new global economic order will need to be established or revamped as soon as possible. The creation of the World Trade Organization is one important step in this respect. Another is the ongoing debate about the role of the World Bank and the IMF in view of the entry of so many new countries into the world market.

> The whole modus operandi of the international economy will have to be reviewed in light of the new strategic parity among North America, Western Europe, and East Asia. As previously noted, the G7 process (on which so many expectations were placed in the 1980s) will have to undergo a fundamental reevaluation. As the trend toward regionalization gains momentum, the key element will be support for whatever policies and initiatives sustain and expand the notion of open regionalization.

A kind of "cultural revolution" will need to be instigated in the developed countries of the West in order to bring about the required adjustment, at the corporate and national levels, to the shift in economic power toward East Asia. The loss of the benefits that these countries once derived from their preeminent position in the world economy need not lead to a long-term decline in living standards, provided that, by adopting the requisite attitudes and policies, these nations can learn to utilize their remaining competitive advantages. At the same time, the newly industrialized countries must show, by their attitudes and initiatives in international economic forums, that they are ready to assume the new responsibilities resulting from their emerging power and status in the global arena.

In recent commemorations of the end of World War II and of the establishment of the subsequent global economic arrangements, much has been said about the merits of the Bretton Woods institutions in creating the conditions for postwar growth and prosperity. Today we can say, in the aftermath of the Cold War and in the midst of a worldwide economic revolution, that we are entering the post-Bretton Woods period. There is no reason to think that in this phase we cannot bring about even greater and more widespread prosperity.

2
Does Third World Growth Hurt First World Prosperity?

Paul Krugman

Only a short while ago, our most influential business writers were warning that the biggest threat to U.S. prosperity was competition from other developed countries. One need only look at the subtitle of Lester Thurow's 1992 best-seller, *Head to Head: The Coming Economic Battle Among Japan, Europe, and America*. But in the last year or so, our supposed economic adversaries have begun to appear a lot less invincible: both the Japanese and the German economies are stuck in intractable recessions, their exports hammered by overvalued currencies and their vaunted labor-market institutions fraying under the impact of economic adversity. In comparison, the U.S. economy, while hardly a picture of glowing prosperity, looks healthy.

But even as many economic writers and corporate executives lose interest in the much-hyped U.S.-Japanese battle, they see a new battle on the horizon—between the advanced economies and the emerging economies of the Third World. There is a striking contrast between the disappointing performance of the advanced nations over the past 20 years and the successes of an increasing number of developing countries. Rapid economic growth, which first began in a few small Asian nations in the 1960s, has now spread across a wide arc of East Asia—not only to relatively well-off Southeast Asian nations like Malaysia and Thailand but also to two poor countries with huge populations: Indonesia and China. There are signs of similarly rapid growth in Chile and perhaps in northern Mexico; centers of rapid development, like the Bangalore software complex, are appearing even in India.

One might have expected everyone to welcome this change in the global landscape, to see the rapid improvement in the living standards of hundreds of millions of people, many of whom had previously been desperately poor, as progress—and as an unprecedented business opportunity. Rather than taking satisfaction in global economic development, however, more and more influential people in the West are regarding economic growth in the Third World as a threat.

These new fears are exemplified in a letter circulated early this year by Klaus Schwab, president of the World Economic Forum, which hosts the famous Davos conferences. Schwab asked a large number of people to provide input for a document he had been asked to prepare for UN secretary general Boutros Boutros-Ghali, entitled "Redefining the Basic Assumptions of Mankind." To indicate what he had in mind, Schwab offered a sample redefinition. Traditionally, he wrote, the world was divided into rich countries with high productivity and high wages and poor countries with low productivity and low wages. But now, he noted, some countries combine high productivity with low wages. The growing presence of those countries in world markets is leading, Schwab argued, to a "massive redeployment of productive assets," which is making it impossible for advanced nations to maintain their standards of living. In other words, competition from the emerging economies of the Third World has become a threat, perhaps *the* threat, to the economies of the First World.

Schwab's views are not unique. No less imposing a figure than Jacques Delors, president of the European Commission, seems to share them. The European Commission's eagerly awaited white paper on European economic difficulties, "Growth, Competitiveness, and Employment," released in December 1993, lists four reasons for the long upward trend in European unemployment rates. According to the report, the most important factor is the rise of nations that are "competing with us—even in our own markets—at cost levels that we simply cannot match": Eurospeak for low-wage competition from the Third World.

Such views are less widespread in the United States. In spite of the Clinton administration's tendency to define economic problems in competitive terms, it has saved its fire for advanced nations like Japan; the 1994 *Economic Report of the President* argues that imports from the Third World have not been a major pressure on the U.S. labor market, at least not so far. Still, such economic writers as *Business Week*'s Robert Kuttner and think tanks like the Economic Policy Institute maintain a steady drumbeat of warnings about the threat that low-wage imports pose to U.S. living standards. The magazine *CEO/International Strategies*, in its December 1993/January 1994 issue, which was devoted to the theme "Redefining the Global Economy," published not one but three pieces on the threat of low-wage competition from developing countries. Some informal polling of noneconomists I know suggests that a majority of them, including many who consider themselves well informed about economic affairs, consider it an established fact that competition from the Third World is a major source of current U.S. economic problems.

The truth, however, is that fears about the economic impact of Third World competition are almost entirely unjustified. Economic growth in low-wage nations is in principle as likely to raise as to lower per capita income in high-wage countries; the actual effects have been negligible. In theory, there are some reasons for concern about the possible impact of Third World competition on the *distribution* (as opposed to the *level*) of income in the West, but there are few signs that such concern is justified in practice, at least so far.

How can so many sophisticated people be so wrong? (And how can I be so sure that they are wrong?) To make sense of the alleged threat from the Third World, it is necessary to begin with a brief discussion of the world economy.

Thinking About the World Economy

The idea that Third World competition threatens living standards in advanced countries seems straightforward. Suppose that somebody has learned to do something that used to be my exclusive specialty. Maybe he or she isn't quite as good at it as I am but is willing to work for a fraction of my wage. Isn't it obvious that I am either going to have to accept a lower standard of living or be out of a job? That, in essence, is the view of those who fear that Western wage rates must fall as the Third World develops.

But this story is completely misleading. When world productivity rises (as it does when Third World countries converge on First World productivity), *average* world living standards must rise: after all, the extra output must go somewhere. This by itself presumes that higher Third World productivity will be reflected in higher Third World wages, not lower First World incomes. Another way to look at it is to notice that in a national economy, producers and consumers are the same people; foreign competitors who cut prices may lower the wage I receive, but they also raise the purchasing power of whatever I earn. There is no reason to expect the adverse effect to predominate.

The world economy is a system—a complex web of feedback relationships—not a simple chain of one-way effects. In this global economic system, wages, prices, trade, and investment flows are out-comes, not givens. Intuitively plausible scenarios based on day-to-day business experience can be deeply misleading about what happens to this system when underlying parameters change, whether the pa-rameters are government policies like tariffs and taxes or more mys-terious factors like the productivity of Chinese labor.

As anyone knows who has studied a complex system, be it global weather, Los Angeles traffic patterns, or the flow of materials through a manufacturing process, it is necessary to build a model to understand how the system works. The usual procedure is to start with a very simplified model and then make it increasingly realistic; in the process, one comes to a more sophisticated understanding of the actual system.

In this article, I will follow that procedure to think about the impact of emerging economies on wages and jobs in the advanced world. I will start with an oversimplified and unrealistic picture of the world economy and then gradually add realistic complications. At each stage, I will also bring in some data. By the end, I hope to have made clear that the seemingly sophisticated view that the Third World is causing First World problems is questionable on conceptual grounds and wholly implausible in terms of the data.

Model 1: A One-Good, One-Input World

Imagine a world without the complexities of the global economy. In this world, one all-purpose good is produced—let's call it chips—using one input, labor. All countries produce chips, but labor is more pro-ductive in some countries than in others. In imagining such a world, we ignore two crucial facts about the actual global economy: it pro-duces hundreds of thousands of distinct goods and services, and it does so using many inputs, including physical capital and the "human capital" that results from education.

What would determine wages and standards of living in such a simplified world? In the absence of capital or differentiation between skilled and unskilled labor, workers would receive what they produce. That is, the annual real wage in terms of chips in each country would equal the number of chips each worker produced in a year—his or her productivity. And since chips are the only good consumed as well as the only good produced, the consumer price index would contain nothing but chips. Each country's real wage rate in terms of its CPI would also equal the productivity of labor in each country.

What about relative wages? The possibility of arbitrage, of shipping goods to wherever they command the highest price, would keep chip prices the same in all countries. Thus the wage rate of workers who produce 10,000 chips annually would be ten times that of workers who produce 1,000, even if those workers are in different countries. The ratio of any two nations' wage rates, then, would equal the ratio of their workers' productivity.

What would happen if countries that previously had low productivity and thus low wages were to experience a large increase in their productivity? These emerging economies would see their wage rates in terms of chips rise—end of story. There would be no impact, positive or negative, on real wage rates in other, initially higher-wage countries. In each country, the real wage rate equals domestic productivity in terms of chips; that remains true, regardless of what happens elsewhere.

What's wrong with this model? It's ridiculously oversimplified, but in what ways might the simplification mislead us? One immediate problem with the model is that it leaves no room for international trade: if everyone is producing chips, there is no reason to import or export them. (This issue does not seem to bother such competitiveness theorists as Lester Thurow. The central proposition of Thurow's *Head to Head* is that because the advanced nations produce the same things, the benign niche competition of the past has given way to win-lose head-to-head competition. But if the advanced nations are producing the same things, why do they sell so much to one another?)

While the fact that countries do trade with one another means that our simplified model cannot be literally true, this model does raise the question of how extensive the trade actually is between advanced nations and the Third World. It turns out to be surprisingly small despite the emphasis on Third World trade in such documents as the Delors white paper. In 1990, advanced industrial nations spent only 1.2% of their combined GDPs on imports of manufactured goods from newly industrializing economies. A model in which advanced countries have no reason to trade with low-wage countries is obviously not completely accurate, but it is more than 98% right all the same.

Another problem with the model is that without capital, there can be no international investment. We'll come back to that point when we put capital into the model. It's worth noting, however, that in the U.S. economy, more than 70% of national income accrues to labor and less than 30% to capital; this proportion has been very stable for the past two decades. Labor is clearly not the only input in the production of goods, but the assertion that the average real wage rate moves almost one for one with output per worker, that what is good for the

United States is good for U.S. workers and vice versa, seems approximately correct.

One last assertion that may bother some readers is that wages automatically rise with productivity. Is this realistic? Yes. Economic history offers no example of a country that experienced long-term productivity growth without a roughly equal rise in real wages. In the 1950s, when European productivity was typically less than half of U.S. productivity, so were European wages; today average compensation measured in dollars is about the same. As Japan climbed the productivity ladder over the past 30 years, its wages also rose, from 10% to 110% of the U.S. level. South Korea's wages have also risen dramatically over time. Indeed, many Korean economists worry that wages may have risen too much. Korean labor now seems too expensive to compete in low-technology goods with newcomers like China and Indonesia and too expensive to compensate for low productivity and product quality in such industries as autos.

The idea that somehow the old rules no longer apply, that new entrants on the world economic stage will always pay low wages even as their productivity rises to advanced-country levels, has no basis in actual experience. (Some economic writers try to refute this proposition by pointing to particular industries in which relative wages don't match relative productivity. For example, shirtmakers in Bangladesh, who are almost half as productive as shirtmakers in the United States, receive far less than half the U.S. wage rate. But as we'll see when we turn to a multigood model, that is exactly what standard economic theory predicts.)

Our one-good, one-input model may seem silly, but it forces us to notice two crucial points. First, an increase in Third World labor productivity means an increase in world output, and an increase in world output must show up as an increase in *somebody's* income. And it does: it shows up in higher wages for Third World workers. Second, whatever we may eventually conclude about the impact of higher Third World productivity on First World economies, it won't necessarily be adverse. The simplest model suggests that there is no impact at all.

Model 2: Many Goods, One Input

In the real world, of course, countries specialize in the production of a limited range of goods; international trade is both the cause and the result of that specialization. In particular, the trade in manufactured goods between the First and Third worlds is largely an exchange of sophisticated high-technology products like aircraft and microprocessors for labor-intensive goods like clothing. In a world in which countries produce different goods, productivity gains in one part of the world may either help or hurt the rest of the world.

This is by no means a new subject. Between the end of World War II and the Korean War, many nations experienced a series of balance-of-payments difficulties, which led to the perception of a global "dollar shortage." At the time, many Europeans believed that their real problem was the overwhelming competitiveness of the highly productive U.S. economy. But was the U.S. economy really damaging the rest of the world? More generally, does productivity growth in one country raise or lower real incomes in other countries? An extensive body of theoretical and empirical work concluded that the impact of productivity growth abroad on domestic welfare can be either positive or negative, depending on the *bias* of that productivity growth—that is, depending on the sectors in which such growth occurs.[1]

Sir W. Arthur Lewis, who won the 1979 Nobel Prize in economics for his work on economic development, has offered a clever illustration of how the effect of productivity growth in developing countries on the real wages in advanced nations can work either way. In Lewis's model, the world is divided into two regions, call them North and South. This global economy produces not one but three types of goods: high-tech, medium-tech, and low-tech. As in our first model, however, labor is still the only input into production. Northern labor is more productive than Southern labor in all three types of goods, but that productivity advantage is huge in high-tech, moderate in medium-tech, and small in low-tech.

What will be the pattern of wages and production in such a world? A likely outcome is that high-tech goods will be produced only in the North, low-tech goods only in the South, and both regions will produce at least some medium-tech goods. (If world demand for high-tech products is very high, the North may produce only those goods; if demand for low-tech products is high, the South may also specialize. But there will be a wide range of cases in which both regions produce medium-tech goods.)

Competition will ensure that the ratio of the wage rate in the North to that in the South will equal the ratio of Northern to Southern productivity in the sector in which workers in the two regions face each other head-to-head: medium-tech. In this case, Northern workers will not be competitive in low-tech goods in spite of their higher productivity because their wage rates are too high. Conversely, low Southern wage rates are not enough to compensate for low productivity in high-tech.

A numerical example may be helpful here. Suppose that Northern labor is ten times as productive as Southern labor in high-tech, five times as productive in medium-tech, but only twice as productive in low-tech. If both countries produce medium-tech goods, the Northern wage must be five times higher than the Southern. Given this wage ratio, labor costs in the South for low-tech goods will be only two-fifths of labor costs in the North for this sector, even though Northern labor is more productive. In high-tech goods, by contrast, labor costs will be twice as high in the South.

Notice that in this example, Southern low-tech workers receive only one-fifth the Northern wage, even though they are half as productive as Northern workers in the same industry. Many people, including those who call themselves experts on international trade, believe that kind of gap shows that conventional economic models don't apply. In fact, it's exactly what conventional analysis predicts: if low-wage countries didn't have lower unit labor costs than high-wage countries in their export industries, they couldn't export.

Now suppose that there is an increase in Southern productivity. What effect will it have? It depends on which sector experiences the productivity gain. If the productivity increase occurs in low-tech output, a sector that does not compete with Northern labor, there is no reason to expect the ratio of Northern to Southern wages to change. Southern labor will produce low-tech goods more cheaply, and the fall in the price of those goods will raise real wages in the North. But if Southern productivity rises in the competitive medium-tech sector, relative Southern wages will rise. Since productivity has not risen in low-tech production, low-tech prices will rise and reduce real wages in the North.

What happens if Southern productivity rises at equal rates in low- and medium-tech? The relative wage rate will rise but will be offset by the productivity increase. The prices of low-tech goods in terms of Northern labor will not change, and thus the real wages of Northern workers will not change either. In other words, an across-the-board productivity increase in the South in this multigood model has the same effect on Northern living standards as productivity growth had in the one-good model: none at all.

It seems, then, that the effect of Third World growth on the First World, which was negligible in our simplest model, becomes unpredictable once we make the model more realistic. There are, however, two points worth noting.

First, the way in which growth in the Third World can hurt the First World is very different from the way it is described in the Schwab letter or the Delors White Paper. Third World growth does not hurt the First World because wages in the Third World stay low but because they rise and therefore push up the prices of exports to advanced countries. That is, the United States may be threatened when South Korea gets better at producing automobiles, not because the United States loses the automobile market but because higher South Korean wages mean that U.S. consumers pay more for the pajamas and toys that they were already buying from South Korea.

Second, this potential adverse effect should show up in a readily measured economic statistic: the *terms of trade*, or the ratio of export to import prices. For example, if U.S. companies are forced to sell goods more cheaply on world markets because of foreign competition or are forced to pay more for imports because of competition for raw materials or a devalued dollar, real income in the United States will fall. Because exports and imports are about 10% of GNP, each 10% decline in the U.S. terms of trade reduces U.S. real income by about 1%. The potential damage to advanced economies from Third World growth rests on the possibility of a decline in advanced-country terms of trade. But that hasn't happened. Between 1982 and 1992, the terms of trade of the developed market economies actually improved by 12%, largely as a result of falling real oil prices.

In sum, a multigood model offers more possibilities than the simple one-good model with which we began, but it leads to the same conclusion: productivity growth in the Third World leads to higher wages in the Third World.

Model 3: Capital and International Investment

Let's move a step closer to reality and add another input to our model. What changes if we now imagine a world in which production requires both capital and labor? From a global point of view, there is one big difference between labor and capital: the degree of international mobility. Although large-scale international migration was a major force in the world economy before 1920, since then all advanced countries have erected high legal barriers to economically motivated immigration. There is a limited flow of very highly skilled people from South to North—the notorious "brain drain"—and a somewhat larger flow of illegal migration. But most labor does not move internationally.

In contrast, international investment is a highly visible and growing influence on the world economy. During the late 1970s, many banks in advanced countries lent large sums of money to Third World countries. This flow dried up in the 1980s, the decade of the debt crisis, but considerable capital flows resumed with the emerging-markets boom that began after 1990.

Many of the fears about Third World growth seem to focus on capital flows rather than trade. Schwab's fear that there will be a "massive redeployment of productive assets" presumably refers to investment in the Third World. The famous estimate by the Economic Policy Institute that NAFTA would cost 500,000 U.S. jobs was based on a completely hypothetical scenario about diversion of U.S. investment. Even Labor Secretary Robert Reich, at the March 1994 job summit in Detroit, attributed the employment problems of Western economies to the mobility of capital. In effect, he seemed to be asserting that First World capital now creates only Third World jobs. Are those fears justified?

The short answer is yes in principle but no in practice. As a matter of standard textbook theory, international flows of capital from North to South could lower Northern wages. The actual flows that have taken place since 1990, however, are far too small to have the devastating impacts that many people envision.

To understand how international investment flows could pose problems for advanced-country labor, we must first realize that the productivity of labor depends in part on how much capital it has to work with. As an empirical matter, the share of labor in domestic output is very stable. But if labor has less capital at its disposal, productivity and thus real wage rates will fall.

Suppose, then, that Third World nations become more attractive than First World nations for First World investors. This might be because a change in political conditions makes such investments seem safer or because technology transfer raises the potential productivity of Third World workers (once they are equipped with adequate capital). Does this hurt First World workers? Of course. Capital exported to the Third World is capital not invested at home, so such North-South investment means that Northern productivity and wages will fall. Northern investors presumably earn a higher return on these investments than they could have earned at home, but that may offer little comfort to workers.

Before we jump to the conclusion that the development of the Third World has come at First World expense, however, we must ask not merely whether economic damage arises in principle but how large it is in practice.

How much capital has been exported from advanced countries to developing countries? During the 1980s, there was essentially no net North-South investment—indeed, interest payments and debt repayments were consistently larger than the new investment. All the action, then, has taken place since 1990. In 1993, the peak year of emerging-markets investment so far, capital flows from all advanced nations to all newly industrializing countries totaled about $100 billion.

That may sound very high, but compared with the First World economy, it isn't. Last year, the combined GNPs of North America, Western Europe, and Japan totaled more than $18 trillion. Their combined investment was more than $3.5 trillion; their combined capital stocks were about $60 trillion. The record capital flows of 1993 diverted only about 3% of First World investment away from domestic use and reduced the growth in the capital stock by less than 0.2%. The entire emerging-market investment boom since 1990 has reduced the advanced world's capital stock by only about .5% from what it would otherwise have been.

How much pressure has this placed on wages in advanced countries? A reduction of the capital stock by 1% reduces productivity by less than 1%, since capital is only one input; standard estimates put the number at about 0.3%. A back-of-the-envelope calculation therefore suggests that capital flows to the Third World since 1990 (and bear in mind that there was essentially no capital flow during the 1980s) have reduced real wages in the advanced world by about 0.15%—hardly the devastation that Schwab, Delors, or the Economic Policy Institute presume.

There is another way to make the same point. Anything that draws capital away from business investment in the advanced countries tends to reduce First World wages. But investment in the Third World has become considerable only in the last few years. Meanwhile, there has been a massive diversion of savings into a purely domestic sink: the budget deficits run up by the United States and other countries. Since 1980, the United States alone has run up more than $3 trillion in federal debt, more than ten times the amount invested in emerging economies by all advanced countries combined. The export of capital to the Third World attracts a lot of attention because it is exotic, but the amounts are minor compared with domestic budget deficits.

At this point, some readers may object that one cannot compare the two numbers. Savings absorbed by the federal budget deficit simply disappear; savings invested abroad create factories that make products that then compete with ours. It seems plausible that overseas investment is more damaging than budget deficits. But that intuition is wrong: investing in Third World countries raises their productivity, and we've seen in the first two models that higher Third World productivity per se is unlikely to lower First World living standards.

The conventional wisdom among many policymakers and pundits is that we live in a world of incredibly mobile capital and that such mobility changes everything. But capital isn't all that mobile, and the capital movements we have seen so far change very little, at least for advanced countries.

Model 4: The Distribution of Income

We seem to have concluded that growth in the Third World has almost no adverse effects on the First World. But there is still one more issue to address: the effects of Third World growth on the distribution of income between skilled and unskilled labor within the advanced world.

For our final model, let's add one more complication. Suppose that there are two kinds of labor, skilled and unskilled. And suppose that the ratio of unskilled to skilled workers is much higher in the South than in the North. In such a situation, one would expect the ratio of skilled to unskilled wages to be lower in the North than in the South. As a result, one would expect the North to export skill-intensive goods and services—that is, employ a high ratio of skilled to unskilled labor in their production, while the South exports goods whose production is intensive in unskilled labor.

What is the effect of this trade on wages in the North? When two countries exchange skill-intensive goods for labor-intensive goods, they indirectly trade skilled for unskilled labor; the goods that the North ships to the South "embody" more skilled labor than the goods the North receives in return. It is as if some of the North's skilled workers migrated to the South. Similarly, the North's imports of labor-intensive products are like an indirect form of low-skill immigration. Trade with the South in effect makes Northern skilled labor scarcer, raising the wage it can command, while it makes unskilled labor effectively more abundant, reducing its wage.

Increased trade with the Third World, then, while it may have little effect on the overall level of First World wages, should in principle lead to greater *inequality* in those wages, with a higher premium for skill. Equally, there should be a tendency toward "factor price equalization," with wages of low-skilled workers in the North declining toward Southern levels.

What makes this conclusion worrisome is that income inequality has been rapidly increasing in the United States and to a lesser extent in other advanced nations. Even if Third World exports have not hurt the average level of wages in the First World, might they not be responsible for the steep declines since the 1970s in real wages of unskilled workers in the United States and the rising unemployment rates of European workers?

At this point, the preponderance of the evidence seems to be that factor price equalization has *not* been a major element in the growing wage inequality in the United States, although the evidence is more indirect and less secure than the evidence we brought to our earlier models.[2] In essence, trade with the Third World is just not that large. Since trade with low-wage countries is only a little more than 1% of GDP, the net flows of labor embodied in that trade are fairly small compared with the overall size of the labor force.

More careful research may lead to larger estimates of the effect of North-South trade on the distribution of wages, or future growth in that trade may have larger effects than we have seen so far. At this point, however, the available evidence does not support the view that trade with the Third World is an important part of the wage inequality story.

Moreover, even to the extent that North-South trade may explain some of the growing inequality of earnings, it has nothing to do with the disappointing performance of average wages. Before 1973, average compensation in the United States rose at an annual rate of more than 2%; since then it has risen at a rate of only 0.3%. This decline is at the heart of our economic malaise, and Third World exports have nothing to do with it.

The Real Threat

The view that competition from the Third World is a major problem for advanced countries is questionable in theory and flatly rejected by the data. Why does this matter? Isn't this merely academic quibbling? One answer is that those who talk about the dangers of competition with the Third World certainly think that it matters; the European

Commission presumably did not add its comments about low-wage competition to its white paper simply to fill space. If policymakers and intellectuals think it is important to emphasize the adverse effects of low-wage competition, then it is at least equally important for economists and business leaders to tell them they are wrong.

Ideas matter. According to recent newspaper reports, the United States and France have agreed to place demands for international standards on wages and working conditions on the agenda at the next GATT negotiations. U.S. officials will doubtless claim they have the interests of Third World workers at heart. Developing countries are already warning, however, that such standards are simply an effort to deny them access to world markets by preventing them from making use of the only competitive advantage they have: abundant labor. The developing countries are right. This is protectionism in the guise of humanitarian concern.

Most worrisome of all is the prospect that disguised protectionism will eventually give way to cruder, more open trade barriers. For example, Robert Kuttner has long argued that all world trade should be run along the lines of the Multi-Fiber Agreement, which fixes market shares for textile and apparel. In effect, he wants the cartelization of all world markets. Proposals like that are still outside the range of serious policy discussion, but when respectable voices lend credence to the wholly implausible idea that the Third World is responsible for the First World's problems, they prepare the way for that kind of heavy-handed interference in world trade.

We are not talking about narrow economic issues. If the West throws up barriers to imports out of a misguided belief that they will protect Western living standards, the effect could be to destroy the most promising aspect of today's world economy: the beginning of widespread economic development, of hopes for a decent living standard for hundreds of millions, even billions, of human beings. Economic growth in the Third World is an opportunity, not a threat; it is our fear of Third World success, not that success itself, that is the real danger to the world economy.

Notes

1. The essential readings are J.R. Hicks on the long-run dollar problem in "An Inaugural Lecture," *Oxford Economic Papers* (New Series), June

1953; and H.G. Johnson, "Economic Expansion and International Trade," *Manchester School of Economic and Social Studies,* May 1955.

2. See Lawrence F. Katz, "Understanding Recent Changes in the Wage Structure," *NBER Reporter,* Winter 1992–93; and Robert Lawrence and Matthew Slaughter, "International Trade and American Wages in the 1980s: Giant Sucking Sound or Small Hiccup?" *Brookings Papers on Economic Activity* 2, 1993.

3

Putting Global Logic First

Kenichi Ohmae

In today's borderless economy, the workings of the "invisible hand" have a reach and strength beyond anything Adam Smith ever could have imagined. In Smith's day, economic activity took place on a landscape largely defined—and circumscribed—by the political borders of nation-states: Ireland with its wool, Portugal with its wines. Now, by contrast, economic activity is what defines the landscape on which all other institutions, including political institutions, must operate. Business and government are just beginning to live with the consequences.

Most visibly, the nation-state itself—that artifact of the eighteenth and nineteenth centuries—has begun to crumble, battered by a pent-up storm of political resentment, ethnic prejudice, tribal hatred, and religious animosity. The most dramatic examples are the former Soviet Union and Czechoslovakia, which both have ceased to exist as nations. But there are many others. In the now unified Germany, the federal government has ceded an unprecedented amount of power to the individual *Länder*. Similarly, Spain's 17 autonomous communities—especially those with deeply entrenched historical identities, such as Catalonia—are gaining the powers of independent states. In Canada, the French-speaking province of Quebec is actively moving to cut its constitutional ties with the largely English-speaking provinces. Even in dirigiste France, the prefects of President François Mitterrand's government can no longer unilaterally veto decisions made in the country's 22 provinces.

To interpret those events in purely political terms would be a mistake. Of course, nearly half a century of cold war tensions cannot end without dramatic changes on all sides: in the absence of the restraints once imposed by the superpowers, long-repressed political aspirations have burst into the open. But there are three other, more fundamental factors at work. First, the often instantaneous movement of people, ideas, information, and capital across borders means that decisions are swayed by the threat that needed resources will go elsewhere rather than by cold war allegiances. With the speed and volume of transactions in the global capital market, national governments cannot control exchange rates or protect their currencies, and political leaders increasingly find themselves at the mercy of people and institutions making economic choices over which they have no control. Remember the recent Maastricht-related bout of speculation against the British pound, the French franc, and the Swedish krona? It demonstrated that currency speculators can affect the value of a particular currency in ways that the government simply cannot counteract, even if it spends billions in an attempt to prop up the exchange rate.

Second, as the flow of information creates a growing awareness among consumers everywhere about how other people live, tastes and preferences begin to converge. Global brands of colas, blue jeans, athletic shoes, and designer ties and handbags are as much on the mind of the taxi driver in Shanghai as they are in the home of the schoolteacher in Stockholm. Over time, the accelerating convergence of tastes puts pressure on governments to make sure their people have access to the best and cheapest products from all over the world. When governments refuse—in the name of national interest or market protection or whatever—people will find a way to vote with their pocketbooks.

Third, the nation-state, which was a powerful engine of wealth creation in its mercantilist phase, has become an equally powerful engine of wealth destruction. To stay in office, elected leaders know they must satisfy the often extortionate demands of powerful special-interest groups, such as the unions, farmers, and fishermen in Japan. To maintain legitimacy, they must freely make available to all citizens a common level of public services and support even though they cost vastly different amounts to provide. Their constituents demand the same civil minimum of services—telephone, electricity, postal service, roads, schools, and harbors—regardless of whether they live in Tokyo or on the remote island of Okinawa.

As a result of the effort to provide a civil minimum of services, 44 of Japan's 47 prefectures are now net recipients of government subsidies. The other 3—all in the Greater Tokyo area—pay for the rest. The imbalance is striking. The cities of Tokyo, Osaka, Fukuoka, Sapporo, and Nagoya create more than 85% of Japan's wealth. Of those five cities, only Tokyo is a net taxpayer; all the others receive more money from the central government than they pay in taxes. Meanwhile, in the city of Aomori, at the northern end of Japan's main island of Honshu, only $300 million of the annual budget of $1.5 billion comes from local taxes. Everything else comes from the central government.

A government may have understandable political, perhaps even social, reasons to defer to special interests and to observe the civil minimum. Economically, however, it makes no sense. Investing money inefficiently never does. In a borderless world, it is also unsustainable. Sooner or later, usually sooner, the invisible hand of the market will move resources or economic activity elsewhere. During the past several years, for instance, the Japanese government has pumped more than $300 billion into the domestic economy in a Keynesian attempt to jump-start demand after the post-Bubble recession. The strategy worked. But it did not boost local supply or create local jobs. As demand increased, supply came from China, Korea, and the rest of the world. Even in Japan, the instruments of central control are losing their force.

That should come as no surprise. Since nation-states were created to meet the needs of a much earlier historical period, they do not have the will, the incentive, the credibility, the tools, or the political base to play an effective role in the borderless economy of today. By heritage and by experience, nation-states are comfortable with the market's invisible hand only when they can control or regulate it. By orientation and by skill, they cannot help but make economic choices primarily in terms of their political, not economic, consequences. By electoral logic and by popular expectation, they must always sacrifice general, indirect, long-term benefits in favor of immediate, tangible, focused payoffs. They are a willing hostage to the past because the future is a constituency that casts no vote. The bottom line is that they have become unnatural—even dysfunctional—as actors in a global economy because they are incapable of putting global logic first in their decisions.

Nation-states are no longer meaningful units in which to think about economic activity. In a borderless world, they combine things at the wrong level of aggregation. What sense does it make, for example, to think of Italy as a coherent economic entity within the European Union? There is no "average" Italy. There is no meaningful social or economic group precisely at the midpoint. There is an industrial north and a rural south, which are vastly different in their ability to contribute and their need to receive. For the public official or the private-sector manager, treating Italy as if it were fairly represented by an average is to mortgage usable insight in return for an economic relic—and a destructive one at that.

Region-States

In a borderless economy, the units that do make sense are what I call region-states—geographical units such as northern Italy; Wales; Baden-Württemberg in Germany; San Diego, California, and Tijuana, Mexico; Hong Kong and southern China; the Growth Triangle of Singapore and its neighboring Indonesian islands; or Osaka and its outlying areas, which are together known as Kañsai. Those are the natural economic zones. They may or may not fall within the boundaries of a particular nation. If they do, it is an accident of history. In practical terms, it does not really matter. What does matter is that each possesses the key ingredients for successful participation in the global economy—not the least of which is the ability and the determination to put global logic first.

Look, for example, at what is happening in Southeast Asia as the Hong Kong economy reaches out to embrace first Shenzhen and then other parts of the Zhu River Delta, often called the Pearl River Delta, in China. Hong Kong, where per capita gross national product is $12,000, is now the driving economic force in the lives of the people in Shenzhen, and its radiating influence has already boosted per capita GNP there to $5,695. Per capita GNP for all of China is only $317. Even today, those linkages extend beyond Shenzhen to Zhuhai, Xiamen, and Guangzhou as well. By the year 2000, that cross-border region-state could raise the standard of living of some 11 million people to more than the $5,000 level.

Chinese government officials have gotten the message and expanded the "special economic zone" concept, which has worked so well for Shenzhen and Shanghai, to 14 other areas, many of them inland. The concept involves a mix of policies allowing for favorable terms for foreign investment, access to credit, transshipment of goods, and so forth. One such project in Yunnan will become a cross-border region-state encompassing Laos and Vietnam. Within Vietnam, Ho Chi Minh City has launched a similar effort, called Sepzone, in order to attract foreign capital. Moreover, Indonesia, Malaysia, and Thailand unveiled a plan in 1992, modeled in part on Singapore's Growth Triangle, to link economically their respective cities of Medan, Penang, and Phuket across the Strait of Malacca.

Other such initiatives are in the works. The Tumen Delta Project cuts across China, North Korea, and Russia. In Japan, government and business have expressed interest in a Northeastern Asia Economic Zone, also called the Sea of Japan Economic Zone, which would link the Russian cities of Nakhodka, Khabarovsk, and Vladivostok with the Japanese city of Niigata. There are also proposals to integrate that economic zone with the Tumen Delta Project. Cold war animosities notwithstanding, the signs are favorable: a ferry is already in service across the Sea of Japan.

As of early 1994, the city of Dalian on China's Liaodong Peninsula, in the north, was home to more than 3,500 active corporations— nearly 2,500 of them with foreign affiliations. The mayor of Dalian knows perfectly well that continued economic growth depends on providing an attractive environment for foreign investment. He also knows that the region's leaders cannot responsibly ignore the needs of foreign operations and instead divert resources to protect indigenous state-owned companies, most of which are losing money. Dalian and its people simply cannot afford it. Much the same is true in the three northeastern provinces of China, which have already reached a steeper learning curve than Japan has in the manufacture both of printed circuit boards for laptop computers and of cylinder heads for videocassette recorders—with higher productivity and at only 2% of Japan's wage levels.

That kind of economic progress is possible only when regions are genuinely open and responsive—in ways nation-states will not and cannot be—to the real flow of economic activity in today's world. Thomas P. "Tip" O'Neill, the late former Speaker of the U.S. House of Representatives, liked to say, "All politics is local." But region-states are economic units, not political ones, and they are anything but local in focus. They may lie within the borders of an established nation, but their primary linkage is with the global economy.

Region-states welcome foreign investment. They welcome foreign ownership. They welcome foreign products. In fact, they welcome whatever will employ their people productively, improve their quality of life, and give them access to the best and cheapest products in the world. They have discovered that people often have better access to low-cost, high-quality products when they do not try to produce them at home. Singaporeans, for example, enjoy better and cheaper agricultural products than do the Japanese, although Singapore has no farmers—and no farms—of its own. Furthermore, region-states welcome the chance to use any surplus that accrues from global trade and investment activities to ratchet up the quality of life even more rather than to fund the civil minimum or prop up distressed industries. Their leaders do not go around to other countries trying to attract factories and investment—and then appear on television back home vowing to protect local jobs and local producers at all costs.

Region-states are the natural economic zones in a borderless world because, by definition, the demands of the global economy shape their contours. They must be large enough to provide an attractive market for leading consumer products but small enough for their citizens to share economic and consumer interests. They must be of sufficient size to justify economies of services—that is, an infrastructure of communications, transportation, and professional services. They must, for example, have at least one international airport and, more than likely, one good harbor with international-class freight-handling facilities. They tend to have between 5 million and 20 million people. The population range is broad, but the extremes are clear: not half a million, not 50 million or 100 million.

When region-states prosper, their prosperity spills over into adjacent areas. Happy economic experiences in and around Bangkok have prompted investors to explore options in other parts of Thailand. The same is true of Kuala Lumpur in Malaysia, Djakarta in Indonesia, and of course, Singapore. It would also be true of the area around São Paulo if the Brazilian government would free it up to participate as a region-state in the global economy. If it does, São Paulo will probably be ready to join the Organization for Economic Cooperation and Development within ten years. If it does not, Brazil itself may fall off the roster of rapidly developing economies.

The Ladder of Development

What defines region-states is their commitment to being a point of entry to the global economy. But what gives each its special form and shape is its position on the ladder of economic development. Moving up that ladder means being able to put the right policies, institutions, and infrastructure in place at the right time. At about $3,000 per capita GNP, a region-state's desire to get more actively involved with the global economy, both as a market for and as a supplier of basic consumer goods, usually increases steadily. In Japan for example, the desire took the form of rapidly expanding consumer demand for color televisions, refrigerators, and low-cost automobiles. Below that level— between, say, $1,500 and $3,000 per capita—the emphasis is more on motorbikes, as it is today in Thailand; below $1,500, it is more on bicycles, as it is in Shanghai, China, and throughout Vietnam. At the $3,000 threshold, it makes sense to begin serious construction of modern highway systems, urban rail systems, and the rest of the infrastructure needed to support a higher level of international commerce: drinking water, electric power, communications, and finance.

At the $5,000 threshold, the requirements for economic development change yet again. The strength of the desire to be part of the global economic system escalates rapidly. The demand for quality automobiles takes off, as does the need for up-to-date international airports and a high-speed railway system. At that stage also, the drive for ever greater material prosperity often begins to crowd out, even for local elites, quality-of-life considerations—such as living in a clean environment, running factories that observe Western-style child-labor laws, and structuring work so as to allow for leisure time—which tend not to return in force until GNP moves well beyond the $10,000 level.

Something else happens at $5,000: linkages with the global economy expand, but the softer aspects of the economy—the currency, as well as banking and communications, for example—are not yet fully open to it. The heavy hand of government regulation and control remains firmly in place. The temptation, of course, is to keep it there. After all, why face the disruption and loss of control that a deregulated and open economy would bring?

Most midsize countries in Europe have given in to that temptation, which explains why they have had to struggle so much to get beyond the $5,000 barrier. By contrast, Taiwan, at a comparable point in its development, aggressively moved to deregulate foreign-exchange and many other markets. As a result, its economy shot up to the $10,000 level in only a few years. Singapore made basically the same kind of leap. So did Hong Kong, which explains why its economy shot by the $5,000 barrier while South Korea's did not, although all four had competed neck and neck until that point.

The evidence, then, is clear: what a government does at $5,000 per capita GNP makes a huge difference in how quickly—and how well— it can join the $10,000 club. If a country genuinely opens itself up to the global system, prosperity will follow. If it does not or if it does so only halfheartedly, relying instead on the heavy, guiding hand of central government, its progress will falter.

Policy Challenges

Policymakers at all levels, public and private, will need to think carefully about how best to avoid government intervention that will stifle the development of region-states. Silicon Valley, the great early juggernaut of much of the microelectronics industry in the United States, has created industry associations, lobbied the federal government, studied competitiveness as a way to get more federal funding for research and development, and become downright protectionist. The result: Japan has now developed a Silicon Island on Kyushu; Taiwan is trying to create a Silicon Island of its own; and Korea is nurturing a Silicon Peninsula. It is the worst of all possible worlds for Silicon Valley—no new money in California and a host of newly energized and well-funded competitors.

Note that far from Silicon Valley, the story is quite different. When Hollywood recognized that it faced a severe capital shortage, it did not throw up protectionist barriers against foreign money. Instead, it invited Rupert Murdoch into Twentieth Century-Fox, C. Itoh and Toshiba into Time Warner, Sony into Columbia Pictures, and Matsushita into MCA. The result was a $10 billion infusion of new capital—and, equally important, $10 billion less for Japan or anyone else to set up its own Hollywood.

Political leaders around the world are just beginning to pay serious attention to those lessons. But they are—and are likely to remain—the most reluctant of converts. That tendency is, of course, perfectly understandable: their power rests on the traditional nation-state, and its inevitable erosion is not something to be accepted lightly over a cup of tea in the afternoon. But accept it they must. Otherwise, as meaningful economic activity migrates to the region-states that lie within and across their countries' borders, they will be left with hollow political shells and constituents calling for the civil minimum.

Quebec, for example, is not the core economic or even political issue for Canada, although it is of great emotional significance. As the North American Free Trade Agreement takes shape, the relationships between U.S. and Canadian regions—Seattle and Vancouver (the Pacific Northwest region-state); and Detroit, Cleveland, and Toronto (the Great Lakes region-state)—will become increasingly important. How will Canada's leaders deal with the new entities? How will they guide the confederation? If they are going to be able to run Canada politically, they will have to find workable answers to such questions.

On present evidence, however, it is not even clear they are asking the questions, because they are so preoccupied with the problems of the past. It simply makes no sense, for instance, for the great public issue in British Columbia to be the teaching of both French and English. That is not because educational or language choices no longer matter. It is because the information and investment on which the British Columbian economy depends, now and increasingly in the future, will be linked much more closely with Asia than with its sister provinces.

Much the same is true for China. If it is going to survive economically and politically, it will have to allow the development of multiple autonomous region-states within its territory. In the twenty-first century, even more than today, governing 1.2 billion people with a single, centrally dictated economic policy will prove impossible. To bring its people effectively into the modern industrial world, the government must educate them. Once they are educated, they will start to think for themselves and to look for information about how the rest of the world behaves. The rest of the world can only hope that plans are in the works for a Commonwealth of China or a Chinese confederation.

What of Taiwan? With the passing of the old Kuomintang generation, Taiwan has to decide where its future lies. If it gets the answer wrong, there is the real possibility of invasion or civil war. If it gets the answer right, Taiwan can readily become a—perhaps even *the*—leading member of a new Commonwealth of China and one of the most important and autonomous economic powers in the world.

The above examples are not isolated ones. Neither are they hypothetical worries based on fictional concerns. Nation-states *are* eroding as economic actors. Region-states *are* taking shape. It is not a question of maybe or perhaps. It *is* happening. No more than Canute's soldiers can we oppose the tides of the borderless world's ebb and flow of economic activity. The only real question, then, for political leaders—the only responsible question—is whether those tides can be harnessed to provide a better life for their people. And that means acknowledging the emergence—and understanding the unique value—of region-states.

PART

III

The New Realities of Trade

1
Who Is Us?

Robert B. Reich

Across the United States, you can hear calls for us to revitalize our national competitiveness. But wait—who is "us"? Is it IBM, Motorola, Whirlpool, and General Motors? Or is it Sony, Thomson, Philips, and Honda?

Consider two successful corporations:

- Corporation A is headquartered north of New York City. Most of its top managers are citizens of the United States. All of its directors are American citizens, and a majority of its shares are held by American investors. But most of Corporation A's employees are non-Americans. Indeed, the company undertakes much of its R&D and product design, and most of its complex manufacturing, outside the borders of the United States in Asia, Latin America, and Europe. Within the American market, an increasing amount of the company's product comes from its laboratories and factories abroad.

- Corporation B is headquartered abroad, in another industrialized nation. Most of its top managers and directors are citizens of that nation, and a majority of its shares are held by citizens of that nation. But most of Corporation B's employees are Americans. Indeed, Corporation B undertakes much of its R&D and new product design in the United States. And it does most of its manufacturing in the U.S. The company exports an increasing proportion of its American-based production, some of it even back to the nation where Corporation B is headquartered.

Now, who is "us"? Between these two corporations, which is the American corporation, which the foreign corporation? Which is more important to the economic future of the United States?

As the American economy becomes more globalized, examples of both Corporation A and B are increasing. At the same time, American concern for the competitiveness of the United States is increasing. Typically, the assumed vehicle for improving the competitive performance of the United States is the American corporation—by which most people would mean Corporation A. But today, the competitiveness of American-owned corporations is no longer the same as American competitiveness. Indeed, American ownership of the corporation is profoundly less relevant to America's economic future than the skills, training, and knowledge commanded by American workers—workers who are increasingly employed within the United States by foreign-owned corporations.

So who is us? The answer is, the American work force, the American people, but not particularly the American corporation. The implications of this new answer are clear: if we hope to revitalize the competitive performance of the United States economy, we must invest in people, not in nationally defined corporations. We must open our borders to investors from around the world rather than favoring companies that may simply fly the U.S. flag. And government policies should promote human capital in this country rather than assuming that American corporations will invest on "our" behalf. The American corporation is simply no longer "us."

Global Companies

American corporations have been abroad for years, even decades. So in one sense, the multinational identity of American companies is nothing new. What is new is that American-owned multinationals are beginning to employ large numbers of foreigners relative to their American work forces, are beginning to rely on foreign facilities to do many of their most technologically complex activities, and are beginning to export from their foreign facilities—including bringing products back to the United States.

Around the world, the numbers are already large—and still growing. Take IBM—often considered the thoroughbred of competitive American corporations. Forty percent of IBM's world employees are foreign, and the percentage is increasing. IBM Japan boasts 18,000 Japanese employees and annual sales of more than $6 billion, making it one of Japan's major exporters of computers.

Or consider Whirlpool. After cutting its American work force by 10% and buying Philips's appliance business, Whirlpool now employs 43,500 people around the world in 45 countries—most of them non-Americans. Another example is Texas Instruments, which now does most of its research, development, design, and manufacturing in East Asia. TI employs over 5,000 people in Japan alone, making advanced semiconductors—almost half of which are exported, many of them back to the United States.

American corporations now employ 11% of the industrial work force of Northern Ireland, making everything from cigarettes to computer software, much of which comes back to the United States. More than 100,000 Singaporians work for more than 200 U.S. corporations, most of them fabricating and assembling electronic components for export to the United States. Singapore's largest private employer is General Electric, which also accounts for a big share of that nation's growing exports. Taiwan counts AT&T, RCA, and Texas Instruments among its largest exporters. In fact, more than one-third of Taiwan's notorious trade surplus with the United States comes from U.S. corporations making or buying things there, then selling or using them back in the United States. The same corporate sourcing practice accounts for a substantial share of the U.S. trade imbalance with Singapore, South Korea, and Mexico—raising a question as to whom complaints about trade imbalances should be directed.

The pattern is not confined to America's largest companies. Molex, a suburban Chicago maker of connectors used to link wires in cars and computer boards, with revenues of about $300 million in 1988, has 38 overseas factories, 5 in Japan. Loctite, a midsize company with sales in 1988 of $457 million, headquartered in Newington, Connecticut, makes and sells adhesives and sealants all over the world. It has 3,500 employees—only 1,200 of whom are Americans. These companies are just part of a much larger trend: according to a 1987 McKinsey & Company study, America's most profitable midsize companies increased their investments in overseas production at an annual rate of 20% between 1981 and 1986.

Overall, the evidence suggests that U.S. companies have not lost their competitive edge over the last 20 years—they've just moved their base of operations. In 1966, American-based multinationals accounted for about 17% of world exports; since then their share has remained almost unchanged. But over the same period, the share of exports from the United States in the world's total trade in manufactures fell from 16% to 14%. In other words, while Americans exported less, the overseas affiliates of U.S.-owned corporations exported more than enough to offset the drop.

The old trend of overseas capital investment is accelerating: U.S. companies increased foreign capital spending by 24% in 1988, 13% in 1989. But even more important, U.S. businesses are now putting substantial sums of money into foreign countries to do R&D work. According to National Science Foundation figures, American corporations increased their overseas R&D spending by 33% between 1986 and 1988, compared with a 6% increase in R&D spending in the United States. Since 1987, Eastman Kodak, W.R. Grace, DuPont, Merck, and Upjohn have all opened new R&D facilities in Japan. At DuPont's Yokohama laboratory, more than 180 Japanese scientists and technicians are working at developing new materials technologies. IBM's Tokyo Research Lab, tucked away behind the far side of the Imperial Palace in downtown Tokyo, houses a small army of Japanese engineers who are perfecting image-processing technology. Another IBM laboratory, the Kanagawa arm of its Yamato Development Laboratory, houses 1,500 researchers who are developing hardware and software. Nor does IBM confine its pioneering work to Japan: recently, two European researchers at IBM's Zurich laboratory announced major breakthroughs into superconductivity and microscopy—earning them both Nobel Prizes.

An even more dramatic development is the arrival of foreign corporations in the United States at a rapidly increasing pace. As recently as 1977, only about 3.5% of the value added and the employment of American manufacturing originated in companies controlled by foreign parents. By 1987, the number had grown to almost 8%. In just the last two years, with the faster pace of foreign acquisitions and investments, the figure is now almost 11%. Foreign-owned companies now employ 3 million Americans, roughly 10% of our manufacturing workers. In fact, in 1989, affiliates of foreign manufacturers created more jobs in the United States than American-owned manufacturing companies.

And these non-U.S. companies are vigorously exporting from the United States. Sony now exports audio- and videotapes to Europe from its Dothan, Alabama factory and ships audio recorders from its Fort Lauderdale, Florida plant. Sharp exports 100,000 microwave ovens a year from its factory in Memphis, Tennessee. Last year, Dutch-owned Philips Consumer Electronics Company exported 1,500 color televisions from its Greenville, Tennessee plant to Japan. Its 1990 target is 30,000 televisions; by 1991, it plans to export 50,000 sets. Toshiba America is sending projection televisions from its Wayne, New Jersey plant to Japan. And by the early 1990s, when Honda annually exports 50,000 cars to Japan from its Ohio production base, it will actually be making more cars in the United States than in Japan.

The New American Corporation

In an economy of increasing global investment, foreign-owned Corporation B, with its R&D and manufacturing presence in the United States and its reliance on American workers, is far more important to America's economic future than American-owned Corporation A, with its platoons of foreign workers. Corporation A may fly the American flag, but Corporation B invests in Americans. Increasingly, the competitiveness of American workers is a more important definition of "American competitiveness" than the competitiveness of American companies. Issues of ownership, control, and national origin are less important factors in thinking through the logic of "who is us" and the implications of the answer for national policy and direction.

OWNERSHIP IS LESS IMPORTANT

Those who favor American-owned Corporation A (that produces overseas) over foreign-owned Corporation B (that produces here) might argue that American ownership generates a stream of earnings for the nation's citizens. This argument is correct, as far as it goes. American shareholders do, of course, benefit from the global successes of American corporations to the extent that such successes are reflected in higher share prices. And the entire U.S. economy benefits to the extent that the overseas profits of American companies are remitted to the United States.

But American investors also benefit from the successes of non-American companies in which Americans own a minority interest— just as foreign citizens benefit from the successes of American companies in which they own a minority interest, and such cross-ownership is on the increase as national restrictions on foreign ownership fall by the wayside. In 1989, cross-border equity investments by Americans, British, Japanese, and West Germans increased 20%, by value, over 1988.

The point is that in today's global economy, the total return to Americans from their equity investments is not solely a matter of the success of particular companies in which Americans happen to have a controlling interest. The return depends on the total amount of American savings invested in global portfolios comprising both American and foreign-owned companies—and on the care and wisdom with which American investors select such portfolios. Already Americans invest 10% of their portfolios in foreign securities; a recent study by Salomon Brothers predicts that it will be 15% in a few years. U.S. pension managers surveyed said that they predict 25% of their portfolios will be in foreign-owned companies within 10 years.

CONTROL IS LESS IMPORTANT

Another argument marshaled in favor of Corporation A might be that because Corporation A is controlled by Americans, it will act in the best interests of the United States. Corporation B, a foreign national, might not do so—indeed, it might act in the best interests of its nation of origin. The argument might go something like this: even if Corporation B is now hiring more Americans and giving them better jobs than Corporation A, we can't be assured that it will continue to do so. It might bias its strategy to reduce American competitiveness; it might even suddenly withdraw its investment from the United States and leave us stranded.

But this argument makes a false assumption about American companies—namely, that they are in a position to put national interests ahead of company or shareholder interests. To the contrary: managers of American-owned companies who sacrificed profits for the sake of national goals would make themselves vulnerable to a takeover or liable for a breach of fiduciary responsibility to their shareholders. American managers are among the loudest in the world to declare that their job is to maximize shareholder returns—not to advance national goals.

Apart from wartime or other national emergencies, American-owned companies are under no special obligation to serve national goals. Nor does our system alert American managers to the existence of such goals, impose on American managers unique requirements to meet them, offer special incentives to achieve them, or create measures to keep American managers accountable for accomplishing them. Were American managers knowingly to sacrifice profits for the sake of presumed national goals, they would be acting without authority, on the basis of their own views of what such goals might be, and without accountability to shareholders or to the public.

Obviously, this does not preclude American-owned companies from displaying their good corporate citizenship or having a sense of social responsibility. Sensible managers recognize that acting "in the public interest" can boost the company's image; charitable or patriotic acts can be good business if they promote long-term profitability. But in this regard, American companies have no particular edge over foreign-owned companies doing business in the United States. In fact, there is every reason to believe that a foreign-owned company would be even more eager to demonstrate to the American public its good citizenship in America than would the average American company. The American subsidiaries of Hitachi, Matsushita, Siemens, Thomson, and many other foreign-owned companies lose no opportunity to contribute funds to American charities, sponsor community events, and support public libraries, universities, schools, and other institutions. (In 1988, for example, Japanese companies operating in the United States donated an estimated $200 million to American charities; by 1994, it is estimated that their contributions will total $1 billion.)[1]

By the same token, American-owned businesses operating abroad feel a similar compulsion to act as good citizens in their host countries. They cannot afford to be seen as promoting American interests; otherwise they would jeopardize their relationships with foreign workers, consumers, and governments. Some of America's top managers have been quite explicit on this point. "IBM cannot be a net exporter from every nation in which it does business," said Jack Kuehler, IBM's new president. "We have to be a good citizen everywhere." Robert W. Galvin, chairman of Motorola, is even more blunt: should it become necessary for Motorola to close some of its factories, it would not close its Southeast Asian plants before it closed its American ones. "We need our Far Eastern customers," says Galvin, "and we cannot alienate the Malaysians. We must treat our employees all over the world equally." In fact, when it becomes necessary to reduce global capacity, we might expect American-owned businesses to slash more jobs in the United States than in Europe (where labor laws often prohibit precipitous layoffs) or in Japan (where national norms discourage it).

Just as empty is the concern that a foreign-owned company might leave the United States stranded by suddenly abandoning its U.S. operation. The typical argument suggests that a foreign-owned company might withdraw for either profit or foreign policy motives. But either way, the bricks and mortar would still be here. So would the equipment. So too would be the accumulated learning among American workers. Under such circumstances, capital from another source would fill the void; an American (or other foreign) company would simply purchase the empty facilities. And most important, the American work force would remain, with the critical skills and capabilities, ready to go back to work.

After all, the American government and the American people maintain jurisdiction—political control—over assets within the United States. Unlike foreign assets held by American-owned companies that are subject to foreign political control and, occasionally, foreign expropriation, foreign-owned assets in the United States are secure against sudden changes in foreign governments' policies. This not only serves as an attraction for foreign capital looking for a secure haven; it also benefits the American work force.

WORK FORCE SKILLS ARE CRITICAL

As every advanced economy becomes global, a nation's most important competitive asset becomes the skills and cumulative learning of its work force. Consequently, the most important issue with regard to global corporations is whether and to what extent they provide Americans with the training and experience that enable them to add greater value to the world economy. Whether the company happens to be headquartered in the United States or the United Kingdom is fundamentally unimportant. The company is a good "American" corporation if it equips its American work force to compete in the global economy.

Globalization, almost by definition, makes this true. Every factor of production other than work force skills can be duplicated anywhere around the world. Capital now sloshes freely across international boundaries, so much so that the cost of capital in different countries is rapidly converging. State-of-the-art factories can be erected anywhere. The latest technologies flow from computers in one nation, up to satellites parked in space, then back down to computers in another nation—all at the speed of electronic impulses. It is all fungible: capital, technology, raw materials, information—all, except for one thing, the most critical part, the one element that is unique about a nation: its work force.

In fact, because all of the other factors can move so easily any place on earth, a work force that is knowledgeable and skilled at doing complex things attracts foreign investment. The relationship forms a virtuous circle: well-trained workers attract global corporations, which invest and give the workers good jobs; the good jobs, in turn, generate additional training and experience. As skills move upward and experience accumulates, a nation's citizens add greater and greater value to the world—and command greater and greater compensation from the world, improving the country's standard of living.

FOREIGN-OWNED CORPORATIONS HELP AMERICAN WORKERS ADD VALUE

When foreign-owned companies come to the United States, they frequently bring with them approaches to doing business that improve American productivity and allow American workers to add more value to the world economy. In fact, they come here primarily because they can be more productive in the United States than can other American rivals. It is not solely America's mounting external indebtedness and relatively low dollar that account for the rising level of foreign investment in the United States. Actual growth of foreign investment in the United States dates from the mid-1970s rather than from the onset of the large current account deficit in 1982. Moreover, the two leading foreign investors in the United States are the British and the Dutch—not the Japanese and the West Germans, whose enormous surpluses are the counterparts of our current account deficit.

For example, after Japan's Bridgestone tire company took over Firestone, productivity increased dramatically. The joint venture between Toyota and General Motors at Fremont, California is a similar story: Toyota's managerial system took many of the same workers from what had been a deeply troubled GM plant and turned it into a model facility, with upgraded productivity and skill levels.

In case after case, foreign companies set up or buy up operations in the United States to utilize their corporate assets with the American work force. Foreign-owned businesses with better design capabilities, production techniques, or managerial skills are able to displace American companies on American soil precisely because those businesses are more productive. And in the process of supplanting the American company, the foreign-owned operation can transfer the superior know-how to its American work force—giving American workers the tools they need to be more productive, more skilled, and more competitive. Thus foreign companies create good jobs in the United States. In 1986 (the last date for which such data are available), the average American employee of a foreign-owned manufacturing company earned $32,887, while the average American employee of an American-owned manufacturer earned $28,954.[2]

This process is precisely what happened in Europe in the 1950s and 1960s. Europeans publicly fretted about the invasion of American-owned multinationals and the onset of "the American challenge." But the net result of these operations in Europe has been to make Europeans more productive, upgrade European skills, and thus enhance the standard of living of Europeans.

Now Who Is Us?

American competitiveness can best be defined as the capacity of Americans to add value to the world economy and thereby gain a higher standard of living in the future without going into ever deeper debt. American competitiveness is not the profitability or market share of American-owned corporations. In fact, because the American-owned corporation is coming to have no special relationship with Americans, it makes no sense for Americans to entrust our national competitiveness to it. The interests of American-owned corporations may or may not coincide with those of the American people.

Does this mean that we should simply entrust our national competitiveness to any corporation that employs Americans, regardless of the nationality of corporate ownership? Not entirely. Some foreign-owned corporations are closely tied to their nation's economic development— either through direct public ownership (for example, Airbus Industrie, a joint product of Britain, France, West Germany, and Spain, created to compete in the commercial airline industry) or through financial intermediaries within the nation that, in turn, are tied to central banks and ministries of finance (in particular the model used by many Korean and Japanese corporations). The primary goals of such corporations are to enhance the wealth of their nations, and the standard of living of their nations' citizens, rather than to enrich their shareholders. Thus, even though they might employ American citizens in their worldwide operations, they may employ fewer Americans—or give Americans lower value-added jobs—than they would if these corporations were intent simply on maximizing their own profits.[3]

On the other hand, it seems doubtful that we could ever shift the goals and orientations of American-owned corporations in this same direction—away from profit maximization and toward the development of the American work force. There is no reason to suppose that American managers and shareholders would accept new regulations and oversight mechanisms that forced them to sacrifice profits for the sake of building human capital in the United States. Nor is it clear that the American system of government would be capable of such detailed oversight.

The only practical answer lies in developing national policies that reward *any* global corporation that invests in the American work force. In a whole set of public policy areas, involving trade, publicly supported R&D, antitrust, foreign direct investment, and public and private investment, the overriding goal should be to induce global corporations to build human capital in America.

TRADE POLICY

We should be less interested in opening foreign markets to American-owned companies (which may in fact be doing much of their production overseas) than in opening those markets to companies that employ Americans—even if they happen to be foreign-owned. But so far, American trade policy experts have focused on representing the interests of companies that happen to carry the American flag—without regard to where the actual production is being done. For example, the United States recently accused Japan of excluding Motorola from the lucrative Tokyo market for cellular telephones and hinted at retaliation. But Motorola designs and makes many of its cellular telephones in Kuala Lumpur, while most of the Americans who make cellular telephone equipment in the United States for export to Japan happen to work for Japanese-owned companies. Thus we are wasting our scarce political capital pushing foreign governments to reduce barriers to American-owned companies that are seeking to sell or produce in their market.

Once we acknowledge that foreign-owned Corporation B may offer more to American competitiveness than American-owned Corporation A, it is easy to design a preferable trade policy—one that accords more directly with our true national interests. The highest priority for American trade policy should be to discourage other governments from invoking domestic content rules—which have the effect of forcing global corporations, American and foreign-owned alike, to locate production facilities in those countries rather than in the United States.

The objection here to local content rules is not that they may jeopardize the competitiveness of American companies operating abroad. Rather, it is that these requirements, by their very nature, deprive the American work force of the opportunity to compete for jobs, and with those jobs, for valuable skills, knowledge, and experience. Take, for example, the recently promulgated European Community nonbinding rule on television-program production, which urges European television stations to devote a majority of their air time to programs made in Europe. Or consider the European allegations of Japanese dumping of office machines containing semiconductors, which has forced Japan to put at least 45% European content into machines sold in Europe (and thus fewer American-made semiconductor chips).

Obviously, U.S.-owned companies are already inside the EC producing both semiconductors and television programs. So if we were to adopt American-owned Corporation A as the model for America's competitive self-interest, our trade policy might simply ignore these EC initiatives. But through the lens of a trade policy focused on the American work force, it is clear how the EC thwarts the abilities of Americans to excel in semiconductor fabrication and filmmaking—two areas where our work force already enjoys a substantial competitive advantage.

Lack of access by American-owned corporations to foreign markets is, of course, a problem. But it only becomes a crucial problem for America to the extent that both American and foreign-owned companies must make products within the foreign market—products that they otherwise would have made in the United States. Protection that acts as a domestic content requirement skews investment away from the United States—and away from U.S. workers. Fighting against that should be among the highest priorities of U.S. trade policy.

PUBLICLY SUPPORTED R&D

Increased global competition, the high costs of research, the rapid rate of change in science and technology, the model of Japan with its government-supported commercial technology investments—all of these factors have combined to make this area particularly critical for thoughtful public policy. But there is no reason why preference should be given to American-owned companies. Dominated by our preoccupation with American-owned Corporation A, current public policy in this area limits U.S. government-funded research grants, guaranteed loans, or access to the fruits of U.S. government-funded research to American-owned companies. For example, membership in Sematech, the research consortium started two years ago with $100 billion annual support payments by the Department of Defense to help American corporations fabricate complex memory chips, is limited to American-owned companies. More recently, a government effort to create a consortium of companies to catapult the United States into the HDTV competition has drawn a narrow circle of eligibility, ruling out companies such as Sony, Philips, and Thomson that do R&D and production in the United States but are foreign-owned. More generally, long-standing regulations covering the more than 600 government laboratories and research centers that are spread around the United States ban all but American-owned companies from licensing inventions developed at these sites.

Of course, the problem with this policy approach is that it ignores the reality of global American corporations. Most U.S.-owned companies are quite happy to receive special advantages from the U.S. government—and then spread the technological benefits to their affiliates all over the world. As Sematech gets under way, its members are busily going global: Texas Instruments is building a new $250 million semiconductor fabrication plant in Taiwan; by 1992, the facility will produce four-megabit memory chips and custom-made, application-specific integrated circuits—some of the most advanced chips made anywhere. TI has also joined with Hitachi to design and produce a super chip that will store 16 million bits of data. Motorola, meanwhile, has paired with Toshiba to research and produce a similar generation of futurist chips. Not to be outdone, AT&T has a commitment to build a state-of-the-art chip-making plant in Spain. So who will be making advanced chips in the United States? In June 1989, Japanese-owned NEC announced plans to build a $400 million facility in Rosedale, California for making four-megabit memory chips and other advanced devices not yet in production anywhere.

The same situation applies to HDTV. Zenith Electronics is the only remaining American-owned television manufacturer, and thus the only one eligible for a government subsidy. Zenith employs 2,500 Americans. But there are over 15,000 Americans employed in the television industry who do not work for Zenith—undertaking R&D, engineering, and high-quality manufacturing. They work in the United States for

Table I.

U.S. TV Set Production, 1988

Company Name	Plant Type	Location	Employees	Annual Production
Bang & Olufsen	Assembly	Compton, Calif.	n.a.[†]	n.a.
Goldstar	Total*	Huntsville, Ala.	400	1,000,000
Harvey Industries	Assembly	Athens, Tex.	900	600,000
Hitachi	Total	Anaheim, Calif.	900	360,000
JVC	Total	Elmwood Park, N.J.	100	480,000
Matsushita	Assembly	Franklin Park, Ill.	800	1,000,000
American Kotobuki (Matsushita)	Assembly	Vancouver, Wash.	200	n.a.
Mitsubishi	Assembly	Santa Ana, Calif.	550	400,000
Mitsubishi	Total	Braselton, Ga.	300	285,000
NEC	Assembly	McDonough, Ga.	400	240,000
Orion	Assembly	Princeton, Ind.	250	n.a.
Philips	Total	Greenville, Tenn	3,200	2,000,000+
Samsung	Total	Saddle Brook, N.J.	250	1,000,000
Sanyo	Assembly	Forrest City, Ark.	400	1,000,000
Sharp	Assembly	Memphis, Tenn.	770	1,100,000
Sony	Total	San Diego, Calif.	1,500	1,000,000
Tatung	Assembly	Long Beach, Calif.	130	17,500
Thomson	Total	Bloomington, Ind.	1,766	3,000,000+
Thomson	Components	Indianapolis, Ind.	1,604	n.a.
Toshiba	Assembly	Lebanon, Tenn.	600	900,000
Zenith	Total	Springfield, Mo.	2,500	n.a.

*Total manufacturing involves more than the assembling of knocked-down kits. Plants that manufacture just the television cabinets are not included in this list.   [†]Not available

Source: Electronic Industries Association, HDTV Information Center, Washington, D.C.

foreign-owned companies: Sony, Philips, Thomson, and others (see Table I). Of course, none of these companies is presently eligible to participate in the United States's HDTV consortium—nor are their American employees.

Again, if we follow the logic of Corporation B as the more "American" company, it suggests a straightforward principle for publicly supported R&D: we should be less interested in helping *American-owned companies* become technologically sophisticated than in helping *Americans* become technologically sophisticated. Government-financed help for research and development should be available to any corporation, regardless of the nationality of its owners, as long as the company undertakes the R&D in the United States—using American scientists, engineers, and technicians. To make the link more explicit, there could even be a relationship between the number of Americans involved in the R&D and the amount of government aid forthcoming. It is important to note that this kind of public-private bargain is far different from protectionist domestic content requirements. In this case, the government is participating with direct funding and thus can legitimately exact a quid pro quo from the private sector.

ANTITRUST POLICY

The Justice Department is now in the process of responding to the inevitability of globalization; it recognizes that North American market share alone means less and less in a global economy. Consequently, the Justice Department is about to relax antitrust policy—for American-owned companies only. American-owned companies that previously kept each other at arm's length for fear of prompting an inquiry into whether they were colluding are now cozying up to one another. Current antitrust policy permits research joint ventures; the attorney general is on the verge of recommending that antitrust policy permit joint production agreements as well, when there may be significant economies of scale and where competition is global—again, among American-owned companies.

But here again, American policy seems myopic. We should be less interested in helping American-owned companies gain economies of scale in research, production, and other key areas, and more interested in helping corporations engaged in research or production within the United States achieve economies of scale—regardless of their nationality. U.S. antitrust policy should allow research or production joint ventures among any companies doing R&D or production within the United States, as long as they can meet three tests: they could not gain such scale efficiencies on their own, simply by enlarging their investment in the United States; such a combination of companies would allow higher levels of productivity within the United States; and the combination would not substantially diminish global competition. National origin should not be a factor.

FOREIGN DIRECT INVESTMENT

Foreign direct investment has been climbing dramatically in the United States: last year it reached $329 billion, exceeding total American investment abroad for the first time since World War I (but be careful with these figures, since investments are valued at cost and this substantially understates the worth of older investments). How should we respond to this influx of foreign capital?

Clearly, the choice between Corporation A and Corporation B has important implications. If we are most concerned about the viability of American-owned corporations, then we should put obstacles in the way of foreigners seeking to buy controlling shares in American-owned companies, or looking to build American production facilities that would compete with American-owned companies.

Indeed, current policies tilt in this direction. For example, under the so-called Exon-Florio Amendment of the Omnibus Trade and Competitiveness Act of 1988, foreign investors must get formal approval from the high-level Committee on Foreign Investments in the United States, comprising the heads of eight federal agencies and chaired by the secretary of the treasury, before they can purchase an American company. The expressed purpose of the law is to make sure that a careful check is done to keep "national security" industries from passing into the hands of foreigners. But the law does not define what "national security" means: thus it invites all sorts of potential delays and challenges. The actual effect is to send a message that we do not look with favor on the purchase of American-owned assets by foreigners. Other would-be pieces of legislation send the same signal. In July 1989, for instance, the House Ways and Means Committee voted to apply a withholding capital gains tax to foreigners who own more than 10% of a company's shares. Another provision of the committee would scrap tax deductibility for interest on loans made by foreign parents to their American subsidiaries. A third measure would limit R&D tax credits for foreign subsidiaries. More recently, Congress is becoming increasingly concerned about foreign takeovers of American airlines. A subcommittee of the House Commerce Committee has voted to give the Transportation Department authority to block foreign acquisitions.

These policies make little sense—in fact, they are counterproductive. Our primary concern should be the training and development of the American work force, not the protection of the American-owned corporation. Thus we should encourage, not discourage, foreign direct investment. Experience shows that foreign-owned companies usually displace American-owned companies in just those industries where the foreign businesses are simply more productive. No wonder America's governors spend a lot of time and energy promoting their states to foreign investors and offer big subsidies to foreign companies to locate in their states, even if they compete head-on with existing American-owned businesses.

PUBLIC AND PRIVATE INVESTMENT

The current obsession with the federal budget deficit obscures a final, crucial aspect of the choice between Corporation A and Corporation B. Conventional wisdom holds that government expenditures "crowd out" private investment, making it more difficult and costly for American-owned companies to get the capital they need. According to this logic, we may have to cut back on public expenditures in order to provide American-owned companies with the necessary capital to make investments in plant and equipment.

But the reverse may actually be the case—particularly if Corporation B is really more in America's competitive interests than Corporation A. There are a number of reasons why this is true.

First, in the global economy, America's public expenditures don't reduce the amount of money left over for private investment in the United States. Today capital flows freely across national borders—including a disproportionately large inflow to the United States. Not only are foreign savings coming to the United States, but America's private savings are finding their way all over the world. Sometimes the vehicle is the far-flung operations of a global American-owned company, sometimes a company in which foreigners own a majority stake. But the old notion of national boundaries is becoming obsolete. Moreover, as I have stressed, it is a mistake to associate these foreign investments by American-owned companies with any result that improves the competitiveness of the United States. There is simply no necessary connection between the two.

There is, however, a connection between the kinds of investments that the public sector makes and the competitiveness of the American work force. Remember: a work force that is knowledgeable and skilled at doing complex things attracts foreign investment in good jobs, which in turn generates additional training and experience. A good infrastructure of transporation and communication makes a skilled work force even more attractive. The public sector often is in the best position to make these sorts of "pump priming" investments—in education, training and retraining, research and development, and in all of the infrastructure that moves people and goods and facilitates communication. These are the investments that distinguish one nation from another—they are the relatively nonmobile factors in the global competition. Ironically, we do not ordinarily think of these expenditures as investments; the federal budget fails to distinguish between a capital and an operating budget, and the national income accounts treat all government expenditures as consumption. But without doubt, these are precisely the investments that most directly affect our future capacity to compete.

During the 1980s, we allowed the level of these public investments either to remain stable or, in some cases, to decline. As America enters the 1990s, if we hope to launch a new campaign for American competitiveness, we must substantially increase public funding in the following areas:

Government spending on commercial R&D. Current spending in this critical area has declined 95% from its level two decades ago. Even as late as 1980, it comprised .8% of gross national product; today it comprises only .4%—a much smaller percentage than in any other advanced economy.

Government spending to upgrade and expand the nation's infrastructure. Public investment in critical highways, roads, bridges, ports, airports, and waterways dropped from 2.3% of GNP two decades ago to 1.3% in the 1980s. Thus many of our bridges are unsafe, and our highways are crumbling.

Expenditures on public elementary and secondary education. These have increased, to be sure. But in inflation-adjusted terms, per pupil spending has shown little gain. Between 1959 and 1971, spending per student grew at a brisk 4.7% in real terms—more than a full percentage point above the increase in the GNP—and teachers' salaries increased almost 3% a year. But since then, growth has slowed. Worse, this has happened during an era when the demands on public education have significantly increased, due to the growing incidence of broken homes, unwed mothers, and a rising population of the poor. Teachers' salaries, adjusted for inflation, are only a bit higher than they were in 1971. Despite the rhetoric, the federal government has all but retreated from the field of education. In fact, George Bush's 1990 education budget is actually smaller than Ronald Reagan's in 1989. States and municipalities, already staggering under the weight of social services that have been shifted onto them from the federal government, simply cannot carry this additional load. The result of this policy gap is a national education crisis: one out of five American 18-year-olds is illiterate, and in test after test, American schoolchildren rank at the bottom of international scores. Investing more money here may not be a cure-all—but money is at least necessary.

College opportunity for all Americans. Because of government cutbacks, many young people in the United States with enough talent to go to college cannot afford it. During the 1980s, college tuitions rose 26%; family incomes rose a scant 5%. Instead of filling the gap, the federal government created a vacuum: guaranteed student loans have fallen by 13% in real terms since 1980.

Worker training and retraining. Young people who cannot or do not wish to attend college need training for jobs that are becoming more complex. Older workers need retraining to keep up with the demands of a rapidly changing, technologically advanced workplace. But over the last eight years, federal investments in worker training have dropped by more than 50%.

These are the priorities of an American strategy for national competitiveness—a strategy based more on the value of human capital and less on the value of financial capital. The simple fact of American ownership has lost its relevance to America's economic future. Corporations that invest in the United States, that build the value of the American work force, are more critical to our future standard of living than are American-owned corporations investing abroad. To attract and keep them, we need public investments that make America a good place for any global corporation seeking talented workers to set up shop.

Notes

1. Craig Smith, editor of *Corporate Philanthropy Report*, quoted in *Chronicle of Higher Education*, November 8, 1989, p. A-34.

2. Bureau of Economic Analysis, *Foreign Direct Investment in the U.S.: Operations of U.S. Affiliates, Preliminary 1986 Estimates* (Washington, D.C.: U.S. Department of Commerce, 1988) for data on foreign companies; Bureau of the Census, *Annual Survey of Manufactures: Statistics for Industry Groups and Industries, 1986* (Washington, D.C., 1987) for U.S. companies.

3. Robert B. Reich and Eric D. Mankin, "Joint Ventures with Japan Give Away Our Future," *Harvard Business Review* March–April 1986, p. 78.

2
Who Is Them?

Robert B. Reich

"We" are seated at a negotiating table. "They" are seated across from us. The outcome of these talks will shape America's future competitiveness and economic well-being. But "us" is not necessarily companies based in the United States. "Them" is not foreign nations. Rather, us is the people—most prominently, the work force—of the United States. And them is the growing cadre of global managers—supranational corporate players, whose allegiance is to enhanced worldwide corporate performance, not to any nation's economic success.

Unlike their preglobal predecessors, global managers feel little allegiance to us. In the global enterprise, the bonds between company and country—between them and us—are rapidly eroding. Instead, we are witnessing the creation of a purer form of capitalism, practiced globally by managers who are more distant, more economically driven—in essence more coldly rational in their decisions, having shed the old affiliations with people and place.

Today corporate decisions about production and location are driven by the dictates of global competition, not by national allegiance. Witness IBM's recent decision to transfer 120 executives and the headquarters of its $10 billion per year communications business to Europe, a move that is partly symbolic—a recognition that globalization must take companies beyond their old borders—and partly practical—an opportunity for IBM to capitalize on the expected growth in the European market.

As this and countless other examples show, business competition today is not between nations. Nor do trade flows between nations accurately keep score of which companies are gaining the lead. For the past two decades, U.S. businesses have maintained their shares of world markets even as *America* has lost its lead.

Nor does a nation's wealth turn on the profitability of corporations in which its citizens own a majority of shares. Cross-border ownership is booming: Americans are buying into global companies based in Europe and East Asia; Europeans and Asians are buying into companies based in the United States. And most corporate profits are plowed back into new investments spread around the world.

Ultimately, our wealth and well-being depend on the value that the world places on the work we do, on our skills and insights. Hence the importance of the negotiations between us and them about what jobs we are to perform in the new global economy.

In this regard, the logic of the global manager is clear: to undertake activities anywhere around the world that will maximize the performance of the company, enlarge its market share, and boost the price of stock. Our logic is just as clear: to get global managers to site good jobs in the United States. Our best interests are served by making it easy, attractive, and productive for them to do so, regardless of the nationality of the company they represent. At the same time, we need to structure the talks between us and them over the kinds of jobs they put here in a way that represents and secures our interests.

The Logic of the Global Manager

The image out of the past is a compelling one. A strong and proud American company is centered in an American community and is run by American managers. The offices, the factories, the community all bear the unmistakable mark of connectedness. But it is an image that is fading, an ideal that is more in our memories than in reality. Gone is the company town, the huge local labor force, the monolithic factory, and the giant vertically integrated corporation that dominated the entire region. Gone is the tight connection between the company, its community, even its country. Vanishing too are the paternalistic corporate heads who used to feel a sense of responsibility for their local community. Emerging in their place is the new global manager, driven by the irrefutable logic of global capitalism to seek higher profits, enhanced market leadership, and improved stock price. The playing field is the world.

This is not to impugn the patriotism of those Americans (or Italians or Germans) who manage globally. In their private lives, global managers are no doubt one of "us": no less patriotic, no less concerned about their countries' futures, no less involved in civic causes or social issues. But it is in business that global managers become "them." Their outlook is cosmopolitan—corporate citizens of the world, wherever they conduct their business. As one top IBM manager told a reporter, "IBM has to be concerned with the competitiveness and well-being of any country or region that is a major source of IBM revenue."

When it comes to global managers, no group of citizens, no government, has a special claim. Edzard Reuter, chairman of Daimler-Benz and one of the most powerful men in German industry, insists that the company has no special duty to invest in the former East Germany. "We are not national or nationalistic pioneers, but entrepreneurs," he has said. "When [there are good returns] in East Germany, we will invest. But not to do some politician a favor."

Regardless of the manager's national background, the principles are the same. The emerging global manager invests in the most promising opportunities and abandons or sells off underperforming assets—no matter how long they have been part of the corporate family or where they may be located. "You can't be bound emotionally to any particular asset," Martin S. Davis, chairman and CEO of Paramount Communications, told a reporter. Charles (Mike) Harper, head of ConAgra, the giant food-processing and commodity-trading company, which is crucial to the economy of Omaha, Nebraska, recently threatened to move the company unless the state changed its tax code. The bonds of loyalty could slip over the weekend, Harper warned: "Some Friday night, we turn out the lights—click, click, click—back up the trucks, and be gone by Monday morning."

While the tone of such a statement may sound menacing, in fact Harper's logic is anything but sinister. The new global manager's job is to exploit the opportunities created by high-powered technologies of worldwide communication and transportation and by the relaxation of national controls over cross-border flows of capital. The global manager efficiently deploys capital all around the world, seeking the highest returns for shareholders or partners. Competition is intense and growing. The global manager who fails to take advantage of global opportunities will lose profits and market share to global managers who do.

In deciding where around the world to do what, the global manager seeks to meet the needs of customers worldwide for the highest value at the least cost. Some production will be done under the company's direct supervision; much will be outsourced. Often design and marketing activities will be sited close to the markets to be served; research and complex engineering, where skilled scientists and engineers can be found; routine fabrication and assembly, where workers are available at lowest cost. But there are exceptions—depending on products, markets, and circumstances. When there is danger that a market might be closed to imports, production might be shifted there. When two or more locations are about the same, the decision will be based on where the global manager can secure the most profitable deal.

The global manager's task is to put it all together, worldwide. For example, Mazda's newest sportscar, the MX-5 Miata, was designed in California, financed from Tokyo and New York, its prototype was created in Worthing, England, and it was assembled in Michigan and Mexico using advanced electronic components invented in New Jersey and fabricated in Japan. Saatchi and Saatchi's recent television advertising campaign for Miller Lite Beer was conceived in Britain, shot on location in Canada, dubbed in Britain and the United States, and edited in New York. An Intel microprocessor was designed in California and financed in the United States and Germany, containing dynamic random-access memories fabricated in South Korea. Chevrolet's best-selling Geo Metro was designed in Japan and built in Canada at a factory managed by Japan's Suzuki. Boeing's next airliner will be designed in Washington state and Japan and assembled in Seattle, with tail cones from Canada, special tail sections from China and Italy, and engines from Great Britain.

The logic of the global manager is not confined to large, well-established global companies. In 1989, in the first six months of its cosmopolitan life, the tiny Momenta Corporation, headquartered in Mountain View, California with 28 employees, had raised almost $13 million from Taiwanese and American investors. A small band of U.S. engineers was designing Momenta's advanced computer; the components would be engineered and produced in Japan; the actual product would be assembled in Taiwan and Singapore. Kamran Elahian, Momenta's Iranian-born founder, said to a reporter that global financing was "one of the only ways we [could] be assured of the $40 million we needed," and global production was required to "make use of the best technology that is available to the company." Switzerland's Logitech, the world's leading supplier of the "point and click" mouse for personal computers, relies on just 20 Swiss and Italian engineers, 520 technicians and marketing specialists in California, and 350 production workers in Ireland and Taiwan. Weng Kok Siew, president of Singapore Technologies, another upstart, has described his worldwide strategy in words that could stand as the global manager's credo: "We plan to manufacture in any country in the world where there is an advantage—to make things in Thailand where the cost is low, in Germany because the market is big, to do R&D in Boston."

As competition globalizes, so must the vision of the manager. The dictates of capitalism are clear: the global manager gains profits and captures markets by putting worldwide resources to their most efficient uses.

The Logic of the Global Web

If the company town, a relic of the 1950s, is vanishing, so too is the old multinational corporation disappearing, a reminder of the 1960s and 1970s. Like the company town, the multinational exuded a sense of hierarchy, place, and order. World headquarters was, very simply, both in the center and at the top of the worldwide corporate pyramid. The location of the headquarters was a reflection of company history (the founder had begun the company in this place) or of industry requirements (headquarters had to be where the biggest factory was located or where the research and engineering was done). Managers in worldwide headquarters made all the crucial decisions, of course. Foreign subsidiaries were just that—*subsidiary* to headquarters. Their work usually consisted of exporting materials and components back to the parent corporation for assembling and finishing or of selling the parent's finished products in a foreign market. The lines of power, of communication, of corporate decision making and corporate governance all led back to headquarters.

THE FADING SIGNIFICANCE OF WORLD HEADQUARTERS

The emerging global manager works within a global web, which operates according to a new and different logic. The location of headquarters is not a matter of great importance; it is not even necessarily in the country where most of the company's shareholders or employees are. Headquarters for the new global web can even be a suite of rooms in an office park near an international airport—a communications center where many of the web's threads intersect.

In 1988, for example, when RJR Nabisco moved its worldwide

headquarters to Atlanta, Georgia from Winston-Salem, North Caro-
lina—where, years before, it had built the city's largest skyscraper,
created a community arts center, and been the chief patron of Wake
Forest University—the citizens of Atlanta were expecting great things.
But the new worldwide headquarters turned out to be leased space in
a suburban mall, housing only 450 executives and staff (about a third
of 1% of the company's worldwide work force). Ross Johnson, then
RJR-Nabisco's president, cautioned Atlantans to expect no more from
the business than they would from any tiny 450-person company in
their midst.

In fact, the global web may have several worldwide headquarters,
depending on where certain markets or technologies are. Britain's
APV, a maker of food-processing equipment, has a different lead country for each of its worldwide businesses. Hewlett-Packard recently
moved the headquarters of its personal computer business to Greno-
ble, France. Siemens A.G., Germany's electronics colossus, is relocat-
ing its medical electronics division headquarters from Germany to
Chicago, Illinois. Honda is planning to move the worldwide headquarters for its power-products division to Atlanta, Georgia. ABB Asea
Brown Boveri, the European electrical-engineering giant based in Zurich, Switzerland, groups its thousands of products and services into
50 or so business areas (BAs). Each BA is run by a leadership team
with global responsibility for crafting business strategy, selecting product-development priorities, and allocating production among countries. None of the BA teams work out of the Zurich headquarters; they
are distributed around the world. Leadership for power transformers
is based in Germany, electric drives are in Finland, process automation
is in the United States.

The global web's highest value-added activities—its most advanced
R&D, most sophisticated engineering and design, most complex fabrication—need not be in the nation where most of the company's shareholders and executives are. Ford's state-of-the-art engine factory is in
Chihuahua, Mexico, where skilled Mexican engineers and technicians
produce more than 1,000 engines per day with quality equal to the
best in the world. Texas Instruments is fabricating some of its most
complex wafers in Japan at its Sendai facility and is building an R&D
center in Japan's science city of Tsukuba. Other recently or soon-to-be
opened research labs in Japan: Procter & Gamble's technical center on
Rokko Island in Kōbe; Ciba-Geigy's facility in Takarazuka; and Carrier
Corporation's engineering center in Shizuoka prefecture. By 1990,
Hewelett-Packard's German researchers were making significant strides

in fiber-optic technologies; its Australian researchers, in computer-aided engineering software; its Singaporean researchers, in laser printers.

A recent study of where U.S.-and European-based global corporations site their high value-added activities confirms the trend. There was little evidence of any bias in favor of the headquarters nation, except in companies that had only recently become multinational and had not yet had an opportunity to site their high value-added activities abroad. Among more advanced companies working to spin their global webs, the tendency is to site high value-added activities all over the world.[1]

THE COSMOPOLITAN MANAGEMENT TEAM

Increasingly, the managers who inhabit the global web come from many different nations. Take, for example, Whirlpool's approach to going global in the white-goods business. Headquartered in Benton Harbor, Michigan, Whirlpool recently formed a joint venture with the Major Appliance Division of Philips, headquartered in Eindhoven, Holland. The administrative headquarters of this U.S.-Dutch joint venture—Whirlpool International—is in Comerio, Italy, where it is managed by a Swede. On the six-person management committee sit managers from Sweden, Holland, Italy, the United States, and Belgium, with a German to be named later. Such cosmopolitanism is equally apparent at the top of the world's leading companies: IBM prides itself on having five different nationalities represented among its highest ranking officers, and three among its outside directors. Four nationalities are represented on Unilever's board; three on the board of Shell Oil. Sony has attempted to address the global team in a characteristically compact fashion: recently named as president and chief operating officer of Sony America was Ron Sommer, who was born in Israel, raised in Austria, and carries a German passport.

The threads of the new global web extend, as well, across the old boundaries of the company to include transactions between global managers in different companies. Investment decisions travel through far-reaching relationships between global companies headquartered on opposite sides of the world. Profit-sharing agreements, strategic alliances, joint ventures, licensing agreements, and supply arrangements tie together units and subunits. In the 1980s, for instance, Corning Glass abandoned its national pyramidlike organization in favor of a global web, giving it the capability to make optical cable through its European partner, Siemens A.G., and medical equipment with Ciba-Geigy. In 1990, these kinds of foreign alliances generated almost half of Corning's earnings. AT&T has also sought to transform itself from a self-sufficient bureaucratic monopoly into a multilateral global web: Japan's NEC helps AT&T supply and market memory chips; Dutch-owned Philips helps AT&T make and market telecommunications switching equipment and application-specific integrated circuits; Mitsui helps it with value-added networks.

No nation or continent is immune to the logic of the global web. In the 1950s and 1960s, for example, Europe sought to create and nurture "national champion" companies in key industries as a way to shelter domestic businesses from the onslaught of U.S. multinationals. Today these same champions are transforming into global webs with no particular connection to their own countries: France's Renault has teamed up with Sweden's Volvo to create Europe's fourth-largest industrial group; Daimler-Benz, Germany's largest industrial group, is discussing a wide assortment of links with Mitsubishi; Fujitsu, Japan's largest computer company, has acquired Britain's ICL; Pilkington, Britain's largest glassmaker, has joined with France's Saint-Gobain and Japan's Nippon Sheet Glass; Italy's Olivetti is distributing mainframe computers for Hitachi and developing laptops with Japan's YE Data.

THE JAPANESE EXCEPTION?

If there is one country that is criticized for not playing by these emerging global rules, it is Japan. But the logic of the global web is so powerful that the Japanese will either be forced to comply over time or else face a stiff penalty from the marketplace, the talent pool, and competitors and governments. For example, in the competition for global talent, corporations that are reluctant to consider foreign nationals for top managerial positions will lose out: the most talented people simply will not join an organization that holds out no promise of promotion. Japanese-owned companies that have been notoriously slow to open their top executive ranks to non-Japanese will operate at a competitive disadvantage.

Similarly, Japanese companies that have traditionally done most of their highest value-added work in Japan now must reconsider the economic and political advisability of this strategy. Indeed, there is evidence suggesting that the leading Japanese companies—those that are already the most international—are beginning to change. Many of the companies that were the earliest to recognize the need to establish manufacturing facilities in Europe and the United States are now investing in R&D laboratories and complex fabrication facilities outside Japan. By 1990, more than 500 U.S. scientists and engineers worked for Honda in Torrance, California; another 200 worked in Ohio. At Mazda's new $23 million R&D center in Irvine, California, hundreds of U.S. designers and engineers are undertaking long-term automotive research. Nissan employs 400 U.S. engineers at its engineering center in Plymouth, Michigan; Toyota employs 140 at its technical research center in Ann Arbor. Fujitsu is now constructing an $80 million telecommunications plant and research center in Texas. NEC has opened a research laboratory in Princeton, New Jersey.

Japanese investment in Europe has also skyrocketed. According to the Bank of Japan, direct investment in the 12 European Community countries totaled $14 billion in 1989 and grew by a factor of eight between 1985 and 1989, even faster than in the United States. And much of this new investment is at the high value-added end. Fujitsu, for example, has established an R&D center in Britain for semiconductors used in communications equipment; Hitachi, a British R&D laboratory for telecommunications switching equipment.

As the Japanese experience shows, to be successful globally, the global manager cannot bias investment decisions in favor of the corporation's home base. Even the appearance of bias is likely to cause political problems for the company in less favored nations—making it more difficult for the global manager to utilize the people, capital, technology, and natural resources across the global web. Successful global competitors like IBM, GE, McDonald's, Ford, Shell, Philips, Sony, NCR, Unilever, The News Corporation, and Procter & Gamble have willingly shed their national identities and become loyal corporate citizens wherever they do business around the world—siting high value-added activities in many nations, hiring foreign nationals for senior positions, and giving local and regional managers substantial discretion. As a result, these companies are usually treated by governments around the world on an equal footing with locally based companies.

By contrast, the worldwide operations of multinational giants like NEC, Fujitsu, and Mitsubishi, and even some European-based companies like Siemens, are still considered to be *foreign* subsidiaries—subunits whose identities derive from the nation where their worldwide headquarters are. As a result, these companies sometimes have difficulty gaining equal treatment with locally based companies. In fact, even the most cosmopolitan Japanese companies are finding that the general reputation of Japanese business for putting Japan's interests first is creating a competitive disadvantage making it increasingly difficult for these companies to export their products or undertake foreign investment around the world without encountering political opposition.

Furthermore, the well-known predilection of Japanese companies to do business with each other and in a way that uniquely benefits Japan has created a backlash among corporate competitors. In recent years, U.S. and European global managers have grown wary of depending too heavily on Japanese companies for critical high-tech components. Specifically, they worry that Japanese suppliers will allocate the parts they make to other Japanese companies first and withhold them from foreign partners or that Japanese companies will use the parts to gain a predatory foothold, gradually displacing their foreign partner as the relationship becomes more and more lopsided.

These concerns of Western managers about Japanese corporate practice are not necessarily yielding more investment in the United States; they are leading to more alliances across the Atlantic or with non-Japanese Pacific Rim partners. For example, IBM's recent efforts to ensure itself a supply of random-access memory semiconductor chips independent of Japanese companies has led it into a spate of investments and alliances across Europe—a joint venture with Siemens, membership in the European Community's semiconductor research consortium called JESSI. IBM's strategy, like that of other Western global corporations, is not pro-United States—it is pro-IBM and non-Japanese.

In fact, as corporations spin their global webs, other corporations, rather than governments, are likely to engage in strategic countermoves. The more companies decentralize their operations, the less authority and control any single government can assert over them. A company that is comfortable investing all over the world can negotiate with governments all over the world and, with enough leverage, dictate the specific terms and conditions of its investment.

The National Interest

They, as global managers, want to increase their world market shares, profits, and share prices. *We*, as citizens of a particular nation, want to secure national wealth and national economic well-being. They parcel activities around the world according to economic criteria, putting them wherever they can get the best return, intentionally playing no favorites to avoid setting off political alarms. But we do play favorites. We feel a special allegiance to our country and to our compatriots. Global corporations exist within world markets; we are members of a society.

Our interests diverge from theirs for two specific reasons: we are concerned about our nation's relative wealth and power, and we want to capture for our nation the public benefits that spill over from global investment.

RELATIVE WEALTH AND POWER

Consider the following two possible scenarios for economic growth between now and the year 2000 for the United States and Japan:

The United States economy grows 20%, but the Japanese economy grows 90%.

The United States economy grows only 8%, and the Japanese economy grows 8.2%.

When I have offered this choice in classes and corporate training seminars, a majority of the Americans in my audience usually select the second option. Many Americans are more concerned with our country's relative wealth and power compared with Japan's than with our country's absolute growth. We not only want global managers to favor the United States—locating their high value-added activities in America—more than they favor Japan, but many would also sacrifice some additional wealth in order to prevent the Japanese from enjoying even greater gains. Whether or not these sentiments should be commended as a principle of international economic behavior, they cannot be ignored. Despite the logic of the global manager and the global web, national wealth and power continue to drive us to think about our national interests not only in absolute terms but also relative to our perceived national competitors.

SPILLOVERS FROM CORPORATE INVESTMENT

Even those of us who select the first option might still want global managers to favor the United States because of national benefits that do not typically appear on the global manager's balance sheets. Specifically, these spillovers might include the jobs that result from having sophisticated factories, laboratories, and equipment in the United States, whose high wages multiply throughout the economy, raising other incomes. Good jobs also generate higher tax receipts, which permit government to invest in public facilities such as improved schools and transportation and also to care for the elderly and the disadvantaged in society. Moreover, on-the-job training and the resulting technical know-how enable Americans to innovate and thus generate more wealth for the United States in the years to come. This know-how spreads beyond individual Americans to create entire regions of U.S. innovation—the San Francisco Bay area and greater Boston in science and engineering; Los Angeles in music and film; New York in law, advertising, and publishing; Minneapolis in medical devices and instruments; Irvine and Pasadena, California in industrial design, and so on.

The logic brings us to this central issue:

Their goal is to maximize profits by siting their production activities around the world for the highest return and investing wherever it is most efficient and strategically profitable.

Our goal is to attract into the United States the most high value-added global activities with the greatest positive spillovers—and to keep and grow them here.

We can pursue our goal by ensuring that we give America's children a first-class education—starting with preschool and extending through college or vocational training—and that our transportation and communications infrastructure is second to none. But even if we make the United States an attractive place for high value-added investments, that alone will not be enough to guarantee the kind of global investment we need. In a world in which every other nation is bidding for high value-added jobs, America must negotiate as well.

The Logic of Global Negotiations

When trade was the primary engine of global economic integration and corporations were rooted in particular countries, negotiations were government-to-government. Each nation's objective was to open foreign markets to the exports of its own companies or to protect its own companies from foreign competition at home. Countries measured their success by the extent to which they were able to sell their goods and services within foreign nations and how much world market share their own companies could command.

But the new global economy renders obsolete these old forms of negotiating and keeping score. Global investment is supplanting merchandise trade as the major engine of world economic integration—and the key to a nation's wealth and well-being. And negotiations between governments and global managers—between the new "us" and the new "them"—are displacing the old government-to-government talks.

THE GROWING IMPORTANCE OF DIRECT INVESTMENT

Between 1983 and 1988, world trade volumes grew at a compounded annual rate of 5%. Over the same period, global direct foreign investment increased by more than 20% annually in real terms. As a result, sales by foreign-owned affiliates within a nation now typically exceed foreign exports to that nation. In fact, when the foreign sales of U.S.-owned companies are calculated against the total purchases by Americans of the products of foreign-owned companies, America's trade deficit turns into a net surplus. The foreign operations of U.S.-owned corporations now account for more than $1 trillion in annual sales around the world, roughly four times the total export of goods made in the United States and about seven to eight times the value of America's recent trade deficits.

Today much of what is actually "traded" across borders are intangible services—research, engineering, design, financial, management, marketing, and sales—transferred within global corporations from one location to another. IBM exports relatively few machines from the United States to the rest of its global web; most of its U.S. "exports" are ideas and insights. Honda now imports relatively few automotive components into the United States from Japan; most of its Japanese "imports" are technological specifications and management know-how. The threads of the new global web are computers, facsimile machines, satellites, high-resolution monitors, and modems—linking up ideas and money from each of the company's worldwide locations with every other. In 1990, some 20,000 privately leased international telephone circuits carried video images, voices, and data instantaneously back and forth among managers, engineers, and marketers working together on different continents.

THE NEW NEGOTIATIONS

This change in the locus of economic activity—from trade to direct investment—implies a change in the nature of negotiations: while we focus our attention on the Office of the United States Trade Representative in Washington, D.C., looking for government-to-government talks to open up foreign markets to the products of "our" companies, that is no longer where the important action really is. Even when these old-fashioned trade talks succeed in opening a foreign market to a U.S. company, the effect on *us*, on our incomes and standard of living, is often tangential. For example, the recent agreement secured with Japan after intense government pressure to permit Toys "R" Us to open a large retail outlet in Tokyo will have almost no effect on the U.S. work force, apart from a few U.S. managers. Almost everything that Toys "R" Us sells in Japan will be conceived, designed, and manufactured outside the United States.

Another sort of negotiation is becoming far more important—one that occurs between a different set of parties. On one side of the bargaining table still sit the government representatives; but on the other side *they* sit—the global managers. The government negotiators represent the citizens of the nation, not the nation's corporations. Their job is to induce the global managers to site certain activities in the nation and thus provide the nation's citizens with good jobs. In return, the government negotiators offer a carrot—an assortment of tax breaks, financial inducements, and public investments. There is also a stick: government negotiators may threaten to close the national market to the company unless it makes the desired investments.

Third World nations have long bargained along these lines with multinationals headquartered in advanced nations. But the logic of the global web means that practically every nation now ends up sitting on that side of the table, including some of the most unlikely parties. Hoping to attract labor-intensive light industries like electronic-parts manufacturers, Vietnam has recently created an industrial zone on the outskirts of Ho Chi Minh City; the government is prepared to negotiate rock-bottom leases to global companies willing to invest in production facilities there. In these types of negotiations, moreover, governments make virtually no distinction between domestic and foreign-owned companies. "There is no flag on capital," says Argentina's President Carlos Menem. "I ask myself, what is national capital? Is it the $50 billion in flight capital that has left the country via Argentine business executives? Or resources used by multinationals to produce here?"

AMERICA'S NEGOTIATORS

Like every other nation, the United States is taking an active part in these new sorts of negotiations. But unlike other countries, we are not represented by a high-ranking federal official like the United States Trade Representative. Instead, we are represented by 50 state governors and hundreds of mayors and city managers. Like the bargaining agents of other nations, these governors and mayors pay no attention to the nationality of the global managers on the other side of the table. In fact, 43 U.S. states maintain permanent offices and staffs in foreign capitals to conduct negotiations with foreign managers full-time. And these offices are not limited to the major commercial centers of the world: 10 states have recently opened offices in Taipei, and 4 more have announced plans to locate there. Just as often, the global managers sitting across the table are American, whose companies are headquartered in the United States—but they drive just as hard a bargain as the global managers from other countries.

The process works in a crude but effective fashion: the possibility of a new factory, laboratory, headquarters, or branch office within a state or a city sets off a furious auction; a casual threat to move an existing facility starts an equally impassioned round of negotiation. The governor or mayor who successfully lures or keeps the jobs is a hero; the one who loses the bidding may soon lose his or her own job.

The problem for us is that our U.S. bargaining agents often compete against themselves. A case in point: in the early 1980s, the Hyster Corporation, a manufacturer of forklift trucks, notified public officials in eight locations where Hyster had factories—five U.S. states, three foreign locations—that some of the facilities would be closed. Hyster invited each political jurisdiction to bid to keep its local jobs. The resulting auction was a great success for Hyster. By the time the bidding had closed, American states and cities had surrendered a total of $18 million to preserve about 2,000 Hyster jobs. The big "winner" was Danville, Illinois—a town with a population of only 39,000. In exchange for 850 blue-collar jobs, Danville and the state of Illinois agreed to provide Hyster with roughly $10,000 in subsidies.

Just as frequently, these kinds of auctions are global affairs. For example, when Diamond Star Motors, the Mitsubishi-Chrysler joint venture, announced in 1985 that it would begin assembling automobiles in the United States, four states competed for the factory. Illinois came out the winner with a bid of ten years of direct aid and incentives worth $276 million—roughly $25,000 for every new job the factory would create in the state. The city of Bloomington, Illinois threw in an additional $10 million of land and $20 million in local tax abatements.

Over time, the bidding has become more ferocious and the incentives more generous. In 1980, Tennessee paid the equivalent of $11,000 per job to entice Nissan to Smyrna. By 1986, Indiana had to spend $50,000 per job to induce Subaru-Isuzu to set up shop in Lafayette. When ConAgra threatened to leave Omaha, the state of Nebraska felt the heat of the bidding war directly. "It's like a poker game," said Donald Pursell, former director of Nebraska's Bureau of Business Research. "Nebraska makes a bid, Iowa ups it."

Bidding to attract new plants or keep existing ones requires that such state and local largess be routinely parceled out. Few global managers expect to pay the same rate of property tax in proportion to the assessed value of their land as local residents pay. Using the threat of the global web, it is relatively easy for global managers to insist on a better deal simply by pointing out to state or local officials that, without more favorable tax treatment, the company will move to one of its other global locations. Partly as a result of this kind of leverage, corporations now contribute a much smaller percentage of local taxes in the United States than they did in the past. In 1957, corporations accounted for about 45% of local revenues; by 1989, corporate taxes comprised only 16%.

Paradoxically, such tax breaks and subsidies make it more difficult for states and communities to finance public education and infrastructure. For example, General Motors's successful effort to cut its annual taxes by $1 million in Tarrytown, New York, where the company has had a factory since 1914, has forced the town to lay off dozens of teachers and administrators and to cut back on school supplies and routine school maintenance. Ultimately, these kinds of "beggar thy neighbor" ploys by some global managers undermine our ability to attract global investments—since the quality of the work force, good transportation facilities, and a good quality of life are ultimately more important lures for attracting global managers' investments than tax concessions and subsidies.

THE ADVANTAGES OF BARGAINING AS A WHOLE

It is simple common sense that large nations that bargain as a whole with global managers—or groups of smaller nations that pool their bargaining strength behind a single agent—have much more clout than small nations or separate states and cities. By avoiding internal bidding contests, they end up paying far less to attract investment and have an easier time getting the jobs they want when and where they want them. For example, the European Commission reviews location incentives offered by member nations in order to minimize bidding by one against the other. As a result, when Honda decided in 1989 to locate its first European plant in Britain, it did not receive a shilling of inducement from Downing Street.

After 1992, a united Europe will be in an even stronger bargaining position in negotiations with global managers. Access to Europe's newly integrated market of 230 million people will itself be a powerful lure. Global managers are already scrambling to set up facilities there in anticipation that Europe's gates will shut. "You can't pick up a piece of paper that says why Intel has got to manufacture in Europe," one Intel executive told a reporter. "The rules don't exist." But when they do, Intel wants to be already well-established inside the gates.

Another illustration of the same principle: for years, before Japan caught up with the West technologically, Japan's Ministry of International Trade and Industry acted as a single bargaining agent for the country, acquiring foreign technology at cut-rate prices. By effectively barring auctions for licenses in Japan, MITI forced foreign licensors to sell at a fraction of the cost of developing the technology originally. According to estimates, between 1956 and 1978 Japan paid some $9 billion to acquire U.S. technologies that cost between $500 billion and $1 trillion to develop.

The Logic of a *United* States of America

Think back to any earlier time. Before the ratification of the U.S. Constitution, every state carried out its own trade policy, negotiating separate trade pacts with foreign nations. This approach allowed the other nations—Britain in particular—to play one state against another, gaining agreements that favored Britain at the expense of the states.

When John Adams, representing the Continental Congress, sought Britain's agreement to open its ports to U.S. shippers, British Foreign Secretary Charles James Fox contemptuously suggested that ambassadors from all 13 states would have to sign any such treaty. As a result, when the founding fathers met in Philadelphia to devise a new constitution, they agreed with little debate that Congress should have the power to "regulate commerce with foreign nations and among the several states." This unprepossessing clause in Article I became the charter of our national economy.

Today no one would seriously propose that each U.S. state conduct its own foreign trade policy. That responsibility is firmly lodged in the federal government. Trade negotiations are centralized in the Office of the United States Trade Representative, with its own expert staff. But today, with direct investment supplanting trade as the engine of world commerce, we lack any similar vehicle to negotiate on our behalf with global managers. As a consequence, we are relatively easy pickings for them.

What is needed is a shift of authority over global investment, from states and cities to the federal government. What little authority the federal government now exercises over global investment is negative. That is, under the Omnibus Trade Act of 1988, the federal government can block foreign investors from gaining a controlling interest in a U.S.-owned corporation if the purchase is likely to "impair national security." Under several other recent statutes, the federal government subsidizes private sector R&D only if it is undertaken by a U.S.-owned company. Even more recently, Congress has sought to impose special tax and disclosure burdens on non-U.S. companies operating in the United States.

Most of these investment disincentives make little sense. Global managers at U.S.-owned companies are no more "us" than are the global managers of non-U.S. companies. And it is in our interests to attract investment from global managers all over the world, rather than raising investment barriers on the faulty basis of national identity. Most important, while other nations are improving their bargaining power to attract global investment, the United States continues both to dissipate its bargaining power by permitting state and local bidding wars and to discourage foreign investment by creating federal barriers.

A UNITED STATES INVESTMENT REPRESENTATIVE

A response that would serve our interests and accede to the logic of the global manager and the global web is both the creation of an Office of the United States Investment Representative, paralleling the United States Trade Representative, and the preemption by federal law of separate state and local laws that authorize their officials to offer investment incentives. In other words, the federal government should effectively bar states and cities from bidding for global capital; just as the USTR negotiates national trade issues, the USIR would negotiate investment issues.

The USIR would determine what sorts of global investments we need in order to enhance our wealth and create important spillovers, but which would not be made without special incentives. Do we want more of the public benefits associated with microelectronic fabrication and manufacturing? More microbiological research? More state-of-the-art auto assembly plants? Just as important, where do we want to see these investments located—in regions of high unemployment and relatively low skills? In regions where there already exist the beginnings of a critical mass of suppliers and relevant skills? The USIR would also monitor major factories, laboratories, and offices in the United States that global managers were planning to close and move abroad. Is it worth trying to keep them here? Why, and at what cost?

The tools available to the USIR in negotiating on our behalf already exist but are now scattered across the national landscape: tax abatements, tax credits, R&D incentives, loans and loan guarantees, use of public lands, public capital investment, and more. Moreover, working with the USTR, the USIR could offer trade concessions in exchange for the investments we seek—lowering tariffs on certain components to be used in the proposed U.S. manufacturing facility, providing relief from voluntary restraint agreements on other parts and components, granting immunity from certain antidumping levies. And if other nations threaten to close off their markets to global corporations unless they make certain investments there, America would be in the position to use similar threats as a means of ensuring its fair share of such investments.

The creation of a USIR would thus solve four problems at the same time. By pooling our now diffuse bargaining power, the USIR could bargain more effectively and at a lower cost on our behalf—thus preserving scarce resources for the important tasks of educating our work force and building a world-class infrastructure. It would bargain only for those global investments that promised large beneficial spillovers and that would not come to our shores automatically. It would seek to guide these investments to locations that would maximize the benefit to us. And it would put America on an equal footing with other large nations and emerging trading blocs that are already bidding effectively for global investment.

Without question, the activities of the USIR would be the subject of intense political interest. State and local governments would still compete against each other, but the competition would be contained among us, rather than channeled as payments to global corporations. And yes, the USIR would be selecting certain technologies and industries as more critical than others—which is exactly what Carla Hills, the United States Trade Representative, does now when she gives priority to certain industries during trade negotiations.

A GATT FOR DIRECT INVESTMENT

Just as we need a United States Investment Representative to parallel the efforts of the United States Trade Representative, so we need a GATT for Direct Investment to parallel the GATT that establishes rules for global trade—and for precisely the same reasons. So long as relative economic wealth and power figure prominently in national calculations, some framework for negotiations is necessary—lest nations fall prey to the same zero-sum investment bidding as America's states now engage in. Moreover, in the absence of such a new international forum, wealthy nations will always have the capacity to outbid poorer ones.

A GATT for Direct Investment would establish international rules by which nations bid for global investment and processes for settling disputes over such bids. For example, threats to close off a domestic market unless certain investments were made in it would be carefully circumscribed—for it is precisely threats such as these that rapidly unravel into zero-sum contests. The amount of permissible subsidies to attract investment might be proportional to the size of the nation's work force, but inversely proportional to its average skills—so that nations with large and relatively unskilled work forces would be allowed greater leeway in bidding for global investments than nations with smaller and more highly skilled work forces.

Other kinds of investment subsidies would be pooled and parceled out to where they could do the most good globally, as the European Community has begun to do regionally. For instance, nations would agree to fund jointly those basic research projects whose fruits are likely to travel across international borders almost immediately—projects such as the high-energy particle accelerator and the exploration of space. How such funds were apportioned and toward what ends would, of course, be subject to negotiation. The rules of the GATT for

Direct Investment would also specify fair allocations of tax payments by companies operating across several borders and would reconcile various regulatory regimes.

Come back to the global negotiating table where we started. We are on one side; they are on the other. There is nothing sinister or hostile about this setting. It is, in fact, an inevitable, practically inexorable extension of the emerging global economy. It is not, however, absolutely true that our interests and theirs conflict. Both sides, for example, benefit from our having a well-educated, well-trained work force; a well-developed, well-maintained public infrastructure; a high-quality environment and a high overall standard of living.

But there are differences as well, places where our interests naturally diverge. Many global managers, more sensitive to the requirements of the bottom line and thus more agile in adapting, have realized the implications of globalization. We and our governments are still struggling to catch up. They are changing the shape, size, location, and operating principles of global businesses. We are mired in the obsolete practices and attitudes of a previous era; our government lags behind the epoch-shaping events unfolding around the globe. Other nations—other groups of "us"—are reacting to these same events: EC'92, Japan's cautious emergence in world councils. Now we must move in the United States to create the new institutions and new attitudes that will permit us to negotiate effectively with them—that will allow us to negotiate as if our future depended on it.

Note

1. John Cantwell, *Technological Innovation and Multinational Corporations* (Oxford: Basil Blackwell, 1989).

3
Global Finance and the Retreat to Managed Trade

David D. Hale

The competitiveness debate that today focuses on America's industrial performance will soon confront something even more fundamental: money. The rise of Japanese financial power and the contradictions of U.S. economic policy are weakening the competitive position of the U.S. financial services industry—one of the few sectors where the United States still regards itself as more creative, more sophisticated, and more aggressive than its foreign rivals. As a consequence, the United States may soon face the same market erosion in financial services that has afflicted its producers of machine tools, automobiles, and semiconductors.

There is already ample evidence of a Japanese challenge in financial services:

> Foreign banks account for a growing share of the U.S. market. As of June 1988, 265 foreign banking institutions from 57 countries operated 673 offices throughout the United States. These banks controlled assets of $617 billion, representing 20% of all commercial banking assets and 25% of the business loan market. Japanese banks control some 20% of the California retail market; 4 of the 10 largest banks in California are Japanese.

> Japan's banks dwarf their U.S. counterparts. Japan's 13 largest commercial banks have a combined stock market capitalization of more than $470 billion. Its 3 long-term credit banks have a combined market value of $140 billion, and its 12 largest regional banks have a combined value of $80 billion. The combined value of the 50 largest U.S. banks is $110 billion. If assets are the benchmark, 9 of the world's 10 largest

banks are Japanese. Citicorp is the only U.S. bank in the top 20. All told, Japan's banks now account for 40% of international bank assets, compared with 20% in 1983.

Japan's Big Four securities houses (Nomura, Daiwa, Yamaichi, and Nikko) have become a major force in global underwriting. Ten years ago, the top 20 Eurobond underwriters did not include any Japanese firms. In 1988, each member of the Big Four ranked in the top 20, as did the Industrial Bank of Japan.

These and other developments raise difficult questions for financial services companies and the United States as a whole: How important is national banking power to a country's investment levels and exports? As foreign market share grows, how much influence can the Federal Reserve wield in the event of a domestic financial crisis? Are there economic and national security risks in allowing U.S. high-technology entrepreneurs to rely on foreign institutions for financing? Since Japanese banks and manufacturing companies have large cross-shareholdings, can they be considered autonomous players when they review sensitive financial information from U.S. corporate borrowers? If Japanese banks use their enormous advantages to dominate lending to blue-chip corporations, will U.S. banks be forced down market and become de facto repositories for "junk" loans?

There are no "right" answers to these questions, just as there are no easy remedies for America's competitive slide. Liberalizing Japan's financial markets—long a goal of Washington—may create more problems than opportunities by denying American banks the specialized niches they have traditionally enjoyed. Adopting policies to enhance long-term financial competitiveness by raising the U.S. savings rate could threaten the short-term profitability of Wall Street and U.S. commercial banks by slowing the leverage boom that drove their expansion in the 1980s. As a result, the United States is likely to embrace a managed trade policy in financial services comparable to policies that developed in many goods-producing industries during the 1980s—an ad hoc, results-oriented process that uses targeted protection, moral suasion by regulatory authorities, and corporate self-restraint to set new political rules for financial competition between the United States, Europe, and Japan.

The financial services industry is experiencing the same process of globalization that has already transformed goods-producing industries. Commercial banks increasingly compete in the domestic lending markets of other countries, not just in offshore wholesale markets like Eurobonds. Most large investment banks now trade stocks, manage funds, and advise on mergers and acquisitions around the world. Reuters and the Chicago Mercantile Exchange will soon offer a 24-hour global trading system linking all the world's markets for derivative instruments.

Yet the speed and ease with which stocks and bonds move between New York, London, and Tokyo does not characterize the political realm. The financial services marketplace resembles a twenty-first century global electronic village; the political marketplace is still rooted in eighteenth century ideas of the nation-state.

The General Agreement on Tariffs and Trade, the 97-nation accord that sets the rules for merchandise flows, never included banking and financial services. Most governments retain strict controls over what businesses they allow their financial services companies to enter. Regulators have long subordinated free markets and consumer choice to the interests of monetary control, prudential banking supervision, and deposit safety.

Because of this unique history, the central political question in financial services is not whether governments will become more protectionist but how much less protectionist they will become in response to technological change and the increasing mobility of capital.

In financial services, free trade is usually synonymous with a "national treatment" policy. Under national treatment, the basis of U.S. policy until very recently, financial institutions operating in a foreign country can enter the same lines of business and provide the same services as comparable domestic firms. More protection-minded officials advocate "reciprocity." Under reciprocity, which has characterized trade policy in continental Europe, foreign firms get access to a country's market only if that country's firms get access to foreign markets on the same terms. Since banking and securities laws, regulations, and practices differ widely among countries, strict reciprocity can provide a convenient rationale for excluding unwanted foreign competition.

So the choice is usually posed as a simple question: Will the United States help shape a system of world finance based on national treatment or reciprocity? In fact, the globalization of financial services will not evolve along a single political track. It will follow models as diverse as those that now govern trade in manufactured goods. The new international order in banking and financial services will include regional free-trade blocks, bilateral forms of reciprocity and national treatment, financial free ports on the periphery exploiting tax and regulatory rigidities in the centers, and covert government support for "national champions" in commercial banking and investment banking. The United States will be an important force behind the emergence of this new "managed trade" system.

No government official is using the term "managed trade" to describe U.S. policy. But the signs are all around us. For the first time in modern history, Congress included a reciprocity provision in the Omnibus Trade and Competitiveness Act of 1988 that required Japan to open government-bond auctions to foreign firms. The trade act also proposes retaliation if Europe adheres to strict reciprocity policies. It instructs the U.S. Trade Representative, upon finding that European Community (EC) financial policies discriminate against U.S. firms, to pursue market-opening measures including restrictions on European firms in the United States. Finally, the United States has traditionally had a de facto managed trade policy in financial services with Japan. Although American banking assets in Japan are only $30 billion, U.S. firms have received small but profitable niches in Japan's protected financial markets in return for a strong foothold in U.S. commercial lending and government securities trading.

It is too early to describe just what managed trade in financial services will look like. But the coming system is likely to have three basic components:

1. Quiet (but effective) moral suasion by the Federal Reserve and Japan's Ministry of Finance to regulate the growth of the Japanese share of the U.S. banking market as well as the behavior of Japanese banks in the United States.

2. Self-restraint by Japanese banks and securities houses in pursuing U.S. market share through aggressive pricing actions that could be perceived as "financial dumping."

3. More active congressional monitoring of how U.S. financial institutions are performing in Europe and Japan, coupled with demands for special policies to improve U.S. market share if financial liberalization alone is inadequate.

Anyone who doubts the likelihood of managed trade in financial services need only examine the record of the Reagan administration. Despite its free market rhetoric, it was the most protectionist administration in modern history. The share of U.S. imports subject to some form of restraint increased from 12% in 1980 to 24% in 1989. The administration also launched an unprecedented number of nonmilitary, high-technology industrial policy initiatives that would be considered illegal under the 1988 trade act if undertaken by foreign governments. If the U.S. government can be persuaded to intervene on behalf of industries as diverse as textiles, steel, and semiconductors, is there any doubt it will act to stem the erosion of banking, securities trading, and other financial services?

Washington's memories of the thrift-industry crisis will also encourage the trend toward managed trade. The thrift crisis demonstrated that the financial sector has a number of characteristics that resemble those of a utility and that require government to set parameters for risk taking in order to prevent destructive business practices. Congress will be doubly sensitive to the danger of American banks reducing their lending standards in order to meet the challenge posed by aggressive foreign competitors.

On the basis of traditional economic theory, the most desirable market structure for financial services should be "free trade." That is, a worldwide commitment to national treatment in which Japan liberalizes its tightly regulated financial marketplace, Europe harmonizes conflicting national traditions and allows foreign firms to compete on an equal footing with domestic firms, and the United States expands its commitment to evenhanded treatment of foreign rivals.

Such a structure is unlikely. Many U.S. officials worry that European economic and financial integration will not produce open financial markets. Europe is home to some of the world's most cosmopolitan financial institutions as well as some of its most parochial. The threat of protection in defense of the continent's weaker players has already produced trade disputes and political compromises that will result in quid pro quos on market access between Europe, the United States, and Japan. (See "Banking on 1992: Europe Embraces Managed Trade.")

Banking on 1992: Europe Embraces Managed Trade

U.S. officials worry that the movement toward European economic and financial integration will not reduce protectionism in banking and financial services. The focal point of these fears is a statement from the EC Commission last year that it would seek "reciprocity" from other countries as a condition of market access to areas not covered by the General

Agreement on Tariffs and Trade (GATT). The United States, in contrast, has emphasized its long-standing policy of "national treatment" and has urged Europe to be mindful of this model.

Ultimately, European policy is unlikely to reflect either strict reciprocity or national treatment. It is likely to be a hybrid model that technically conforms to any new GATT agreement in financial services but is "results oriented" in its application by central banks to achieve particular objectives—for example, retaining strong market positions for European institutions that would otherwise fall victim to U.S. and Japanese competitors, and negotiating a "fair share" of other countries' financial markets.

The United States and Japan have been alarmed about European calls for reciprocity because the Glass-Steagall Act and its Japanese equivalent, Article 65, separate commercial and investment banking. No such separation exists in Europe, where commercial banks are allowed to underwrite stocks and bonds, provide advice on mergers and acquisitions, and offer a range of other services. So long as these laws are operative, Europe could use them as a pretext to restrict the growth of U.S. and Japanese financial institutions in the Community.

Last spring, however, the European Community tried to calm outside fears about the rigid application of reciprocity. It issued a new directive with the following provisions:

> As originally drafted, the Commission planned to apply a foreign reciprocity test to each future application by a foreign bank to establish or acquire a subsidiary in the Community. Under the new plan, the Commission will be notified of such authorization requests, but there will be no automatic suspension of the license.
>
> The Commission will monitor the treatment of European banks by foreign countries. This country-by-country review process will affect how the Community will look at new license applications by foreign banks.
>
> As for the definition of reciprocity, the Commission proposes to open negotiations only where equivalent treatment is not granted. It may suspend or limit expansion or acquisitions by foreign banks if European banks do not secure "effective market access" in other countries.

This new directive was not drafted solely to satisfy foreign objections to a closed European market. Internal politics also played a role. Member countries with relatively open financial systems, like Great Britain, advocate a national treatment approach. They worry that more mercantilist EC members might use strict reciprocity as an excuse to exclude U.S. and Japanese banks from Europe. Such protectionism would seriously damage London's role as an international banking center but have only modest consequences for other European centers. Moreover, a protectionist trade policy in financial services would deny European consumers the productivity and price benefits that the EC Commission has argued should result from creation of a larger internal market. In fact, the original White Paper on unification contended that financial services would produce nearly one-fourth of the output gains from European integration.

For several reasons, then, managed trade rather than strict reciprocity or national treatment is the likely outcome. First, European countries have such differing and constraining regulatory traditions in trade and finance that it would be impossible for all of them to accept a new policy without many elements of conditionality. London has been a global financial center for 200 years; Italy and Spain ceased to be important financial powers after the seventeenth century.

Second, European financial institutions need time to consolidate and become cost effective. Europe is significantly overbanked on the basis of conventional productivity ratios. It has 20% more bank branches and only half the deposits per capita of the United States. Unfettered banking competition would mean draconian adjustments.

Third, Japan is likely to become a larger player in European financial services during the 1990s. The Japanese have 8% of the British lending market, but their share elsewhere in Europe is still insignificant. The Europeans will want to reserve some leverage for negotiating access to potentially profitable niches in the Japanese marketplace. The Community can probably extract new concessions as Japan's banks expand on the Continent. The French may even try to link financial-sector concessions to trade policy for industrial goods.

Finally, it seems increasingly likely that the United States will respond to Japanese economic power by pursuing managed trade in both financial services and manufactured goods. Surely it is unrealistic to expect Europe, with its long history of protected financial markets, to engage in free-market policies that the United States itself eschews.

An even more potent force behind the rise of managed trade is Japan's new status as a world financial superpower. Under current economic conditions, "free trade" in financial services would dramatically increase Japan's share of the U.S. market. Japanese banks hold two decisive advantages over their U.S. rivals: a low cost of capital and a system of cross-shareholdings with their large industrial clients that makes it easy to raise large amounts of equity at high price-earnings multiples.

These advantages grow out of Japan's high savings rate and corporatist economic system. Corporatist systems, like capitalist ones, have private ownership and use the marketplace as a screening device to allocate resources. But they do so within a framework that tries to achieve targeted objectives rather than trusts the market alone to ensure that national interests are served. Japan's economic system emerged out of its nineteenth century experience as a developmental state, in which the government played a major role importing foreign institutions and technology in order to encourage rapid modernization and lower the risk of European encroachment on the country's sovereignty. Because of its success at achieving rapid economic development, Japan was one of only three nonwhite societies to avoid partial European occupation during the nineteenth century. As a result of this unique historical experience, Japan has been far more successsful than other modern nations in implementing corporatist trade and industrial policies.

In contrast to pure command economies, Japan's public expenditures as a share of GNP are comparatively modest and the bureaucracy does not direct investment decisions. Rather, government plays a pre-scriptive role by using a mix of tax incentives, subsidies, and active coordination of private decisions to encourage new high-value-added industries and the orderly contraction of declining industries. Companies are not required to comply with government plans. But the incentives for cooperation are strong because government strategies are usually market conforming and well integrated with other aspects of economic policy.

Meanwhile, the Japanese corporate sector has a system of owner-ship that differs radically from the Anglo-Saxon form of capitalism. In contrast to the United States, where companies are controlled by individual investors and institutions seeking to maximize profits in the short term, Japanese companies are members of industrial groups with extensive cross-shareholding networks. Under this system, the return on equity investments is not measured solely on the basis of dividends and capital appreciation but also by how it enhances business relationships. As a result, companies are immune to hostile takeover bids and can sell equity to strengthen balance sheets without depressing share prices. This is a model that the United States has little leverage to modify and that U.S. financial services companies are not in a position to emulate.

Although analysts have long noted the unique features of Japanese capitalism, they were not thought to be of international significance. They will now emerge as a trade issue because of the explosive growth

Figure I.

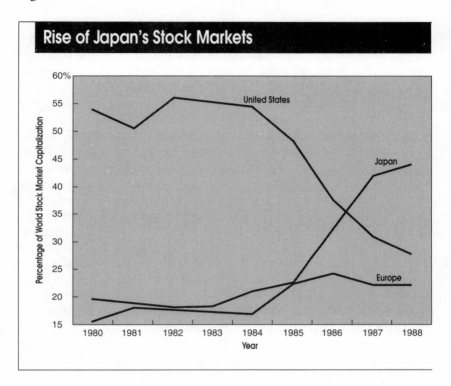

of the Tokyo stock market in the 1980s. There have been two major upheavals in the distribution of world stock market capitalization in the last 100 years. The first was during the early twentieth century. Rapid growth of the U.S. economy and the crippling effects of World War I allowed New York to displace London as the world's dominant capital market. The second was in 1987 and 1988. Japan's share of world stock market capitalization shot up to 45%, while the U.S. share fell to below 30% from 55% at the start of the decade. Some of the decline in the U.S. share reflects the spread of takeovers, leveraged buyouts, and share repurchases. But even using a broader definition of corporate capital that includes bonds as well as equity, U.S. corporations today have a market value of about $3 trillion, compared with $4 trillion for Japan's corporations. (See Figure I.)

Commentators often point to the United States's new status as a debtor nation as a sign of economic weakness. In fact, the shift in stock market capitalization is much more sobering. Whether a country is a debtor or a creditor says little about its economic performance, except that it has less savings than investment. During the early twentieth century, despite large-scale external borrowing, the United States overtook Great Britain in both national income and stock market capitalization. That's because foreign borrowing was used to finance expansion of the U.S. capital stock. In the 1980s, the United States borrowed on twice the scale (in terms of GNP share) as during the 1880s. But the growth rate of its capital stock did not accelerate, and its share of world stock market capitalization was halved. Practically all the decline in market capitalization was matched by growth in Japan's share.

The extraordinary growth of Japanese economic power during the Reagan years (a record that continues in the Bush years) is of great consequence for what it portends for the future management of the world economy. The history books may remember the 1980s as the triumph of neoconservative economic policies. But the dramatic expansion of Japan's economic power is anything but an endorsement of laissez-faire capitalism and the free-market dogma that President Reagan and his Chicago-trained economists brought to Washington in 1981.

To be sure, much of the rise in the Tokyo stock market can be explained by traditional economic variables such as liquidity and profits. Since 1950, Japan has enjoyed a high rate of personal savings and a low cost of capital. Japanese citizens save because tax laws encourage it and a whole range of policies discourage consumption. In the mid-1980s, excess liquidity in the Japanese financial system swelled to record levels because of an export boom and a collapse of imported commodity prices. Corporate earnings grew, share-price multiples nearly tripled, and stock market capitalization expanded dramatically. Although the price-earnings multiple for consolidated profits on the Tokyo Stock Exchange (TSE) now hovers around 35, down from a high of 52 in 1986, it is still much higher than the aggregate multiple of 12 on the New York Stock Exchange (NYSE)—despite the fact that Japanese interest rates are now 6% to 7%, compared with 8% in the United States.

Of course, many countries have enjoyed good economic records without sparking such dramatic increases in their stock markets. Germany, for example, has run current-account surpluses of between 3% and 4% of GNP for the last several years and has an extensive system of cross-ownership. But its stock market multiple hovers around 15.

Another factor behind the rise of the Tokyo market is its emergence as a major source of funds for the Japanese economy. The TSE has become a big source of funds for the privatization-minded Japanese government, banks, and manufacturing companies restructuring their operations to cope with the strong yen. In 1988, new equity financing equaled nearly 5.5% of GNP (¥16 trillion), compared with 1% to 2% of GNP per year through the 1970s.

As with Japanese industrial policy, official guidance of the TSE is usually prescriptive rather than proscriptive. The players know their roles without the government having to use overt controls. Four brokerage firms control 50% to 60% of the trading volume directly or through affiliates. (The MOF recently requested that Nomura restrain its market share to 30% of monthly trading volume in any given stock.) This level of concentration is unusually high when compared with other stock markets. Moreover, unlike in the United States or Britain, Japanese brokerage houses still enjoy fixed commissions, which provide them with profits large enough to offset trading losses incurred supporting the markets during periods of stress. The fact that Japan's securities industry is autonomous from its banks has played a major role in encouraging development of the equity market. Indeed, when trading volume is adjusted for the cross-shareholding system, share turnover is three to four times higher than in London, despite Tokyo's fixed commission structure. (See Table I.)

Other features of the Tokyo market have been conducive to sharply rising share prices. More than half of all equity is tied up in cross-shareholdings, and new issues have been far less common than in other countries. Between 1980 and 1988, only 207 companies went public despite the buoyancy of the Tokyo market—compared with 717 companies in the United States and 748 in Britain. Since new issues historically commanded a big scarcity premium in the after-market, brokerage houses used them to reward investors who helped support the share prices of troubled companies.

Meanwhile, the institutional investment business in Tokyo is nearly as concentrated as the brokerage business. The United States has more than 14,000 commercial banks; Japan has 158. The United States has more than 1,500 life insurance companies; Japan has 24. The United States has nearly 1,800 property-casualty insurers; Japan has 23. This compact structure allows the Ministry of Finance to have a large impact on stock prices by influencing the decisions of only a few fund managers.

Finally, the Japanese government will intervene directly to bolster the market if financial pressures threaten to overwhelm the capacity of the brokerage houses and large institutions to protect share prices. In the aftermath of the October 1987 crash, for instance, the MOF

Table I.

Japanese Brokerage Houses Dwarf Their U.S. Rivals

(in millions of dollars; figures have been rounded)

Category (1988)	Nomura Worldwide	Daiwa Securities	Nikko Securities[1]	Yamaichi Securities	Total Big Four	The 18 Largest U.S. Brokers
Brokerage Commissions	$4,629	$2,396	$2,202	$2,554	$11,780	$ 8,750
Underwriting and Distribution	1,400	835	774	940	3,949	4,750
Net Gain on Trading	1,024	306	474	5	1,809	5,750
Interest and Dividends	1,401	1,398	67	694	3,560	23,150
Other	62	183	180	211	636	5,250
Total Revenues	8,516	5,118	3,697	4,404	21,735	47,650
Total Expenses	3,885	2,800	1,821	2,236	10,742	45,350
Income Before Taxes	4,631	2,318	1,876	2,168	10,993	2,300
Pretax Margin[2]	60%	58%	54%	54%	56%	9%
Average Shareholders' Equity	$6,950	3,413	$3,287	$3,197	$16,845	$19,000
Pretax Return on Equity	67%	67%	58%	68%	65%	12%

Source: Sanford C. Bernstein & Co.

1. Financial statement excludes unconsolidated subsidiaries.
2. Revenues include net interest.

revised accounting standards for the country's *tokkin* funds, the corporate stock and bond portfolios managed by outside firms. Instead of reporting their assets at the lower of cost or market, tokkin managers were allowed to report fund values at the higher of cost or market—a change that lessened the danger of reporting trading losses that could have sparked a new wave of selling. Japanese brokers and investment institutions also worked together to prevent the price break in New York on Friday, October 13, 1989 from causing a collapse in Tokyo Monday morning, even though share prices slumped worldwide in sympathy with New York.

In the 1980s, Japanese banks benefited from the buoyancy of the Tokyo market and the impact of the cross-shareholding system on their ability to sell equity at attractive prices. Cross-ownership is just that: banks hold equity positions in the companies to which they lend, and the companies hold equity positions in the main bank of their *keiretsu* industrial group. In a December 1987 paper on Japanese banking, Akio Mikuni, who heads Tokyo's only independent credit-rating agency, described the intimate links between Japan's city banks and its largest industrial companies:

"In their halcyon days of high growth, our banks enjoyed a lender's market. That was the root of their cartel power. In fact, they possessed funds surplus to needs, and they created families of industrial firms—covering each new industry—simply as a means of putting the money to work. Mitsubishi, Sumitomo, Fuji, Sanwa, Mitsui, and Dai-Ichi Kangyo all formed comprehensive groups in auto, machinery, plant engineering, chemicals, steel, mining, oil refining, construction, trading, and so on. The main banks served as queen bees to large groups that in turn provided markets for member firms. A company belonging to one of the groups could count on 8% to 10% of the Japanese market straight off: a vital platform for entering a new industry."

It's impossible to quantify precisely how much these cross-shareholdings benefit Japanese banks in terms of their stock market value. But bank share prices do seem to correlate with the level of corporate holdings. For example, Kyowa Bank, which is scaling back low-return corporate lending in favor of consumer lending, has one of the lowest price-earnings multiples among the 13 big commercial banks—despite its strong balance sheet and excellent earnings growth. Because of its strategic shift away from corporate lending, Japanese companies are shedding their Kyowa holdings; its 1988 multiple was only 45 compared with the large-bank aggregate of 70. If shares in Japan's 13 largest banks were priced at Kyowa's multiple, their combined market value would be only $305 billion rather than $470 billion.

Cooperative self-leveraging of the Tokyo stock market is a great source of strength for Japan's financial services companies. It allows banks to raise large amounts of cheap equity capital. This makes them formidable competitors in corporate lending, where margins are thin and competition intense. To earn an adequate spread over the cost of deposits, banks must charge an interest rate high enough to cover the cost of equity, operating expenses, loan loss reserves, and an adequate pool of low-yielding liquid reserves. Four years ago, First Manhattan Consulting estimated that U.S. banks on average needed a 240 basis-point spread over deposit costs to earn an adequate return on a loan. Japanese banks needed only 110 basis points, creating a substantial advantage of 130 basis points. This differential reflected lower bank capital/asset ratios and reserve requirements in Japan as well as lower noninterest operating costs. With capital/asset ratios now in the process of becoming equalized across countries, some of the Japanese price advantage will erode. But First Manhattan estimates that Japanese banks still enjoy a substantial 50 basis-point advantage.

In December 1987, central bankers from the Group of Ten countries adopted guidelines requiring that all major commercial banks attempt to achieve an 8% capital/asset ratio by 1992. This new regulatory emphasis on expanding bank capital plays directly to Japan's TSE-based strengths. Japanese banks raised $50 billion of equity capital (¥6.7 trillion) from 1987 through 1989. In the United States, such heavy fund raising would have depressed share prices. In Japan, brokers and bank customers helped to ramp up share prices in order to ensure that the banks were recapitalized on attractive terms.

A report by Morgan Stanley reviewed the self-levitating properties of Japanese bank shares earlier in the 1980s, after a decade in which they had languished relative to the stock market as a whole. The financial networking described in this report still pertains today and would be considered illegal in the United States:

"Until the end of 1983, share prices of the Japanese city banks were held down to the low average level of ¥380 per share by the banks' antipathy to increasing the number of shareholders and their fears of speculative plays on their stock. However, in early 1984, under the aegis of the MOF and encouraged by the securities firms, the major banks changed their policy. This brought about an immediate and rapid upsurge in bank share prices, to an average of ¥770 in March 1984. In mid-1984, the major city banks made substantial equity offerings, which again prompted a sharp rise in stock prices to an average of ¥930 at the close of the year. . . . Subsequently, two years of modest rises accompanied by rather narrow fluctuations resulted in average stock prices of ¥1,160 for the city banks at the close of November 1986."

Banks that can more easily meet tougher guidelines enjoy a big competitive advantage. Put simply, there are two ways to meet tougher standards: increase capital or scale back assets (loans). Japan's banks are increasing their capital. (The G-10 guidelines also allow Japanese banks to include 45% of their unrealized gains on equity holdings and real estate as part of their capital, another big advantage.)

Many U.S. banks, in contrast, are curtailing lending growth or relying more heavily on loans to lower quality borrowers (assets that generate higher returns) and are expanding their fee-generating activities. New York's Loan Pricing Corporation maintains a data bank on the prices at which deals are sold in the U.S. secondary market for bank loans. It reports that during the first ten months of 1989, the ten largest U.S. banks purchased $225 billion worth of loans over 184 deals at an average spread of 175 basis points above the benchmark LIBOR rate. Loan purchases by the six largest Japanese banks ($97 billion worth of loans over 180 deals) had an average spread of 166 basis points. This difference may well reflect a migration "down market" and toward smaller companies on the part of U.S. banks. Such are the consequences of differences in global capital costs.

The low cost of capital could also emerge as an important factor for Japan's securities houses if international regulators institute capital-asset ratios for the securities industry. Nomura has a market capitalization of roughly $45 billion; the other Big Four firms have a combined market value of $55 billion. Already, the Big Four have become powerful competitors in the Eurobond market, with an aggressive market-share strategy made possible in part by their access to cheap funds. Indeed, these firms are sharply increasing their share of stock and bond underwriting around the world. In the first quarter of 1989, the Big Four's combined global underwriting share rose to nearly 40% from less than 22% a year earlier. Although the bulk of this underwriting was for Japanese companies, the Big Four are gaining ground with non-Japanese companies.

The conclusion is inescapable: if the United States commits itself to developing truly free markets, the foreign share of U.S. banking and financial services could expand dramatically. Japanese banks have traditionally concentrated on looking after their Japanese clients in the United States and buying shares of blue-chip lending syndicates and letters-of-credit guarantees. But there are plenty of new opportunities for competitive entry. Once barriers to interstate banking come down, the Japanese could use their existing California base to move into retail banking throughout the western states or other states with a large Japanese industrial presence. The proliferation of leveraged buy-outs has created a new niche for commercial banks prepared to bid aggressively for large volumes of low- or medium-grade corporate paper. Japanese commercial banks have reportedly supplied one-third of the financing for some of the largest LBOs in 1988 and 1989, and their receptiveness is increasingly important to the success or failure of proposed deals. Finally, some major American commercial banks are so capital deficient that they would welcome a large Japanese investor to restore their balance sheets. Manufacturers Hanover recently sold 5% of its equity and a large share of its CIT subsidiary to Dai-Ichi Kangyo, Japan's largest bank.

Free traders argue that Japan's increasing presence in the United States should not be cause for alarm so long as U.S. firms enjoy the same degree of market access in Japan. And in recent years, the country has pursued liberalization. The MOF is steadily reducing interest rate controls on bank deposits. The commercial paper market is expanding rapidly. The Japanese government is selling 40% of its new bond issues through competitive auctions, and it plans to introduce a Treasury-bill instrument for the first time. Indeed, as a result of these and other measures, the MOF estimates that Japan's money market (Treasury bills, commercial paper, unrestricted bank certificates of deposit) will soon be 50% of GNP, compared with only 30% for the United States. Eight years ago, the Japanese money market was only 10% of GNP.

The United States applauded this market opening. After all, Treasury officials initiated talks in the mid-1980s to encourage just such a process. They argued that financial liberalization would lessen the danger of Japan manipulating its exchange rate to maximize export competitiveness. By the early 1990s, though, the U.S. government may be much less enthusiastic. Liberalization could increase competition in some of the niches that were specially created to compensate foreign banks for the entry barriers in Japan's primary banking markets.

For example, the Japanese government has allowed foreign commercial banks to enter the trust bank business. Nine non-Japanese banks own such institutions, even though Japanese commercial banks are excluded from this sector. During 1988 and 1989, foreign securities firms received a guaranteed share of government bond syndicates; that share recently increased from 2.5% to 8%. Under prodding from Shearson Lehman Hutton, the Japanese government is studying the feasibility of giving foreign firms access to new licenses to operate investment trust management companies.

The potential problem with further liberalization is that it could give Japanese banks access to niches once reserved for foreigners. (Indeed, as a result of liberalization, the foreign share of Japanese banking profits has dropped to 1% from 3% ten years ago.) In a paper for the Council on Foreign Relations, Eric Hayden, a former managing director of the Bank of Boston, has described the effects of increased local competition on the market for foreign currency or "impact" loans, once the exclusive preserve of non-Japanese banks:

"Once we began clamoring in the late 1970s for a more open financial system, the authorities decided to 'level the playing field' for the domestic banks and permitted them for the first time to compete head-on with the foreigners in providing impact loans. This turn of events was entirely unexpected by Tokyo's foreign banking community, and it proved to be a quick lesson in the double-edged sword of liberalization. Within the space of two years, the foreign banking community had lost virtually the entire market for foreign currency loans and, with it, a significant portion of profits. That event more than any other has been responsible for the continuing earnings deterioration of the foreign banks in recent years."

Liberalization of the stock and bond markets may also be a mixed blessing. Last spring, the Japanese government held its first truly competitive bond auction. The Big Four bid so aggressively that some foreign firms are worried they will not be competitive under the new regime. The emergence of a futures market in equities might also cut into foreign profits—despite the fact that the U.S. firms enjoy a head start in using and developing such derivative instruments. Tokyo's high commission structure is encouraging foreign buyers of Japanese stocks (many of whom funnel their orders through U.S. firms) to shift more of their trading from the cash market to derivatives. This shift will hurt foreign firms more than local firms, which can rely on millions of loyal Japanese retail customers to remain in the cash market.

Even the U.S. Treasury may become reluctant to encourage further Japanese liberalization. The more open Japan's financial system becomes, the harder it will be for the MOF to protect Washington from the consequences of America's low savings rate and irresponsible fiscal policies. Japan's corporatist financial system has played a big role in propping up the dollar and financing the U.S. current account deficit. The absence of a large and active money market in Tokyo has helped keep the yen from emerging as a reserve currency to challenge the dollar. Because of its ability to use credit controls, the Bank of Japan was able to pursue a monetary policy in support of the dollar during 1987 and 1988 without losing control of domestic credit growth. The MOF has often helped maintain U.S. financial stability by discouraging Japanese life insurance companies from dumping U.S. bonds during periods of exchange rate tension.

Indeed, historians may someday note with ironic delight that at the end of the 1980s, it was graduates of the University of Tokyo Law School presiding over the finance ministry of the industrial world's least deregulated economy that helped to rescue the United States from currency misalignments, trade imbalances, and financial crises produced by fiscal and monetary policies engineered by economics graduates of the University of Chicago.

As Japan's presence in the U.S. banking market becomes more conspicuous and as liberalization in Tokyo fails to boost the U.S. presence there, bankers and political leaders may start demanding protection. The Treasury has not yet focused on the policy implications of the Tokyo market's unique institutional features, but consider some of the questions that might arise:

Should one firm be permitted to control 20% of Tokyo's trading volume and thus implicitly 10% of the world's? What advantages do fixed commissions give Japanese brokerage firms in managing markets?

Since real estate prices are an important prop to the Tokyo stock market, should the United States and other countries lobby for deregulation of the Japanese real estate market?

Does the implicit cost of capital subsidy that Japanese banks enjoy from official guidance of the stock market and corporate cross-shareholdings encourage them to engage in overseas "financial dumping"—accepting low profit margins for loans, securities trading, and other financial activities in order to expand market share?

Have the BIS capital requirements inadvertently caused Japanese banks to become overcapitalized relative to their true needs in Japan, and thus increased the pressure on them to pursue aggressive expansion overseas? Will they now export asset inflation to other countries as a result of the balance-sheet strength they enjoy through inflated prices on real estate and the Tokyo Stock Exchange?

Are Japanese banks true free agents or are they financial appendages of octopuslike industrial groups with no real counterpart in United States?

Such questions are not totally new. Germany's universal banking system has long been characterized by corporate cross-shareholdings and an equity market dominated by the banks. But Germany has never posed as great a competitive challenge to the financial and industrial power of the United States as Japan does today.

Japan recognizes the potential for trade tensions in financial services. As its share of the U.S. lending market expands, the MOF will probably attempt to develop new niches for U.S. financial service players. Some MOF officials even want to encourage a foreign bank to purchase one of the smaller Japanese regional banks with a good retail network, but current share prices make such a deal prohibitive.

Japanese banks and securities houses will also attempt to calm protectionist forces through covert forms of managed trade. They will pursue more joint ventures with U.S. firms, develop modest cross-shareholding relationships, and voluntarily forgo some business in the interests of political harmony.

Even with Japanese self-restraint, however, it is easy to imagine the United States concluding that banking and financial services are strategic sectors that deserve government support. But moving from abstract concerns about financial competitiveness to an effective agenda for action is much easier said than done.

First, there is no simple way to define America's potential comparative advantage. The country's high cost of capital means its advantage in financial services is likely to be in providing specialist fee services (such as structuring mergers and acquisitions, loan syndications, securitization, and designing swaps) than in businesses requiring deep pockets. But Japan's rapid growth in the Eurobond market testifies that securitization and trading are not immune from cost of capital factors. If the Japanese are prepared to spend heavily on staffing or joint ventures with top U.S. firms, they could well achieve success in the fee-generating "financial engineering" business. The alliances of Nomura with Wasserstein Perella, of Nikko with the Blackstone Group, and of Dai-Ichi Kangyo with Clayton & Dubilier point to the direction in which more Japanese firms are heading.

The obvious response to this scenario is for the United States to adopt policies that reduce its cost of capital. That requires major fiscal policy changes to raise the national savings rate. While bankers love to make speeches about the virtues of higher savings, they are unlikely to welcome the changes needed in the tax system to get them.

The U.S. tax system has been highly benign for the banking community and Wall Street. It includes the most generous tax allowances in the industrial world for home mortgages. This encourages households to maximize their use of mortgage debt, which either can be retained by financial institutions or sold in an active secondary market. It is also the only tax system in the industrial world to provide no credits to offset the double taxation of dividends. This creates strong incentives for corporations to use debt rather than equity and helps to encourage growth of the junk bond market.

Consumer lending, takeover activity, and balance-sheet restructuring in favor of debt were the chief growth locomotives of the U.S. financial service industry during the 1980s. Any coherent fiscal reform program would have to strike directly at the tax allowances that subsidize overconsumption and overinvestment in residential real estate and that encourage firms to leverage their balance sheets. Few bankers are likely to embrace such a political agenda.

As a result, it is difficult to imagine fiscal reforms far-reaching enough to reduce the cost of U.S. capital during the 1990s. Under these conditions, the logical policy response would be to encourage the development of U.S. universal banks. These institutions could retain a foothold in commercial lending but grow primarily through the development of non-capital-intensive service activities. Indeed, U.S. banks have already pursued such a growth strategy in offshore markets.

But there are problems here too. The concept of universal banks runs directly counter to U.S. banking traditions of geographic decentralization and functional compartmentalization. Moreover, Wall Street firms remain opposed to granting banks additional powers to underwrite corporate debt and equity, one reason the debate over the Glass-Steagall Act has festered for so long. The U.S. banking system is likely to retain its dual structure well into the 1990s.

Nor is there any guarantee that the rise of universal banks would reverse U.S. competitive fortunes. Several large insurance companies bought brokerage houses in the early 1980s. They have yet to show positive results either in terms of either profits or in market penetration. Some of the most spectacular business strategy failures in London and Tokyo during the late 1980s were among U.S. commercial banks that tried to turn small or medium-sized brokerages into engines of global expansion. Seldom has so much money been wasted attempting to blend such divergent business cultures. It is striking testimony to the sophistication of the Japanese firms that they have expanded their foreign business gradually or by buying shares of other firms' syndications, rather than paying high prices for British and U.S. securities houses on the eve of major bear markets in equity prices and commissions.

Finally, the U.S. banking system may need large injections of Japanese capital during the early 1990s. The U.S. stock market will have trouble generating the funds required to recapitalize the thrift industry and strengthen bank balance sheets, especially if interest rates rise sharply and if highly leveraged companies experience solvency problems. In contrast, Japanese banks have strong equity bases and a long history of working with corporate managements to reorganize troubled companies. The United States can't simultaneously keep out Japanese banks and avail itself of their financial resources.

It is one of the great paradoxes of the 1980s that the big comparative advantage of U.S. financial institutions is their flexibility in coping with the disadvantages created by a fiscal system that inflates the cost of equity capital and encourages overconsumption. No other country has gone as far as the United States in securitizing mortgages, consumer debt, and low-grade corporate paper. America has also been unique in creating private insurance guarantees for many financial instruments. As larger secondary markets develop for such instruments outside the United States, the U.S. experience should be exportable in a variety of ways. Of course, the contradiction in this strategy is the long-term macroeconomic consequences of encouraging so much financial innovation to boost consumption, cannibalize corporate equity, and maximize use of leverage.

U.S. financial institutions are not directly responsible for the dramatic changes in the country's international financial position. But as with the Latin American debt crisis, they have been one of the key agents through which government policy operated. When OPEC ran a huge current-account surplus and the U.S. domestic savings rate was much higher, Washington encouraged the money-center banks to grow by exporting capital or recycling it from the Persian Gulf. In the 1980s, the interaction between massive budget deficits at home and restrictive fiscal policies abroad turned the United States into the world economy's borrower and spender of last resort. So U.S. banks became aggressive domestic lenders.

The linkages between proconsumption tax allowances, permissive financial regulation, and large trade deficits mean U.S. banks could face some potentially perverse trade-offs. If the Bush administration takes effective action to raise the domestic savings rate, the consumer-lending sector will be less buoyant than during the 1980s, and corporations will become more self-funding, but the drift toward protection will slow. If, by contrast, U.S. policy retains its bias toward low savings and high consumption, protectionist sentiment will flourish. Although powerful U.S. banks would get their fair share of the rents produced by managed trade in financial services, continued large budget and trade deficits and financial protectionism augur poorly for America's economic standing in the world.

4
Japan & the USA: Wrangling Toward Reciprocity

Kazuo Nukazawa

To my way of thinking, the U.S. economy is like a tough stomach. It digests everything new and foreign and converts it to an element of strength. Japanese-style management is just one such element—admired briefly from a distance, then quickly studied and made part of American business culture. This extraordinary power of assimilation has made American business diverse and strong.

The world economy, rapidly becoming one vast marketplace, is beginning to learn from America's example. More and more private-sector economic activities are beginning to extricate themselves from narrow national confines and contribute to the global expansion of employment and income. More and more countries are adopting the businesses and business practices of other nations, even other continents. This mutual penetration of investments, goods, services, and business cultures can save societies from self-suffocation.

Japan's past obduracy in not allowing this process to occur is one of the factors underlying the severe international economic conflicts we see today between Japan and its trading partners.

Arrogance and Insensitivity

In all fairness, I must point out that Japan is not the only country to have failed to pursue such efforts vigorously. Europe has long neglected serious study of the Orient as an economic partner and a cultural equal. Only now is the United States beginning to include Japanese as a part of its linguistic curriculum.

Nevertheless, Japan is today the principal target of criticism. Increasingly, the Japanese are accused of arrogance and insensitivity. I have conflicting thoughts on this subject.

On one hand, it is probably true—though probably also temporary. But almost every nation has gone through an arrogant period in its history. Caution is necessary to keep the phenomenon under control, but preaching is not likely to be of much help. Instead, policymakers and economists should try to direct this psychological energy and put it to a good use. Lamenting arrogance is often just an expression of impotence.

Since the economic regime we have chosen—capitalism—uses self-interest as the mainspring of social progress, we must spend more time examining the ways and means to use this drive. One way is to play a more responsible role, and thus increase our voting power, in international organizations. Another might be to implement the recent proposal for a new Japanese Marshall Plan to increase foreign aid, support international peace-keeping efforts, and assist debt-ridden countries—all the while expanding domestic demand. The key domestic challenge of the day in Japan is to make this idea more appealing to the public and to enlist the support of Japanese constituencies.

On the other hand, if Japan's problem is the arrogance of efficiency, that is a more serious matter. In the course of trying to catch up with modern civilization, the Japanese have been inspired more by the material success than by the spirit of the Western world, and some of us may have mistaken Western economic and technical efficiency and diligence for greatness.

Simply put, efficiency is merely a way of doing a three-day task in two, while diligence assures quality and delivery. All well and good, but the creative genius of a Beethoven, a Shakespeare, or a Bashō goes beyond both of these, and *theirs* are the immortal achievements. Until we understand this fact and begin to appreciate foreign values, we Japanese will never integrate harmoniously into the international community. All countries are deficient in this area, but an island nation clearly has to work harder to avoid measuring others on a single scale.

Appreciating different cultures is a basic requirement for international understanding and lasting peace. A stone comb I once saw in a Turkish museum initially struck me as nothing more than a rudimentary tool, made thousands of years ago by a virtual savage. A moment's reflection, however, led me to think of the months of labor some man put into making it, and of the sweetheart he made it for.

We Japanese have complained over the years that Americans drag their moral universe behind them wherever they go, disregarding different value standards, advising all and sundry with missionary zeal to discard irrational practices. Some have called *that* arrogance. Maybe. But I cannot help feeling that the American "Can do!" belief in progress has done the world a great service.

Many Americans have discovered ways to be outspoken without being arrogant, frank without being insensitive. We should emulate them, study their record, and, where possible, try to do even better. The heart of the effort is a reconciliation of values. For conceptual purists this reconciliation is impossible, but the rest of us succeed a little every day. We need to succeed a little more.

For hundreds of years the Japanese have suffered from a parochial fear that foreign goods and capital will rend the traditional fabric of Japanese society and culture. Ever since the 1850s, when the foreign invasion actually began, many of my countrymen have cried out stridently in protest.

But our culture has proven more resilient than these xenophobes believed. As we allowed foreign imports and investment to penetrate, we found that they became Japanese—in the same way that sushi has become American and Japanese corporations in the United States have had to adopt many local employment practices. We found cultural interaction to be a source more of strength than of weakness. It is a lesson we need to remember as we deal with what seem to be more pressing problems.

The Japanese Economy

Japanese industrialists today see themselves on a treadmill, running faster and faster to overcome the appreciation of the yen but knowing all the while that success will only drive the yen up further still and force them to run faster yet.

The only way off the treadmill is to make so-called exchange-rate-neutral investments in the United States or elsewhere abroad. But to invest abroad may be to stop running and start swimming—in a totally new environment and with a lot of local tricks to learn fast. Coping with local unions is only the tip of a single iceberg.

We know that many U.S. industries have deserted their own shores and moved their production bases out of the United States in the face of high wages, exaggerated product liability, and other adverse domestic factors. Japanese investors realize that they may not be able to deal with such problems any better than their American counterparts. Even where quick profits *are* reported, the rise of the yen has drowned the dollar-term gain.

Yet direct overseas investment seems to be a landslide. In fiscal 1986 (April 1986–March 1987), Japan invested $22 billion abroad, and the sum is expected to have exceeded $30 billion in fiscal 1987 (April 1987–March 1988). The Japanese feel pressed in every market as they hear the footsteps of new Asian dragons.

By the end of this century, Japanese overseas production will grow from 4% currently to almost 20% of total manufacturing output. So people are discussing, somewhat prematurely, the hollowing of Japan. Steel, shipbuilding, coal mining, aluminum, and other industries have announced employment reductions. Local governments—prefectures and municipalities—have redoubled their efforts to attract foreign investment.

The yen-based export figure slipped from ¥42 trillion in 1985 to ¥35 trillion in 1986 and ended 1987 at ¥33 trillion. Meanwhile, the country's export dependency declined from 13.2% of GNP in 1985 to 10.6% in 1986, to 9.7% last year.

THE MAEKAWA REPORT

Japan's huge trade surplus and current-account balance led, in 1985, to the formation of a private group to study possible structural adjustments to the economy. Its findings and recommendations—called the Maekawa report after the former governor of the Bank of Japan who was the group's chairman—were submitted to then prime minister Yasuhiro Nakasone in April 1986. The report proposed a number of basic changes.

One of the goals established by the Maekawa report was to reduce the ratio of current-account surplus to GNP. The ratio (to nominal GNP) went up from 3.8% in fiscal 1985 to 4.5% in fiscal 1986, but for fiscal 1987 the figure is expected to go down to around 3.3%, and the forecast for fiscal 1988 runs at about 2.5% to 2.7%.

The appreciation of the yen, not government intervention, is taking care of the report's other targets for structural industrial adjustment.

Expansion of domestic demand to absorb Japanese and foreign products, another Maekawa goal, has been greatest in housing. Housing starts ran at about 1.7 million units in 1987 (compared with 1.5 million in the United States, which has twice Japan's population). Other efforts to reduce Japan's current-account surplus include an increase in budgetary outlays for infrastructure construction, a reduction in the official discount rate to 2.5% (the lowest since World War II), stimulation of private-sector economic activities by deregulation and privatization, a change in land and housing taxes, removal of import-related red tape, and elimination of the tax break for savings (which will reduce the savings ratio).

Despite outstanding long- and short-term government liabilities of nearly $2.2 trillion—roughly equal to four-fifths of its GNP—Japan was forced in May 1987 to resort to Keynesian prescriptions to boost its economy. It both cut taxes and expanded government outlays. Defeat of a sales tax proposal also gave the economy a short-term boost.

In designing the basic shape of the fiscal 1988 budget late last summer, the Nakasone government and the ruling Liberal Democratic Party (LDP) chose to maintain their budget-balancer facade by selling off government assets.

To satisfy domestic and foreign constituencies, the LDP has promised to study construction of several new deficit-producing railways, to expand foreign aid, and to increase military expenditures—scrapping the 20-year-old ceiling of 1% of GNP.

The American Economy

Even though it is now losing steam, the U.S. economy has run faster in recent years than those of most other countries including Japan, and domestic employment has risen. Between 1980 and 1985, U.S. employment grew by 7.8 million and Japan's grew by 2.6 million, while employment actually shrank in Great Britain, France, and West Germany by a total of 3.6 million. This trend continues. Almost miraculously, but helped by oil price reductions, inflation in the United States seems reasonably under control.

The price of this good news has been the fiscal and current-account deficits. But after a rather long lag due to continued confidence in the dollar and faster U.S. economic growth, the exchange rate adjustment was finally triggered by the G5 (United States, Japan, West Germany, Britain, and France) agreement of September 1985. Now, though the remaining misalignment vis-à-vis non-G5 currencies and the U.S. savings rate continue to be important factors, the slow but steady reduction of the current-account deficit is likely.

The United States reduced its budget deficit in 1987, but this year's reduction will be more difficult. There is, by the way, some inconsistency between the domestic arguments of American budget balancers about U.S. fiscal health (raise taxes, reduce expenditures) and America's advice to Japan about fiscal stimulus (increase expenditures, cut taxes).

AMERICAN ENTERPRISE

The American industries in decline are the ones the country is graduating from—textiles, steel, automobiles. The economy's vitality is in other sectors. For example, the United States overwhelms Japan and Europe in most super high-tech and sophisticated service areas, and most countries are seriously concerned about widening technology gaps.

In visits to more than a dozen states in 1986 and 1987, I was greatly impressed by the dynamism of American enterprises. Take *Federal Express*, for instance. The company hub in Memphis, Tennessee essentially operates for 2 hours and 25 minutes a day—from 11:45 P.M. to 2:10 A.M. About 60 planes from all over the nation and from foreign countries land there every night and unload mail, documents, and parcels, which are then sorted and labeled electronically, put back into containers, and reloaded. All planes leave again before 4 A.M., and the parcels arrive at their destinations by 10 the next morning.

In Japan, such a business would be very difficult to operate. But in the United States, night-landing regulations are not as tight, the restrictions on carrying public mail are less strict, and customs officials cooperate in providing middle-of-the-night service. (In fact, *Federal Express* pays their overtime.)

In Ann Arbor, Michigan, I visited Domino's Farms and its owner, Tom Monaghan, a man who began life in an orphanage and rose to rule a fastfood kingdom—the largest pizza delivery company in the world. Several years ago Monaghan bought the Detroit Tigers, and he is now constructing a 300-acre corporate education center and training facility. His enterprise impressed me immensely; it is the Land of Opportunity in action.

AMERICAN VULNERABILITY

American competitiveness cannot be measured by the balance-of-payments table. Many U.S. companies are producing a host of goods abroad and sending them back home. Such companies are already among the most competitive and integrating elements in the European economic scene. U.S. companies in Japan show much higher profit rates than Japanese companies in the States.

The United States is not hollowing, it is replenishing. It is not deindustrializing, it is only shedding a set of outgrown clothing. During the process, it looks off guard and sometimes vulnerable, but now that it has realized a fairly extensive currency realignment, now that competitiveness has again captured its attention, American dynamism will surely rise to the challenge.

The lead will not come from Washington but from the hundreds of industrial parks and research labs where the interdisciplinary studies and the rich cross-fertilization of ideas are taking place. New Japanese companies are being attracted to this only-in-America environment. Japanese managers, engineers, and their families are now becoming an integral part of the American scene. And though the road is bumpy, the direction is clear.

A Level Playing Field

The United States and Japan are the two strongest promoters of the new Uruguay Round of the General Agreement on Tariffs and Trade (GATT). At the same time, the United States is building free-trade relationships with Israel and Canada, and the U.S. ambassador to Japan, Mike Mansfield, has repeatedly proposed an American-Japanese free-trade agreement—a proposal I think should be more seriously studied.

However contradictory on the surface, U.S. bilateral, multilateral, and unilateral moves are linked by the American belief that the United States cannot lose if it is allowed to play on a level field. But as Julia Child said of the tomato, this concept hides a lot of grief.

To begin with, the underlying premise that American domestic production is competitive has now become valid for many industries, thanks to the exchange-rate correction. In fact, many U.S. factories are now operating at nearly full capacity. This is one of the reasons many foreign businesses have established plants in the United States.

But even if the U.S. playing field is level, it is nevertheless a bit muddy. It is much too litigious, for example; and its rules differ from state to state. Its voluntary export restraints impose a de facto quota system on some trading partners. It also forces quarterly evaluations of corporate batting averages and requires enormously expensive product liability insurance.

As for the international playing field, the legal framework of the GATT and other trade organizations permits one nation to demand most-favored-nation treatment of another but makes no allowance for the kind of reciprocity that the United States currently demands of most other countries. While America can request flexibility of Japan, it has no internationally acknowledged right to demand change or to attempt to twist our arms by unilateral action.

U.S. UNILATERALISM

The attention of trade policy observers all over the world is focused on the U.S. comprehensive trade bill. But the actions taken so aggressively by the U.S. administration since the fall of 1985 (in accordance with Section 301 of the Trade Act of 1984) have already given trade interests in the United States a means of bypassing the traditional method of seeking relief, i.e., by proving injury to domestic industry at the International Trade Commission.

The ITC is politically neutral and almost free of political pressures, and much of the evidence used to reach judgment is made public, ensuring scrutiny. In bypassing this process, the Reagan administration is single-handedly acting as prosecutor and judge, against the most deeply rooted traditions of American justice.

The ITC is an excellent institution, one Japan would do well to emulate. Undermining the ITC will only permit narrow interests to pursue mercantilist goals at the expense of the national interest.

JAPANESE PROTECTIONISM

For years, Western scholars, business executives, and government officials have preached the virtues of the free market to the Japanese.

The free play of market forces based on comparative advantage, we are told, will bring about the most efficient allocation of resources, while protectionism will reduce national income and raise unemployment in any country where it is practiced.

Imagine our consequent confusion when we are told by Americans that Japan is now enjoying undue benefits by maintaining protectionist barriers and rejecting the law of comparative advantage! If the sermons are correct, and if Japan is exercising protectionism on a broad scale, then Japan must be greatly reducing its own efficiency, income, and employment rate. How can this be called reaping the benefits of protectionism? And how has Japan actually achieved high growth?

One might argue that Japan's protectionism has succeeded, despite textbook economics, because of freer markets abroad. But if freer overseas markets rewarded state controls, then Russia and other centrally planned economies would be economic giants. Those who believe that governments can allocate resources better than the free market should espouse their socialism openly and stop delivering lectures on the virtues of the market economy.

To the extent that Japan twice distorted price mechanisms, first to satisfy immediate and dire postwar needs, then to nurture the industries the government thought important, it aided certain inefficient industries at significant cost. That cost was paid by the more efficient segments of the national economy. In most nations, inefficient industries employ more people than efficient ones, and, alas, most of these people vote for protectionism.

Later, in the 1960s, when Japan progressively liberalized trade and then foreign investment—in both directions—economic growth accelerated. The Japanese economy has tried, is still trying, to overcome the die-hard, residual market rigidities that are the legacy of the immediate postwar crisis. Granted, the Japanese economy is still much more heavily regulated than the U.S. economy, but the Japanese as well as foreign participants in the Japanese market all play on the same rocky, regulatory playing field.

JAPANESE AGRICULTURE: THE DAWN OF REALISM

Japan's agricultural policies have extracted a heavy price from Japanese households and corporations. Explicit and implicit agricultural subsidies, more expensive raw materials for the food-processing industries, exorbitant land prices—all have placed terrible burdens on the manufacturing and service sectors, as well as on families. This protectionism has kept food prices high—much higher than in the United States—and blocked a large portion of household disposable income from other uses. Expensive food and land keep industrial workers' real wages artificially low, while the need to maintain acreage and keep rice from perennial oversupply obstructs technological advances like high-yield rice.

Market forces, along with a likely increase in the property tax on farmland in urban areas, will probably lead to a reduction in land prices. This development would permit housing policies to be vigorously pursued without straining the relative equality of income distribution. At the same time, less developed countries would gain from the widened opportunity to export agricultural products to Japan.

Domestically, the proportion of household income spent on food would go down drastically, and the unleashed disposable income would find outlet in other goods and services. Further, mounting agricultural imports would check the meteoric rise of the yen.

Japan will soon become a surplus nation in invisible trade because the growing influx of dividend and interest earnings will more than absorb the traditional deficits in transport and tourist payments. (More than six million Japanese go abroad each year.) If this pushes the exchange rate prohibitively high for exporters, voices for agricultural liberalization will make themselves heard from many quarters.

After all, the flexible exchange rate conceals a valuable self-correcting mechanism. With an appreciating currency and a steady loss of price advantage, many economic sectors will cry out for elimination of protection and subsidies for their less competitive compatriots.

ISSUES IN PRIVATE PROCUREMENT

In the nonagricultural area, it is often argued that Japanese markets are legally open but effectively closed. Underlying this observation is the persistent perception that Japanese society is closed. Many anecdotes are produced to corroborate this view. Some of these stories were true years ago and some of them still are. Others are simply myths.

Anecdotes are also offered to play up the importance of association rules, school ties, corporate affiliations, and the like. To the extent that such relationships enjoy administrative support and thus contribute to institutional intractability, their elimination would lessen market rigidity. The present efforts for deregulation and privatization not only stimulate domestic private-sector economic activity but also work in favor of better integration of the Japanese economy into the world economy. As for noninstitutional, nonadministrative market rigidities such as business fraternity, two points must be made.

First, the GATT has set the ground rules for government procurement for the simple reason that governments are outside the free play of the market. A government may buy goods and services from inefficient suppliers and still not go bankrupt. The GATT procurement rule disciplines governments against inefficient procurement practices, saves taxpayers money, and prevents the use of procurement policy to protect domestic industry.

No such rules exist for private-sector procurement because we do not need civil and commercial codes to force companies to buy from the cheapest sources of supply. Free market winds and currents cause inefficient purchasers and suppliers to lose commercial headway.

Second, governments and the GATT have stopped short of legislating in the area of private procurement because doing so would interfere with civil and commercial freedom. When buying a bouquet of flowers, we are free to choose a street vendor for convenience, a supermarket for price, or the flower shop of a childhood friend for sentiment. This sometimes irrational freedom of choice exists in most common business transactions. We can view it as the cost of unwritten insurance against uniformity. When the premium becomes excessive, we eventually find convenience and sentiment overwhelmed by thrift.

The important thing is to keep the winds of the marketplace blowing vigorously. I strongly oppose government intervention in private business affairs. If an outsider wants to influence a company's sourcing policy, he or she has to buy the company's stock and argue for a change of policy at the shareholders' meeting. All other propositions, it seems to me, are armchair attempts to influence other people's use of money without risking one's own.

In all fairness, I must say that the Japanese business system is a difficult one for new entrants, Japanese or foreign. We must make it easier for new participants to try their wits and fortunes. At the same time, I find it unconscionable that in their eagerness to make entry easier, the United States is pressing Japanese government agencies to exercise power that will only strengthen administrative and bureaucratic control.

Trade MAD

Propelled by market forces, international trade may in time develop a mechanism analogous to the military's Mutually Assured Destruction. In the trade version, both partners of a bilateral trade relation would suffer equally in the event of a sudden uncoupling of their linkages.

A stable, interdependent relationship requires symmetrical vulnerability, whether real or perceived. If we want to build a less ambivalent relationship between the United States and Japan, we must assiduously pursue our efforts to improve this symmetry. Otherwise, the outbalanced partner will always feel it has to eat from the hand of its larger companion.

A Trade MAD could lead Japan to welcome greater penetration of American food, goods, and services and to support many U.S. military and political initiatives. A Trade MAD could lead the United States to accept dependence on Japan even for strategically important goods and services.

Needless to say, in today's world no single partnership can stand alone. A network of interdependence would substantially diminish the present psychological ambivalence among the allies. Currently, they accept American leadership because they know that crisis management cannot function entirely on the basis of democratic consultation. But they nevertheless dislike American unilateralism.

The fundamental concept behind Trade MAD must be mutual trust and the establishment of psychological symmetry, not the balance of fear that permeates the military version. This kind of relationship could eventually be broadened to include the entire free world.

INTERDEPENDENCY

As the international flow of capital and individuals becomes increasingly free, market forces will begin to shape national institutions. Corporations and individuals compare all kinds of locally available economic resources and their prices—labor force; raw materials; quality of soil, air, and water; communications; transportation; and public sector services and disservices including tariffs, taxes, and economic and social regulation.

Corporations shy away from countries with high taxes, copious red tape, and overregulated economic activity for the same reason that ships avoid ports with poor services. International investment brings about some of the necessary governmental reforms that so many industrial democracies have failed to achieve internally. Government services and disservices will be arbitrated in the market.

People choose, too. The best and the brightest seek a better quality of life, a better research environment, richer opportunities for intellectual activity. If countries and corporations do not meet these needs, people will simply choose another home and employer.

Japan's financial and capital markets will become more and more international or be left out in the cold as Japanese industries, savers, lenders, and borrowers seek satisfaction elsewhere.

Obviously the path to this world marketplace of capital, labor, and government will not be smooth. Labor unions will scream about the exodus of job opportunities. Governments may join them, concerned about the loss of tax revenue. And the changes for human beings will be painful unless we can educate our children and properly retrain ourselves to adjust to the changing economic and technological environment.

Japan and the United States will continue to wrangle and compete in many fields. But when we approach the year 2000, we will be able to look back with pride at the way our two nations have set an example of international understanding, partly as a result of such noisy exercises in mutual accommodation.

Christmas in Wyoming

Years ago, Denver Post editor Bill Hosokawa told me a story I have always found moving.

In the early days of the second world war, he and his family were moved from their home on the Pacific Coast to a detention camp in northern Wyoming. December 1942 brought their first bleak Christmas as "enemy aliens," and parties were organized in each barrack to relieve the gloom.

Quite unexpectedly, in the middle of the evening, a truck pulled up outside and a Santa Claus strode into the barrack with an enormous bag of presents for the children. The presents were meager enough—a pad and pencil, a pair of mittens, five cents worth of candy—but they had been donated in churches all across America for the children of people who thought themselves forgotten or despised, and they lifted the spirits of everyone present for years to come.

Such openheartedness is not totally foreign to the Japanese. There is a Hachi-no-ki story, for example, about a samurai who burns his cherished bonsai to give a traveler warmth.

Such stories, from whatever source, must become the model for an integrated world community.

PART

IV

The Management Agenda

1
The Post-Capitalist Executive: An Interview with Peter F. Drucker

T George Harris

For half a century, Peter F. Drucker, 83, has been teacher and adviser to senior managers in business, human service organizations, and government. Sometimes called the godfather of modern management, he combines an acute understanding of socioeconomic forces with practical insights into how leaders can turn turbulence into opportunity. With a rare gift for synthesis, Drucker nourishes his insatiable mind on a full range of intellectual disciplines, from Japanese art to network theory in higher mathematics. Yet, he learns most from in-depth conversations with clients and students: a global network of men and women who draw their ideas from action and act on ideas.

Since 1946, when his book, *Concept of the Corporation*, redefined employees as a resource rather than a cost, Drucker's works have become an ever-growing resource for leaders in every major culture, particularly among Japan's top decision makers in the critical stages of their rise to world business leadership. A goodly share of productive organizations worldwide are led by men and women who consider Drucker their intellectual guide, if not their personal mentor.

Drucker's most productive insights have often appeared first in the *Harvard Business Review*. He has written 30 *HBR* articles, more than any other contributor. HBR editors sent T George Harris, a Drucker collaborator for 24 years, to the Drucker Management Center at the Claremont Graduate School in California for two days of intensive conversation about the book's practical implications for today's executives.

HBR: *Peter, you always bring ideas down to the gut level where people work and live. Now we need to know how managers can operate in the post-capitalist society.*

Peter F. Drucker: You have to learn to manage in situations where you don't have command authority, where you are neither controlled nor controlling. That is the fundamental change. Management textbooks still talk mainly about managing subordinates. But you no longer evaluate an executive in terms of how many people report to him or her. That standard doesn't mean as much as the complexity of the job, the information it uses and generates, and the different kinds of relationships needed to do the work.

Similarly, business news still refers to managing subsidiaries. But this is the control approach of the 1950s or 1960s. The reality is that the multinational corporation is rapidly becoming an endangered species. Businesses used to grow in one of two ways: from grassroots up or by acquisition. In both cases, the manager had control. Today businesses grow through alliances, all kinds of dangerous liaisons and joint ventures, which, by the way, very few people understand. This new type of growth upsets the traditional manager who believes he or she must own or control sources and markets.

How will the manager operate in a work environment free of the old hierarchies?

Would you believe that you're going to work permanently with people who work for you but are not your employees? Increasingly, for instance, you outsource when possible. It is predictable, then, that ten years from now a company will outsource all work that does not have a career ladder up to senior management. To get productivity, you have to outsource activities that have their own senior management. Believe me, the trend toward outsourcing has very little to do with economizing and a great deal to do with quality.

Can you give an example?

Take a hospital. Everybody there knows how important cleanliness is, but doctors and nurses are never going to be very concerned with how you sweep in corners. That's not part of their value system. They need a hospital maintenance company. One company I got to know in Southern California had a cleaning woman who came in as an illiterate Latino immigrant. She is brilliant. She figured out how to split a bed sheet so that the bed of a very sick patient, no matter how heavy, could be changed. Using her method, you have to move the patient about only six inches, and she cut the bed-making time from 12 minutes to 2. Now she's in charge of the cleaning operations, but she is not an employee of the hospital. The hospital can't give her one single order. It can only say, "We don't like this; we'll work it out."

The point is, managers still talk about the people who "report" to them, but that word should be stricken from management vocabulary. Information is replacing authority. A company treasurer with outsourced information technology, IT, may have only two assistants and a receptionist, but his decisions in foreign exchange can lose—or make—more money in a day than the rest of the company makes all year. A scientist decides which research *not* to do in a big company lab. He doesn't even have a secretary or a title, but his track record means that he is not apt to be overruled. He may have more effect than the CEO. In the military, a lieutenant colonel used to command a battalion, but today he may have only a receptionist and be in charge of liaisons with a major foreign country.

Amidst these new circumstances, everybody is trying to build the ideal organization, generally flat with few layers of bosses and driven directly by consumer satisfaction. But how do managers gear up their lives for this new world?

More than anything else, the individual has to take more responsibility for himself or herself, rather than depend on the company. In this country, and beginning in Europe and even Japan, you can't expect that if you've worked for a company for 5 years you'll be there when you retire 40 years from now. Nor can you expect that you will be able to do what you want to do at the company in 40 years time. In fact, if you make a wager on any big company, the chances of it being split within the next 10 years are better than the chances of it remaining the way it is.

This is a new trend. Big corporations became stable factors before World War I and in the 1920s were almost frozen. Many survived the Depression without change. Then there were 30 or 40 years when additional stories were built onto skyscrapers or more wings added onto corporate centers. But now they're not going to build corporate skyscrapers. In fact, within the past ten years, the proportion of the work force employed by *Fortune* 500 companies has fallen from 30% to 13%.

Corporations once built to last like pyramids are now more like tents. Tomorrow they're gone or in turmoil. And this is true not only of companies in the headlines like Sears or GM or IBM. Technology is changing very quickly, as are markets and structures. You can't design your life around a temporary organization.

Let me give you a simple example of the way assumptions are changing. Most men and women in the executive program I teach are about 45 years old and just below senior management in a big organization or running a midsize one. When we began 15 or 20 years ago, people at this stage were asking, "How can we prepare ourselves for the next promotion?" Now they say, "What do I need to learn so that I can decide where to go next?"

If a young man in a gray flannel suit represented the lifelong corporate type, what's today's image?

Taking individual responsibility and not depending on any particular company. Equally important is managing your own career. The step-ladder is gone, and there's not even the implied structure of an industry's rope ladder. It's more like vines, and you bring your own machete. You don't know what you'll be doing next, or whether you'll work in a private office or one big amphitheater or even out of your home. You have to take responsibility for knowing yourself, so you can find the right jobs as you develop and as your family becomes a factor in your values and choices.

That's a significant departure from what managers could expect in the past.

Well, the changes in the manager's work are appearing everywhere, though on different timetables. For instance, I see more career confusion among the many Japanese students I've had over the years. They're totally bewildered. Though they are more structured than we ever were, suddenly the Japanese are halfway between being totally managed and having to take responsibility for themselves. What frightens them is that titles don't mean what they used to mean. Whether you were in India or France, if you were an Assistant Director of Market Research, everybody used to know what you were doing. That's not true any more, as we found in one multinational. A woman who had just completed a management course told me not long ago that in five years she would be an assistant vice president of her bank. I'm afraid

I had to tell her that she might indeed get the title, but it would no longer have the meaning she thought it did.

Another rung in the ladder?

Yes. The big-company mentality. Most people expect the personnel department to be Papa—or Ma Bell. When the AT&T personnel department was at its high point 30 years ago, it was the power behind the scenes. With all their testing and career planning, they'd know that a particular 27-year-old would be, by age 45, an Assistant Operating Manager and no more. They didn't know whether he'd be in Nebraska or Florida. But unless he did something quite extraordinary, his career path until retirement was set.

Times have certainly changed. And, in fact, the Bell people have done better than most, because they could see that change coming in the antitrust decision. They couldn't ignore it. But most people still have a big-company mentality buried in their assumptions. If they lose a job with Sears, they hunt for one with K mart, unaware that small companies create most of the new jobs and are about as secure as big companies.

Even today, remarkably few Americans are prepared to select jobs for themselves. When you ask, "Do you know what you are good at? Do you know your limitations?" they look at you with a blank stare. Or they often respond in terms of subject knowledge, which is the wrong answer. When they prepare their resumes, they still try to list positions like steps up a ladder. It is time to give up thinking of jobs or career paths as we once did and think in terms of taking on assignments one after the other.

How does one prepare for this new kind of managerial career?

Being an educated person is no longer adequate, not even educated in management. One hears that the government is doing research on new job descriptions based on subject knowledge. But I think that we probably have to leap right over the search for objective criteria and get into the subjective—what I call *competencies*. Do you really like pressure? Can you be steady when things are rough and confused? Do you absorb information better by reading, talking, or looking at graphs and numbers? I asked one executive the other day, "When you sit down with a person, a subordinate, do you know what to say?"

Empathy is a practical competence. I have been urging this kind of self-knowledge for years, but now it is essential for survival.

People, especially the young, think that they want all the freedom they can get, but it is very demanding, very difficult to think through who you are and what you do best. In helping people learn how to be responsible, our educational system is more and more counterproductive. The longer you stay in school, the fewer decisions you have to make. For instance, the decision whether to take French II or Art History is really based on whether one likes to get up early in the morning. And graduate school is much worse.

Do you know why most people start with big companies? Because most graduates have not figured out where to place themselves, and companies send in the recruiters. But as soon as the recruits get through training and into a job, they have to start making decisions about the future. Nobody's going to do it for them.

And once they start making decisions, many of the best move to midsize companies in three to five years, because there they can break through to top management. With less emphasis on seniority, a person can go upstairs and say, "I've been in accounting for three years, and I'm ready to go into marketing." Each year I phone a list of my old students to see what's happening with them. The second job used to be with another big company, often because people were beginning to have families and wanted security. But with two-career families, a different problem emerges. At a smaller organization, you can often work out arrangements for both the man and the woman to move to new jobs in the same city.

Some of the psychological tests being developed now are getting better at helping people figure out their competencies. But if the world economy is shifting from a command model to a knowledge model, why shouldn't education determine who gets each job?

Because of the enormous danger that we would not value the person in terms of performance, but in terms of credentials. Strange as it may seem, a knowledge economy's greatest pitfall is in becoming a Mandarin meritocracy. You see creeping credentialism all around. Why should people find it necessary to tell me so-and-so is really a good researcher even though he or she doesn't have a Ph.D.? It's easy to fall into the trap because degrees are black-and-white. But it takes judgment to weigh a person's contribution.

The problem is becoming more serious in information-based organizations. As Michael Hammer pointed out three years ago in Harvard Business Review, when an organization reengineers itself around information, the majority of management layers becomes redundant. Most turn out to have been just information relays. Now, each layer has much more information responsibility. Most large companies have cut the number of layers by 50%, even in Japan. Toyota came down from 20-odd to 11. GM has streamlined from 28 to maybe 19, and even that number is decreasing rapidly. Organizations will become flatter and flatter.

As a result, there's real panic in Japan, because it's a vertical society based on subtle layers of status. Everybody wants to become a *kachō*, a supervisor or section manager. Still, the United States doesn't have the answer either. We don't know how to use rewards and recognition to move the competent people into the management positions that remain. I don't care for the popular theory that a generation of entrepreneurs can solve our problems. Entrepreneurs are monomaniacs. Managers are synthesizers who bring resources together and have that ability to "smell" opportunity and timing. Today perception is more important than analysis. In the new society of organizations, you need to be able to recognize patterns to see what is there rather than what you expect to see. You need the invaluable listener who says, "I hear us all trying to kill the new product to protect the old one."

How do you find these people?

One way is to use small companies as farm clubs, as in baseball. One of my ablest friends is buying minority stakes in small companies within his industry. When I said it didn't make sense, he said, "I'm buying farm teams. I'm putting my bright young people in these companies so they have their own commands. They have to do everything a CEO does in a big company."

And do you know the biggest thing these young executives have to learn in their new positions? My friend continued, "We have more Ph.D.'s in biology and chemistry than we have janitors, and they have to learn that their customers aren't Ph.D.'s, and the people who do the work aren't." In other words, they must learn to speak English instead of putting formulas on the blackboard. They must learn to listen to somebody who does not know what a regression analysis is. Basically, they have to learn the meaning and importance of respect.

A difficult thing to learn, let alone teach.

You have to focus on a person's performance. The individual must shoulder the burden of defining what his or her own contribution will be. We have to demand—and "demand" is the word, nothing permissive—that people think through what constitutes the greatest contribution that they can make to the company in the next 18 months or 2 years. Then they have to make sure that contribution is accepted and understood by the people they work with and for.

Most people don't ask themselves this question, however obvious and essential it seems. When I ask people what they contribute to an organization, they blossom and love to answer. And when I follow with, "Have you told other people about it?" the answer often is "No, that would be silly because they know." But of course "they" don't. We are 100 years past the simple economy in which most people knew what others did at work. Farmers knew what most farmers did, and industrial workers knew what other factory workers did. Domestic servants understood each other's work, as did the fourth major group in that economy: small tradesmen. No one needed to explain. But now nobody knows what others do, even within the same organization. Everybody you work with needs to know your priorities. If you don't ask and don't tell, your peers and subordinates will guess incorrectly.

What's the result of this lack of communication?

When you don't communicate, you don't get to do the things you are good at. Let me give you an example. The engineers in my class, without exception, say they spend more than half their time editing and polishing reports—in other words, what they are least qualified to do. They don't even know that you have to write and rewrite and rewrite again. But there are any number of English majors around for that assignment. People seldom pay attention to their strengths. For example, after thinking for a long time, an engineer told me he's really good at the first design, at the basic idea, but not at filling in the details for the final product. Until then, he'd never told anybody, not even himself.

You're not advocating self-analysis alone, are you?

No. You not only have to understand your own competencies, but you also have to learn the strengths of the men and women to whom you assign duties, as well as those of your peers and boss. Too many managers still go by averages. They still talk about "our engineers." And I say, "Brother, you don't have engineers. You have Joe and Mary and Jim and Bob, and each is different." You can no longer manage a work force. You manage individuals. You have to know them so well you can go and say, "Mary, you think you ought to move up to this next job. Well, then you have to learn not to have that chip on your shoulder. Forget you are a woman; you are an engineer. And you have to be a little considerate. Do not come in at 10 minutes to 5 on Friday afternoon to tell people they have to work overtime when you knew it at 9 A.M."

The key to the productivity of knowledge workers is to make them concentrate on the real assignment. Do you know why most promotions now fail? One-third are outright disasters, in my experience, while another third are a nagging backache. Not more than one in three works out. No fit. The standard case, of course, is the star salesman promoted to sales manager. That job can be any one of four things—a manager of salespeople, a market manager, a brand manager, or a super salesman who opens up an entire new area. But nobody figures out what it is, so the man or woman who got the promotion just tries to do more of whatever led to the promotion. That's the surest way to be wrong.

Expand on your idea of information responsibility and how it fits into post-capitalist society.

Far too many managers think computer specialists know what information they need to do their job and what information they owe to whom. Computer information tends to focus too much on inside information, not the outside sources and customers that count. In today's organization, you have to take responsibility for information because it is your main tool. But most don't know how to use it. Few are information literate. They can play "Mary Had a Little Lamb" but not Beethoven.

I heard today about a brand manager in a major OTC drug company who tried to get the scientific papers on the product he markets. But the corporate librarian complained to his superior. Under her rules, she gives hard science only to the company's scientists and lawyers. He had to get a consultant to go outside and use a computer database to pull up about 20 journal articles on his product, so he'd know how to develop honest advertising copy. The point of the story is that this brand manager is way ahead of the parade: 99 out of 100 brand managers don't know they need that kind of information for today's consumers and haven't a clue how to get it. The first step is to say, "I need it."

And many people don't recognize the importance of this step. I work with an information manager at a large financial institution that has invested $1.5 billion in information. He and I talked all morning with his department's eight women and ten men. Very intelligent, but not one began to think seriously about what information they need to serve their customers. When I pointed this out, they said, "Isn't the boss going to tell us?" We finally had to agree to meet a month later so that they could go through the hard work of figuring out what information they need and—more important—what they do not need.

So a manager begins the road to information responsibility first by identifying gaps in knowledge.

Exactly. To be information literate, you begin with learning what it is you need to know. Too much talk focuses on the technology, even worse on the speed of the gadget, always faster, faster. This kind of "techie" fixation causes us to lose track of the fundamental nature of information in today's organization. To organize the way work is done, you have to begin with the specific job, then the information input, and finally the human relationships needed to get the job done.

The current emphasis on reengineering essentially means changing an organization from the flow of things to the flow of information. The computer is merely a tool in the process. If you go to the hardware store to buy a hammer, you do not ask if you should do upholstery or fix the door. To put it in editorial terms, knowing how a typewriter works does not make you a writer. Now that knowledge is taking the place of capital as the driving force in organizations worldwide, it is all too easy to confuse data with knowledge and information technology with information.

What's the worst problem in managing knowledge specialists?

One of the most degenerative tendencies of the last 40 years is the belief that if you are understandable, you are vulgar. When I was growing up, it was taken for granted that economists, physicists, psychologists—leaders in any discipline—would make themselves understood. Einstein spent years with three different collaborators to make his theory of relativity accessible to the layman. Even John Maynard Keynes tried hard to make his economics accessible. But just the other day, I heard a senior scholar seriously reject a younger colleague's work because more than five people could understand what he's doing. Literally.

We cannot afford such arrogance. Knowledge is power, which is why people who had it in the past often tried to make a secret of it. In post-capitalism, power comes from transmitting information to make it productive, not from hiding it.

That means you have to be intolerant of intellectual arrogance. And I mean intolerant. At whatever level, knowledge people must make themselves understood, and whatever field the manager comes from, he or she must be eager to understand others. This may be the main job of the manager of technical people. He or she must not only be an interpreter but also work out a balance between specialization and exposure.

Exposure is an important technique. For an exotic example, look at weather forecasting, where meteorologists and mathematicians and other specialists now work with teams of experts on satellite data. Europeans, on the one hand, have tried to connect these different disciplines entirely through information managers. On the other hand, Americans rotate people at an early stage. Suppose you put a Ph.D. in meteorology on a team that is to work on the new mathematical model of hurricanes for three years. He isn't a mathematician, but he gets exposed to what mathematicians assume, what they eliminate, what their limitations are. With the combination of exposure and translation, the American approach yields forecasts that are about three times more accurate than the European, I'm told. And the exposure concept is useful in managing any group of specialists.

Is the fact that some teams provide exposure as well as interpreters a reason why the team has become such a hot topic?

There's a lot of nonsense in team talk, as if teams were something new. We have always worked in teams, and while sports give us hundreds of team styles there are only a few basic models to choose from. The critical decision is to select the right kind for the job. You can't mix soccer and doubles tennis. It's predictable that in a few years, the most traditional team will come back in fashion, the one that does research first, then passes the idea to engineering to develop, and then on to manufacturing to make. It's like a baseball team, and you may know I have done a little work with baseball-team management.

The great strength of baseball teams is that you can concentrate. You take Joe, who is a batter, and you work on batting. There is almost no interaction, nothing at all like the soccer team or the jazz combo, the implicit model of many teams today. The soccer team moves in unison but everyone holds the same relative position. The jazz combo has incredible flexibility because everyone knows each other so well that they all sense when the trumpet is about to solo. The combo model takes great discipline and may eventually fall out of favor, especially in Japanese car manufacturing, because we do not need to create new models as fast as we have been.

I know several German companies that follow the baseball-team model, whether they know it or not. Their strength is clear: they are fantastic at exploiting and developing old knowledge, and Germany's midsize companies may be better than their big ones simply because they concentrate better. On the other hand, when it comes to the new, from electronics to biotech, German scientists may do fine work, but their famous apprenticeship system discourages innovation.

So, beyond all the hype, teams can help the executive navigate a post-capitalist society?

Thinking about teams helps us highlight the more general problem of how to manage knowledge. In the production of fundamental new knowledge, the British groups I run into are way ahead of anybody. But they have never done much with their expertise, in part because many British companies don't value the technically oriented person enough. I don't know of a single engineer in top management there. My Japanese friends are just the opposite. While they still do not specialize in scientific advances, they take knowledge and make it productive very fast. In this country, on the other hand, we have not improved that much in existing industries. The automobile business, until recently, was perfectly satisfied doing what it did in 1939. But, as we are discovering in computers and in biotech, we may be at our very best when it comes to ground-breaking technology.

Where is the lesson in all this for the manager?

The lesson is that the productivity of knowledge has both a qualitative and a quantitative dimension. Though we know very little about it, we do realize executives must be both managers of specialists and synthesizers of different fields of knowledge—really of knowledges, plural. This situation is as threatening to the traditional manager, who worries about high-falutin' highbrows, as it is to the intellectual, who worries about being too commercial to earn respect in his or her discipline. But in the post-capitalist world, the highbrow and the low-brow have to play on the same team.

That sounds pretty democratic. Does a post-capitalist society based more on knowledge than capital become egalitarian?

No. Both of these words miss the point. Democratic bespeaks a narrow political and legal organization. Nor do I use the buzzword participative. Worse yet is the empowerment concept. It is not a great step forward to take power out at the top and put it in at the bottom. It's still power. To build achieving organizations, you must replace power with responsibility.

And, while we're on the subject of words, I'm not comfortable with the word manager any more, because it implies subordinates. I find myself using executive more, because it implies responsibility for an area, not necessarily dominion over people. The word boss, which emerged in World War II, is helpful in that it can be used to suggest a mentor's role, someone who can back you up on a decision. The new organizations need to go beyond senior/junior polarities to a blend with sponsor and mentor relations. In the traditional organization— the organization of the last 100 years—the skeleton, or internal structure, was a combination of rank and power. In the emerging organization, it has to be mutual understanding and responsibility.

2
Fast Heat: How Korea Won the Microwave War

Ira C. Magaziner and Mark Patinkin

On my first visit to Samsung's Suwŏn complex, the headquarters of the company's electronics and appliance division was even more Third World than I expected. The factory floors were bare concrete. People hand-wheeled parts to and from the production line. The research lab reminded me of a dilapidated high-school science classroom. But the work going on at Suwŏn—what they were doing with televisions, for example—was intriguing. At the time, there wasn't a single TV station in Korea that could broadcast in color. But Samsung's engineers had gathered color televisions from every leading company in the world—RCA, GE, Hitachi—and were using them to design a model of their own.

I spoke with the chief engineer, a young graduate of a U.S. university. I asked him about Samsung's color television strategy, telling him I presumed the company planned to buy parts overseas and do only assembly in Korea. Not at all, he replied. The company was going to make everything itself, even the color picture tube. They'd already picked the best foreign models and signed agreements for technical assistance. Soon, he said, Samsung would be exporting around the globe. I wasn't convinced. Maybe in 10 or 15 years, I thought, but not much sooner. To be a world player, you need world-class engineers, and that was something Korea was short on.

What I didn't realize was that Samsung's chairman, Lee Byung Chull, was investing not just in better technology but in better minds as well. Slowly he was building what was soon to become the biggest company engineering pool in any developing country. Had I looked in all the corners of the Samsung lab that day in 1977, I might have seen Yun Soo Chu, one of those engineers, just beginning work on a microwave oven prototype.

When Chu joined Samsung in 1973, the company had just taken on a manufacturing challenge decades old for America but new to Korea: making home appliances. Chu started by designing washing machines, then moved to electric skillets. In 1976, he received an unexpected assignment. That year, on a visit to the United States, a Samsung vice president named J.U. Chung had become intrigued by a new kind of oven, heated not by electricity or gas but by microwaves. Chung knew there was no way he could market such an oven at home—few Koreans could afford it. But that wasn't a concern. In Korea, when a company considers a new product, the first question is, can we export it?

Knowing that Americans like convenience, Chung thought the microwave oven was perfect for that market, the world's largest. When he got back to Korea, he asked Chu to form a team to design a Samsung microwave. Chu knew his company was starting well behind Japanese and U.S. producers, but he felt Samsung had two advantages: low-wage workers and a willingness to wait for a payback. The company's first priority, he knew, wasn't high profits but high production. And Samsung was especially interested in modern products. For Korean industry, that was almost unprecedented.

Traditionally, low-wage countries have been content to let their factories lag a decade behind countries like the United States. They make bicycles in the age of the automobile, black-and-white televisions in the age of color. Samsung was one of the first Third World companies to take a new approach, to compete directly in modern products.

Chu began by ordering the Jet 230, a new microwave model made by General Electric, America's leading appliance company. Before long, he was looking at his first microwave oven. Chu took it apart but still had no idea how it worked. The plastic cavity seemed simple enough, as did the door assembly and some of the wiring. But there were several complex parts, especially the device that generated the microwaves—the magnetron tube. To build it, he knew, required expertise Samsung lacked. He began to tinker anyway.

Chu's team was given 15 square feet in the corner of an old lab. The lab served the company's entire electronics division, which at the time consisted of three Quonset-hut factories. It seemed absurd that such a place could consider challenging giant U.S. and Japanese corporations, and Chu knew it. But he also knew Samsung's senior managers cared little at the moment about marketing. They'd told him they wanted only one thing—production. They'd worry about selling the oven later.

Soon, Chu had gathered a number of the world's top models and was choosing the best parts of each for his prototype. One thing that drove him was his failure in his last assignment, designing an electric skillet. He just hadn't been able to make it work right. This time, he told himself, he had to succeed.

Samsung didn't have all the manufacturing equipment he needed, so Chu began visiting press vendors, plastic vendors, toolmakers. When he couldn't find anyone in Korea to do the kind of welding he wanted, he decided to seal the oven prototype with caulking instead. Slowly, it came together—brackets, outer panel, door. But when he got to the magnetron tube, he was lost. There was no way Samsung could make or subcontract it locally. At the time, only three manufacturers in the world had that ability, two in Japan, one in Rhode Island. Chu decided to buy the magnetron tube outright—to source it—from Japan.

As the months passed, he drove himself even harder, often working in the lab all night. It took him a year of 80-hour weeks to finish the prototype, but finally he was ready to test it. He pushed the "on" button. In front of his eyes, the plastic in the cavity melted. So much for a year's work.

Chu spent more 80-hour weeks rebuilding his prototype, readjusting it, redesigning it. Again he turned it on. This time the stir shaft melted. Even his wife began to question his obsessiveness. "You must be mad," she'd tell him. At times, he agreed with her. The Japanese and Americans, he knew, were now selling over 4 million microwave ovens a year, and he couldn't even get a single prototype to work.

Microwave-oven technology was pioneered in the late 1940s by a U.S. defense contractor, Raytheon. While experimenting with radar microwaves, a Raytheon researcher noticed that a candy bar in his pocket melted when exposed to the waves. That led to the idea of an oven. Raytheon and another defense-oriented company, Litton, tried to sell the product in the United States without much success. Few U.S. appliance makers saw promise in it. Even though it was the first new major appliance in a generation, it seemed unnecessary. Most U.S. households already had an oven. Who would want two?

The product seemed ideal for Japan, however, a nation of small houses and small kitchens. Moreover, Japanese cooking relied heavily on reheating, a strong point of microwaves. But even though a few U.S. companies saw the microwave's sales potential in Japan, they weren't interested. Exporting to distant markets wasn't worth the trouble.

That's how the Japanese became the first big manufacturers of microwave ovens. They seized the technology, began perfecting it, and soon went beyond their backyard. They saw export as an opportunity, not a burden. They pushed the product overseas, harvesting a windfall when the world market took off, going from 600,000 ovens in 1970 to 2.2 million in 1975. Finally, in the late 1970s, U.S. appliance makers like GE began investing seriously in microwave ovens. But they paid a price for being late. By 1979, when the U.S. market finally eclipsed Japan's, Japanese companies already controlled over 25% of it.

June 1978—and in the corner of his Suwŏn lab, Chu finally finished another prototype. Ready for the worst, he turned it on for a test. This time, nothing melted. His bosses were encouraged. They knew Chu's oven was still too crude to compete in the world market, but they told him to make more anyway. Chu himself had few global hopes. At best, he thought, Samsung would find a small, low-priced niche in the United States. But that didn't discourage him. The company's preeminent goal was production.

Samsung management sent out a few salespeople with the prototypes. They didn't have much success, but headquarters decided to put together a makeshift production line anyway. Management wanted to be ready in case an order came. It was one of the company's rules: never, ever keep a customer waiting.

The production team began making one oven a day, then two. Soon, it was up to five. By mid-1979, when over 5 million ovens were sold around the world, Samsung had finished making only 1,460 of them. That's when the company decided to try its first real sales push. It chose to focus on the local market. Unfortunately, its low scale meant high prices—an exorbitant $600 per oven—half the yearly income of an average Korean family. Almost no one bought. Still, management was upbeat. The machines worked. Having no sales was no reason to stop development.

With the domestic push a washout, Samsung's salespeople began to look abroad. They sent out brochures and hired distributors in dozens of countries. They offered to cut the price and were ready to fill the smallest order. The first came from Panama—for 240 ovens. By the time it had shipped them, Samsung had lost money. But there was celebration in Suwŏn. They'd broken through. And besides, this would be a good way to learn what customers wanted. They could refine the product in a few small markets before trying big ones.

The Panama sales gave Samsung the confidence to apply for the Underwriters' Laboratory approval needed for exports to the United

States. Late in 1979 they got it. For Samsung, America wasn't a totally foreign market. Many of the company's managers had gone to school there; they knew the country, knew English. And Samsung was ready to do something few U.S. manufacturers were doing: tailor its product to foreign tastes. If that meant retooling production back in Suwŏn, it would spend the money. Instead of planning on a single line of ovens for the world, its strategy was to make unique models for unique markets.

Microwave ovens were then selling for $350 to $400 each in the United States. One of the country's biggest retailers, J.C. Penney, had been searching for a cheaper model, but hadn't had any luck in either Japan or the United States. Then Penney heard about Samsung and saw an opportunity—a low-wage country capable of building a high-tech product. In 1980, the retailer asked Samsung if it could build a microwave oven to sell in the United States for $299.

By then, world sales were up to 4.7 million units a year. Samsung was being asked for a few thousand ovens only. On top of that, Penney's order would mean designing a whole new oven and taking heavy losses, all in the name of gaining a fraction of 1% of the U.S. market. But in Suwŏn, Samsung's managers were ecstatic. They promised Penney anything it wanted. To deliver, they promised Chu any investment he needed. They still put no pressure on him for profits. All they wanted was production and a doorway into a major foreign market.

Penney's technical people would help Chu with product quality, but Chu knew the greatest burden would be on Samsung. The challenge now was to turn a still-primitive assembly room into an efficient factory almost overnight. And he and his team would have to get it right the first time. This wasn't another Panama. The machines would be going to Americans, the most sophisticated consumers in the world.

Chu's boss was a quiet mechanical engineer named Kyung Pal Park. Ask him why he chose manufacturing, and he'll tell you about U.S. soldiers during the Korean War. Everything about them suggested wealth: their clothes, their equipment, their vehicles. How, Park wondered, had the United States achieved that? In time, he saw that production was the answer. America was wealthy because it made things. Park wanted that for Korea too—a nation not of rice paddies, but factories. In 1969 he joined Samsung. In 1980, at the age of 39, he was named head of home appliances. Delivering the Penney order was his responsibility.

Soon, Park came up with his plan for organizing a team. In the

United States, product designers would normally head such a team; factory engineers would come second. At Samsung, production is king. So Park merged his product and factory people, stressing that design should be done with manufacturing in mind. He gave the team one unbreakable rule: no matter what, it would deliver on every deadline, not a day later. The responsibility for following through would fall to Park's chief lieutenant, I.J. Jang, a production engineer just transferred from Samsung's motor division.

Before his transfer, Jang had managed the production of millions of motors a year on four separate lines. Now he found himself in a division making five or six ovens a day. He didn't see it as a demotion. "There is one thing more valued at Samsung than high production," he explains, "the potential of high production." The best engineers aren't placed with boom products but with products yet to take off.

Jang immersed himself in learning the product, spending hours talking with designers like Chu, then journeying overseas to Matsushita, Sanyo, and GE. Once he'd learned world standards, he began to make sure Samsung was living up to them. He studied the prototype test results, pausing on the high microwave leakage numbers. He asked if they could be fixed and was told the seal design made it hard to get a better weld. So Jang, one of Samsung's most senior production managers, went to the welding vendor to help him upgrade his process. Of the 100 outside vendors working on the project, Jang ended up visiting 30 of them himself.

Then he turned his attention to building the assembly line. He started with an empty factory room and a delivery date only months away. His senior people often began at dawn, worked until 10:30 P.M., then took a brief nap, and went back to work for the rest of the night. Even Jang's boss, Park—one of the highest executives at Suwŏn—kept the same hours. There was only one sign of privilege—a few cots scattered around the factory. The executives got those—the others grabbed their naps in chairs.

The line took shape and production began; inevitably, there were bugs. They couldn't afford to lose production, however, so they manufactured by day, then ran the line all night to fine-tune it. Production improved to 10 ovens a day, then 15. Soon they were making 1,500 a month, enough to meet Penney's order of several thousand.

Penney liked the ovens and soon asked for more. Could Samsung deliver 5,000 in another month? The company made that deadline too, but there wasn't time for celebration. Now Penney wanted another 7,000. There was only work. "Like a cow," Jang would say later.

The production team thought it wise to install more assembly lines and asked management for the money. "It was no problem," Jang said. By the end of 1981, Samsung had increased microwave production a hundredfold over the previous year, from just over 1,000 to over 100,000. Still, that was only a fraction of the world market. And almost none of the giants in the United States or Japan noticed. They still couldn't see Korea as a serious competitor in such sophisticated technology. But they were overlooking a crucial factor: the role the Korean government was playing in the country's development.

Around this time, in 1981, I returned to Korea and spent several days meeting with both corporate managers and government economic planners. Korea's progress, I found, was driven by government, the key player being the Economic Development Board. Its job was to think about where Korea's economy should be headed and give incentives to help companies get there. The board built industrial parks, subsidized utilities, provided tax rebates for export, and made low-cost loans for investment in selected new products. The incentives were particularly helpful to big companies like Samsung, whose managers met frequently with government officials, plotting strategy, trading ideas, and discussing projects.

Both business and government understood the country couldn't depend on low-wage industries for long, not with even cheaper labor in countries next door. Just as the United States had lost thousands of jobs in the apparel industry to Korea, soon, the Koreans knew, they would lose such jobs to Malaysia and China. To prepare, the government consulted with companies and developed incentives for investing in new industries. By 1980, the country had gone beyond textiles into steel and ships. Now it was making automobiles. And it had begun moving toward world-class electronics. Korea was developing faster than I had expected.

Samsung's microwave production in 1982 topped 200,000, double what it had produced the previous year. But Park and his team didn't think it was enough. They knew that, in microwaves, Samsung was still a global afterthought. U.S. manufacturers were making over 2 million ovens a year and the Japanese were making even more—2.3 million at home and another 820,000 in their U.S. plants. Matsushita had 17% of the world market. Sanyo had 15%.

Moreover, the big producers were bringing their prices down, narrowing Samsung's key advantage. If Samsung were to keep growing, it had to lower its own prices even more. Samsung's managers pored over their cost structure. The highest item was the magnetron tube, which they were still buying from the Japanese. Could they make it themselves? It would mean millions of dollars of investment for a new, highly complex factory. They approached Japan's magnetron producers for technical assistance but were turned down. That left only one other company to approach—Amperex, the Rhode Island company that was America's sole manufacturer. But that plant, Samsung found, was going out of business. It had been unable to compete with Japan.

That same year in Louisville, Kentucky, Bruce Enders—the head marketing manager for GE Appliances—was beginning to see warning signs in his microwave-oven division. Because GE had come into microwave ovens so late, it had not yet made money on them. Now the losses began to get worse; the Japanese were chipping away at GE's U.S. share, pushing it down from over 16% in 1980 to 14% in 1982. No one at GE was thinking about conceding ground, though. Japan's wage rates were no lower than GE's, and GE was just completing a multimillion dollar modernization at its microwave-oven factory in Columbia, Maryland. Just as important, Enders knew that his company understood the U.S. consumer better than any other appliance maker. GE had just scored a tremendous success with the Spacemaker, for example, the industry's first under-the-shelf model. If the Maryland modernization could make GE cost-competitive, he knew that they could make the business profitable.

But in late 1982, the Japanese began to export a new midsize line of ovens at an alarmingly low price—even below GE's cost at its modernized plant. Enders' manufacturing people insisted that the Japanese must be dumping. Enders wanted to know for sure. He asked me to do a study.

The study was supposed to focus on Japan, so I spent three weeks there. But I knew Samsung had begun to make microwaves, so before coming home, I flew to Korea for a two-day visit. It was my first glimpse of Samsung since 1977. It was soon clear that there had been big changes.

In Suwŏn, the three Quonset huts had been replaced by a dozen new buildings. I was taken on a tour, which began in the basement of the microwave building where the machining was done. That wasn't so impressive. Most of the equipment was old. Then my guides took me to the second floor where the microwaves were being assembled. It was a little better but still backward. Samsung's wage rates, I thought, could perhaps outcompete GE, but its technology couldn't.

Then my guides invited me to see the TV plant. The old one, I remembered, had long lines of women plugging in parts by hand. But this was different—as automated as any TV plant I'd seen in the United States. Next, they invited me to see the new television-tube factory. It was much larger and more modern than I'd expected. The biggest surprise was a highly complex TV-glass plant being put up in partnership with America's Corning Glass Works. Clearly Samsung had been serious about producing every color television part by itself.

Finally I went to the R&D lab. It had gone from an old high-school science room to a large modern operation. Instead of a handful of engineers, there were 500. Everything Samsung had said in 1977 that it would do, it had done. I understood they weren't showing me all this out of pride alone. Management knew I was doing a study for GE and hoped I'd bring back a message: Samsung could do in microwaves what it had done in TVs.

As I was leaving Suwŏn, I saw a truck pull up and men begin to unload equipment. I looked at it, then looked closer. Months before, I'd visited Amperex, America's last magnetron plant. Now, here in Korea, Amperex's equipment was coming off the truck. Park and the others had decided to build their own magnetrons after all. In an almost disturbingly symbolic strategy, they were going to transplant a U.S. factory that could no longer compete, and sell its goods—now made in Korea—back to U.S. consumers.

Early in 1983, I gave my initial impressions to GE. The Japanese weren't dumping. Their plants and product designs were so efficient they could indeed land microwave ovens in the United States cheaper than those coming off GE's new assembly line. Moreover, GE's share was falling even as the world market grew. Global sales had gone from 5 million in 1980 to 7 million in 1983, but GE's U.S. market share had shrunk to 12%. Other U.S. producers had declined even more. The shift had almost all gone to the Japanese.

GE had two options. One was to invest, as the Japanese had, in hundreds of engineers. But GE was already pouring enormous investment into refrigerators and dishwashers, products in which it was a leader. Microwaves were a lower priority. That brought us to the second option—get product from overseas through sourcing or a joint venture.

While I was finishing my final report, GE decided to explore a joint-venture factory with the Japanese to be built in the United States. Its hope was to work with Matsushita, the biggest producer. Enders traveled to Japan to negotiate and seemed to be getting close.

He even got Samsung's management to agree that a co-venture would be highly profitable for both. But in the end, Matsushita declined because it would mean losing some of the U.S. market to GE. Foreign market share is a key priority, one of the company's key executives explained. "Enders-san," he said, "you have to understand. In Japan, it's our destiny to export. If we don't export, we don't survive."

That left GE with one other option: sourcing—buy Japanese products and put the GE label on them. No one in Louisville was ready to shut down the new Maryland plant, but maybe it made sense to source a few lines.

In April 1983, I finished my full report. In it, I raised a Korean option. If GE sourced only with Matsushita, it would be at the mercy of a direct competitor. Korean costs, however, were potentially low enough to undercut the Japanese. And because the Koreans were anxious for volume, it would be easier to negotiate a good deal with them.

Louisville was skeptical. The Koreans? Perhaps they were making a few ovens for Penney, but they were a Third World country. A high-quality company like GE—selling a million ovens—couldn't risk depending on Korea.

But then we looked at the cost differences. In 1983, it cost GE $218 to make a typical microwave oven. It cost Korea's Samsung only $155. Then we broke the costs down: assembly labor cost GE $8 per oven; Samsung, only 63 cents. The differences in overhead labor—supervision, maintenance, setup—were even more astounding: for GE it was $30 per oven; for Samsung, 73 cents. GE was spending $4 on materials handling for each oven; Samsung, 12 cents. The biggest area of difference was in GE's line and central management—that came to $10 per oven. At Samsung, it was 2 cents. What the companies got for their money was the most disturbing figure of all. Samsung workers were paid less but delivered more. GE got four units per person each day. Samsung got nine. And once their volume increased, Korean costs could go even lower.

The GE managers continued to waver. Japanese costs, though not at Korean levels, were better than those at GE. And Japan's products were clearly high quality. Many thought it was more prudent to source there. To explore the option further, Enders decided to go to Korea himself. At the end of his first day, he asked Samsung's managers for a proposal, including a cost breakdown, a delivery schedule, and a description of how they would build the GE ovens. In the United States, it takes companies four to six weeks to develop that kind of plan. The next morning, Enders had a final breakfast meeting with Samsung executives.

"A group of engineers came in," Enders recalls, "and they gave us their proposal. Their hair was messed up—their eyes were bloodshot. Those guys had worked all night. And it met our target. I couldn't believe it."

A few weeks later, Roger Schipke, the head of GE Appliances, decided to go to Korea. He was walking down a Samsung corridor with his hosts when a crowd of white coats came bustling the other way. He had to stand against the wall to let them by. There were dozens of them, all very young. When they'd passed, he asked who they were. "Those are our new microwave-oven engineers," his host told him. There were more of them than Schipke had working in his whole microwave division, and these were just Samsung's newest hires. Louisville, he realized, was probably outengineered ten to one. He asked where the new hirees were trained. The answer came back: Purdue, the University of Southern California, the University of Washington.

"I'm a simple guy," Schipke would say later. "I just looked around. And I said, 'Wow, I'm not getting into that game.'"

Louisville decided in June 1983 to begin sourcing small and midsize microwave ovens from the Far East. GE would continue to make the full-size models in the United States. The biggest order went to Japan. But GE did give Samsung a much smaller order—only about 15,000. It wanted to see whether the Koreans could deliver high-quality goods at a price America's biggest appliance maker could no longer match.

General Electric sent technical people to Korea to outline its standards for the ovens. From GE's perspective, this was simply quality control for a second-rate supplier. But in Suwŏn, Kyung Pal Park, head of home appliances, saw things differently. If he was a good student, he would learn world-class skills. Once again, there was one unbreakable rule: every deadline had to be met. To make it, he knew he would have to depend on his foot soldiers as well as his lieutenants—the disciplined workers who give 70-hour weeks. Who exactly are they?

At the Suwŏn complex, more than half the basic assemblers are women. Most stay four or five years, arriving with high-school educations and leaving with husbands. Jo Yon Hwang and Jang Mee Hur are in their early twenties. Both applied to Samsung because of its reputation for being good to its workers. They were among the one-third of all applicants accepted. Upon arrival, they were given blue uniforms and two weeks of training. Then they were put to work on the microwave line, 11 hours a day, 27 days a month. Everyone, even the senior people, works the same schedule. The two women say it's why they feel so committed to the company—their bosses make the same sacrifices they do. In 1988, their base wage was just over $350 a month—a little over $1.20 an hour. Male assembly workers are paid the same. Medical services are free, so is lunch. Dinner and breakfast, offered in company dining areas, cost 15 cents each. The workers receive gifts several times a year: clothes, shoes, hiking bags, tape recorders. The recorders are made by Samsung.

Hwang and Hur get five days off in winter and another five in summer, which they can spend at a beach camp on the coast run by Samsung. Like most of Suwŏn's female employees, Hwang lives free in a company dormitory. There are 15 such dormitories, housing 420 women each, 6 to a room. Hur lives outside the complex, in an apartment with a girlfriend. Rent is not a problem: Samsung loaned her $2,000, which she gave to the landlord who invested it and keeps whatever interest it yields. Hur, meanwhile, pays Samsung 10% interest on the loan. When she leaves, she'll give the $2,000 back to the company. Hur and Hwang usually get up at 6 A.M. and have breakfast at 7 A.M. Hwang walks to her factory; Hur comes by company bus. At day's end, Hwang has to be back in the dorm by 9:30 P.M., even on the three Sundays a month she is off.

The subject both women are most enthusiastic about is quality. Hwang is convinced no workers in the world pay as close attention to products as workers at Samsung. She checks her own work one last time even after an inspector has double-checked it. Her task is to attach serial numbers and name-brand labels to microwave ovens. If you own a GE Spacemaker, chances are that Hwang attached the label. She puts on 1,200 GE labels a day. Hur attaches microwave doors, also about 1,200 a day. It's the same simple function, hour after hour, but they see their jobs as a challenge to personal discipline, even integrity. Doing it perfectly each time is a way of teaching themselves excellence. "I put my spirit, my soul, in this product," explains Hwang.

Like everyone, they would love higher salaries, but they also see themselves as planting seeds for both company and country. They still remember a Korea of dirt roads, few cars, and many slums, and though they can't analyze all the reasons for the change, they know manufacturing has been a big one. As factory workers, they feel they're part of that, part of something historic.

Suwŏn's second biggest regiment is its engineers. The company has hundreds, all working the same 68 hours a week. S.D. Lee is typical—a smart, energetic young man who's committed to staying with Samsung. He knows if he works hard, his managers will promote him when he's ready. Although he's a junior engineer, Samsung has already schooled him with extra knowledge. The company has given him 20 days of full-time quality control instruction and once sent him to Japan for two weeks to learn technology from Toshiba. Before that trip, he was given three months of Japanese language training. "Three years after college," he explains, "you forget what you learned. Reeducation is needed."

What are Samsung's most lasting lessons? Two things, Lee says. First, management by target. Set a goal, then meet it no matter what—even if it means working through the night for a week. Second, always think several years ahead; ask where things will be next decade. The assignment Lee himself has illustrates that philosophy. Although Samsung's microwave ovens have the lowest cost in the world, Lee is working on factory automation to make them lower still.

Does he know that Americans work only eight hours a day, five days a week? He smiles. He is envious of that. So why is it worth working so much harder, for less money? Because you don't measure by money alone, he says, you measure by life-style. And his is rising faster than he ever expected. His father could never afford a car. He plans to buy one soon. He sees even greater promise for his children. "If our generation doesn't work hard," he says, "the next generation will suffer."

At first, Samsung's ovens were not up to GE standards. But with the help of GE's quality engineers, things soon got better. Bruce Enders grew more and more impressed and eventually put in another order. Sales steadily improved. It was the GE label customers reached for but Korean workmanship that satisfied them. On his next trip to Suwŏn, Enders was surprised at the changes. The assembly line had gone from roller conveyors to automatic transfer mechanisms. Clearly, Samsung had the capacity to deliver more than GE had been asking for. Enders put in a bigger order. Sales kept improving. Around that time, in mid-1983, the Suwŏn workers hit a milestone. They shipped their five-hundred thousandth oven. For the first time since they'd begun four years before, Park said it was time to celebrate. They paused for a brief party. When the party was over, they went back to work.

By the end of 1983, Samsung's annual microwave production topped 750,000. By 1984 it passed one million. The factory expanded as well. In four years, it had gone from a few prototypes to ten mass-production lines. The product that had begun with melted plastic in an old lab was becoming a major performer in America's market. But for Samsung, that wasn't good enough.

The company had grown concerned over some new market projections. From 1982 to 1986, U.S. microwave sales were expected to keep growing at a healthy rate, but for the four years after that, things would slow. It was time to seek out other markets. The European market, expected to grow by 20% a year, offered the most promise. Among those assigned to the new market was a young executive named J.K. Kim, soon to be named head of appliance export sales.

Like many Samsung executives, Kim is fluent in foreign languages. Like many, he graduated from a U.S. university. Although his parents had little money, they found the means to send him to Berkeley. In Korea, he will tell you, education and family come before everything. Even in the poorer sections of the countryside, over 95% of the population is literate—far higher than in the United States. Kim still remembers arriving in California for school. The size of America's cities, the number of cars, the wealth of the people—all of it astounded him. He returned to Korea determined to help build his own country.

With his prestigious degree, Kim had many career options. Although it paid far less than banking or law, he chose manufacturing. "I thought it could help more the totality of Korea," he explains. "If I work for a lawyer's office, I can get my job and my secretary's job. In Samsung, I can contribute 10,000 jobs."

Kim found Samsung an ideal home. The hours were long, to be sure, but he liked the idea of working for Korea's biggest company. Part of it was the three weeks of training he got each year; another was the company's willingness to invest. Samsung seemed to blend the risk-taking mentality of a startup with the resources of a great corporation. Most of all, Kim liked the company's drive to be a world player. Now, with the European strategy, he was being asked to be part of that.

Curiously, the United States had taught Kim how to succeed abroad. It taught him what not to do. As most Koreans know, U.S. manufacturers rarely customize. "They just send us products made for Americans and say, 'Why don't you Koreans buy them?'" he says. So when Kim began to focus on Europe, he looked at how it differs from America. Europeans, he found, like colder dishes. And they prefer fish to meat and chicken. This information was fed back to Suwŏn's design division. Soon it began designing new European models. In 1983, Samsung microwaves broke into Germany and Norway. In 1984, they added France, Finland, Australia, and Belgium. And, all along, they kept pushing for a bigger piece of the United States.

In most companies, only the sales force travels. Samsung, like many foreign companies, sends engineers abroad to learn buyers' habits too. That's why Jang, head of production, was sent on regular marketing trips to the United States. Jang remembers flying in with a dozen other engineers from Suwŏn for an electronics show in Las Vegas. At one point, he took a side trip on his own, visiting stores such as Sears and talking to salespeople. He asked what models were most popular, what features attracted consumers. Spotting a woman buyer, he asked her what she looked for in a microwave oven.

Why couldn't he rely on Samsung's marketing people? An engineer has to see some things for himself, he explains. You can't describe color by phone or fax. Being told to make a model red isn't enough. He wants to know what kind of red. What size, exactly, the knobs on an oven should be. He seeks more than technical knowledge—something subtler, a feel for America's tastes, its character, its people.

General Electric began shifting more of its orders to Samsung. Soon, GE's Korean models were selling as well as those GE itself made in the United States, and at a much higher profit. Some in Louisville began to wonder whether it was time to source everything. Before going that far, Enders asked if the Columbia, Maryland factory could be further streamlined. The plant's defenders delivered an impressive proposal. They were able to get much lower costs than Enders expected. Still, even if the company went through with the plan, its costs would remain far higher than those in Korea. Management had little choice. In May 1985, GE publicly announced it would stop U.S. production of microwave ovens. From now on, GE would be doing the sales and service side of the product; Samsung, the manufacturing. Soon, the people in Suwŏn would be the biggest makers of microwave ovens in the world.

In deciding to source, GE made a prudent choice. The company had discovered the potential for microwave ovens too late. By the time it invested, the Japanese were way ahead. Going to the Koreans was a good way to leap past the Japanese and fight back. It could have been different, though. If GE or other U.S. appliance companies had acted earlier, not at the height of market demand but ahead of it, they could have built enough scale to afford more product research and factory investment when competition got intense. Dollar-an-hour countries can be beaten. U.S. technology can often overwhelm low wages. But only if we're among the first in the arena. We can no longer afford to spend years analyzing new products. Too many other nations, like Korea, are willing to seize them immediately.

Often, those nations do it with our help. Samsung would have had a hard time succeeding so quickly in microwave ovens without Penney and GE. The Americans helped bring Samsung world-class design, quality, scale, and legitimacy with other world customers, and GE got a good deal in return. But how long can a U.S. company thrive by sourcing? And how long will Samsung be content to be a supplier? Its final vision, as with all great corporations, is to emerge as another General Electric, to become a household name. In some ways, that's already happening. Most luggage carts in West Germany's Frankfurt airport bear an advertisement for Samsung. Drivers on New York's Broadway, Chicago's Loop, London's M1, and even Tokyo's Keio Highway are beginning to see billboards with the same name—Samsung. Someday, Korea will no longer need to market its products through U.S. labels; it will sell them directly, as Hyundai now does its cars.

Back in Suwŏn, it's hard for Yun Soo Chu, Samsung's microwave-oven designer, to sit still for an interview. He'd rather be working. His office is no longer the corner of a primitive lab, it's a vast room filled with dozens of desks. Another dozen rooms for research and testing surround it. Behind his desk are five clocks, each marking the time at Samsung offices: LA, Chicago/Mexico, London/Madrid, Frankfurt/Paris, NYC/Miami. At the moment, Chu has a map of Sweden on his desk. Samsung began exporting there last year. He is organizing trips to Sweden for his staff—not marketing staff but engineers. He wants them to go there as often as possible, to know their customers.

Ask Yun Soo Chu what he works for, and he will tell you his highest goal is to give his children a better standard of living than his own. So each morning, he dons his company jacket, stands for the company song, and then goes back to work, designing the next line of microwave ovens for the modern world's kitchens. On most nights he is likely to be at the office very late.

3
Do You Really Have a Global Strategy?

Gary Hamel and C.K. Prahalad

The threat of foreign competition preoccupies managers in industries from telecommunications to commercial banking and from machine tools to consumer electronics. Corporate response to the threat is often misdirected and ill timed—in part because many executives don't fully understand what global competition is.

They haven't received much help from the latest analysis of this trend. One argument simply emphasizes the scale and learning effects that transcend national boundaries and provide cost advantages to companies selling to the world market.[1] Another holds that world products offer customers the twin benefits of the low-cost and high-quality incentives for foreign customers to lay aside culture-bound product preferences.[2]

According to both of these arguments, U.S. organizations should "go global" when they can no longer get the minimum volume needed for cost efficiency at home and when international markets permit standardized marketing approaches. If, on the other hand, they can fully exploit scale benefits at home and their international export markets are dissimilar, U.S. executives can safely adopt the traditional, country-by-country, multinational approach. So while Caterpillar views its battle with Komatsu in global terms, CPC International and Unilever may safely consider their foreign operations multidomestic.

After studying the experiences of some of the most successful global competitors, we have become convinced that the current perspective on global competition and the globalization of markets is incomplete and misleading. Analysts are long on exhortation—"go international"—but short on practical guidance. Combine these shortcomings with the prevailing notion that global success demands a national industrial policy, a docile work force, debt-heavy financing, and forbearing investors, and you can easily understand why many executives feel they are only treading water in the rising tide of global competition.

World-scale manufacturing may provide the necessary armament, and government support may be a tactical advantage, but winning the war against global competition requires a broader view of global strategy. We will present a new framework for assessing the nature of the worldwide challenge, use it to analyze one particular industry, and offer our own practical guidelines for success.

Thrust & Parry

As a starting point, let's take a look at what drives global competition. It begins with a sequence of competitive action and reaction:

> An aggressive competitor decides to use the cash flow generated in its home market to subsidize an attack on markets of domestically oriented foreign competitors.

> The defensive competitor then retaliates—not in its home market where the attack was staged—but in foreign markets where the aggressor company is most vulnerable.[3]

As an example, consider the contest between Goodyear and Michelin. By today's definitions, the tire industry is not global. Most tire companies manufacture in and distribute for the local market. Yet Michelin, Goodyear, and Firestone are now locked in a fiercely competitive—and very global—battle.

In the early 1970s, Michelin used its strong European profit base to attack Goodyear's American home market. Goodyear could fight back in the United States by reducing prices, increasing advertising, or offering dealers better margins. But because Michelin would expose only a small amount of its worldwide business in the United States, it has little to lose and much to gain. Goodyear, on the other hand, would sacrifice margins in its largest market.

Goodyear ultimately struck back in Europe, throwing a wrench in Michelin's money machine. Goodyear was proposing a hostage trade. Michelin's long-term goals and resources allowed it to push ahead in the United States. But at least Goodyear slowed the pace of Michelin's attack and forced it to recalculate the cost of market share gains in the United States. Goodyear's strategy recognized the international scope of competition and parried Michelin's thrust.

Manufacturers have played out this pattern of cross-subsidization and international retaliation in the chemical, audio, aircraft engine, and computer industries. In each case international cash flows, rather than international product flows, scale economies, or homogeneous markets, finally determined whether competition was global or national. (For a detailed explanation, see "What is cross-subsidization?")

What is cross-subsidization?

When a global company uses financial resources accumulated in one part of the world to fight a competitive battle in another, it is pursuing a strategy we call "cross-subsidization." Contrary to tried-and-true MNC policy, a subsidiary should not always be required to stand on its own two feet financially. When a company faces a large competitor in a key foreign market, it may make sense for it to funnel global resources into the local market share battle, especially when the competitor lacks the international reach to strike back.

Money does not always move across borders, though this may happen. For a number of reasons (taxation, foreign exchange risk, regulation) the subsidiary may choose to raise funds locally. Looking to the worldwide strength of the parent, local financial institutions may be willing to provide long-term financing in amounts and at rates that would not be justified on the basis of the subsidiary's short-term prospects. One note of caution: if competitors learn of your subsidiary's borrowing needs, you may reveal strategic intentions by raising local funds and lose an element of competitive surprise.

Cross-subsidization is not dumping. When a company cross-subsidizes it does not sell at less than the domestic market price. Rather than risk trade sanctions, the intelligent global company will squeeze its competitor's margins just enough to dry up its development spending and force corporate officers to reassess their commitment to the business.

With deteriorating margins and no way of retaliating internationally, the company will have little choice but to sell market share. If your competitor uses simple portfolio management techniques, you may even be able to predict how much market share you will have to buy to turn the business into a "dog" and precipitate a sell-off. In one such case a beleaguered business unit manager, facing an aggressive global competitor, lobbied hard for international retaliation. The corporate response: "If you can't make money at home, there's no way we're going to let you go international!" Eventually, the business was sold.

The Goodyear vs. Michelin case helps to distinguish among:

Global competition, which occurs when companies cross-subsidize national market share battles in pursuit of global brand and distribution positions.

Global businesses, in which the minimum volume required for cost efficiency is not available in the company's home market.

Global companies, which have distribution systems in key foreign markets that enable cross-subsidization, international retaliation, and world-scale volume.

Making a distinction between global competition and a global business is important. In traditionally global businesses, protectionism and flexible manufacturing technologies are encouraging a shift back to local manufacturing. Yet competition remains global. Companies must distinguish between the cost effectiveness based on off-shore sourcing and world-scale plants and the competitive effectiveness based on the ability to retaliate in competitors' key markets.

Identifying the Target

Understanding how the global game is played is only the first step in challenging the foreign competitor. While the pattern of cross-subsidization and retaliation describes the battle, world brand dominance is what the global war is all about. And the Japanese have been winning it.

In less than 20 years, Canon, Hitachi, Seiko, and Honda have established worldwide reputations equal to those of Ford, Kodak, and Nestlé. In consumer electronics alone, the Japanese are present in or dominate most product categories.

Like the novice duck hunter who either aims at the wrong kind of bird or shoots behind his prey, many companies have failed to develop a well-targeted response to the new global competition. Those who define international competitiveness as no more than low-cost manufacturing are aiming at the wrong target. Those who fail to identify the strategic intentions of their global competitors cannot anticipate competitive moves and often shoot behind the target.

To help managers respond more effectively to challenges by foreign companies, we have developed a framework that summarizes the various global competitive strategies (see the Exhibit). The competitive advantages to be gained from location, world-scale volume, or global brand distribution are arrayed against the three kinds of strategic intent we have found to be most prevalent among global competitors: (1) building a global presence, (2) defending a domestic position, and (3) overcoming national fragmentation.

Using this framework to analyze the world television industry, we find Japanese competitors building a global presence, RCA, GE, and Zenith of the United States defending domestic dominance, and Philips of the Netherlands and CSF Thomson of France overcoming national fragmentation. Each one uses a different complement of competitive weapons and pursues its own strategic objectives. As a result, each reaps a different harvest from its international activities.

LOOSE BRICKS

By the late 1960s, Japanese television manufacturers had built up a large U.S. volume base by selling private-label TV sets. They had also established brand and distribution positions in small-screen and portable televisions—a market segment ignored by U.S. producers in favor of higher margin console sets.

In 1967, Japan became the largest producer of black-and-white TVs; by 1970, it had closed the gap in color sets. While the Japanese first used their cost advantages primarily from low labor costs, they then moved quickly to invest in new process technologies, from which came the advantages of scale and quality.

Japanese companies recognized the vulnerability of competitive positions based solely on labor and scale advantages. Labor costs change as economies develop or as exchange rates fluctuate. The world's low-cost manufacturing location is constantly shifting: from Japan to Korea, then to Singapore and Taiwan. Scale-based cost advantages are also vulnerable, particularly to radical changes in manufacturing technology and creeping protectionism in export markets. Throughout the 1970s, Japanese TV makers invested heavily to create the strong dis-

Exhibit   A global competitive framework

	Build global presence	Defend domestic dominance	Overcome national fragmentation
1965	Access volume		
		Response lag	Response lag
1970	Redefine cost-volume relationships		
		Match costs	
1975	Cross-subsidize to win the world		Reduce costs at national subsidiary
		Amortize world-scale investments	
1980	Contiguous segment expansion		Rationalize manufacturing
		Gain retaliatory capability	
1985			Shift locus of strategic responsibility
1990			

tribution positions and brand franchises that would add another layer of competitive advantage.

Making a global distribution investment pay off demands a high level of channel utilization. Japanese companies force-fed distribution channels by rapidly accelerating product life cycles and expanding across contiguous product segments. Predictably, single-line competitors have often been blind-sided, and sleepy product-development departments have been caught short in the face of this onslaught. Global distribution is the new barrier to entry.

By the end of the decade, the Japanese competitive advantage had evolved from low-cost sourcing to world-scale volume and worldwide brand positions across the spectrum of consumer electronic products.

RCA AT HOME

Most American television producers believed the Japanese did well in their market simply because of their low-cost, high-quality manufacturing systems. When they finally responded, U.S. companies drove down costs, began catching up on the technology front, and lobbied heavily for government protection.[4] They thought that was all they had to do.

Some could not even do that; the massive investment needed to regain cost competitiveness proved too much for them and they left the television industry. Stronger foreign companies purchased others.

Those that remained transferred labor-intensive manufacturing offshore and rationalized manufacturing at home and abroad. Even with costs under control, these companies (RCA, GE, and Zenith) are still vulnerable because they do not understand the changing nature of Japanese competitive advantage. Even as American producers patted themselves on the back for closing the cost gap, the Japanese were cementing future profit foundations through investment in global brand positions. Having conceived of global competition on a product-by-product basis, U.S. companies could not justify a similar investment.

Having conceded non-U.S. markets, American TV manufacturers were powerless to dislodge the Japanese even from the United States.

While Zenith and RCA dominated the color TV business in the United States, neither had a strong presence elsewhere. With no choice of competitive venue, American companies had to fight every market share battle in the United States. When U.S. companies reduced prices at home, they subjected 100% of their sales volume to margin pressure. Matsushita could force this price action, but only a fraction of it would be similarly exposed.

We do not argue that American TV manufacturers will inevitably succumb to global competition. Trade policy or public opinion may limit foreign penetration. Faced with the threat of more onerous trade sanctions or charges of predatory trade tactics, global competitors may forgo a fight to the finish, especially when the business in question is mature and no longer occupies center stage in the company's product plans. Likewise, domestic manufacturers, despite dwindling margins, may support the threatened business if it has important interdependencies with other businesses (as, for example, in the case of Zenith's TV and data systems business). Or senior management may consider the business important to the company's image (possible motivation for GE) for continuing television production.

The hope that foreign companies may never take over the U.S. market, however, should hardly console Western companies. TVs were no more than one loose brick in the American consumer electronics market. The Japanese wanted to knock down the whole wall. For example, with margins under pressure in the TV business, no American manufacturer had the stomach to develop its own videocassette recorder. Today, VCRs are the profitability mainstay for many Japanese companies. Companies defending domestic positions are often shortsighted about the strategic intentions of their competitors. They will never understand their own vulnerability until they understand the intentions of their rivals and then reason back to potential tactics. With no appreciation of strategic intent, defensive-minded competitors are doomed to a perpetual game of catch-up.

LOOSE BRICKS IN EUROPE, TOO

Philips of the Netherlands has become well known virtually everywhere in the world. Like other long-standing MNCs, Philips has always benefited from the kind of international distribution system that U.S. companies lack. Yet our evidence suggests that this advantage alone is not enough. Philips has its own set of problems in responding to the Japanese challenge.

Japanese color TV exports to Europe didn't begin until 1970. Under the terms of their licensing arrangements with European set makers, the Japanese could export only small-screen TVs. No such size limitation existed for Japanese companies willing to manufacture in Europe, but no more than half the output could be exported to the rest of Europe. Furthermore, because laws prohibited Japanese producers from supplying finished sets for private-label sale, they supplied picture tubes. So in 1979, although Europe ran a net trade deficit of only 2 million color televisions, the deficit in color tubes was 2.7 million units. By concentrating on such volume-sensitive manufacturing, Japanese manufacturers skirted protectionist sentiment while exploiting economies of scale gained from U.S. and Japanese experience.

Yet just as they had not been content to remain private-label suppliers in the United States, Japanese companies were not content to remain component suppliers in Europe. They wanted to establish their own brand positions. Sony, Matsushita, and Mitsubishi set up local manufacturing operations in the United Kingdom. When, in response, the British began to fear a Japanese takeover of the local industry, Toshiba and Hitachi simply found U.K. partners. In moving assembly from the Far East to Europe, Japanese manufacturers incurred cost and quality penalties. Yet they regarded such penalties as an acceptable price for establishing strong European distribution and brand positions.

If we contrast Japanese entry strategies in the United States and Europe, it is clear that the tactics and timetables differed. Yet the long-term strategic intentions were the same and the competitive advantage of Japanese producers evolved similarly in both markets. In both Europe and the United States, Japanese companies found a loose brick in the bottom half of the market structure—small-screen portables. And then two other loose bricks were found—the private-label business in the United States and picture tubes in Europe.

From these loose bricks, the Japanese built the sales volume necessary for investment in world-scale manufacturing and state-of-the-art product development; they gained access to local producers, who were an essential source of market knowledge. In Europe, as in the United States, Japanese manufacturers captured a significant share of total industry profitability with a low-risk, low-profile supplier strategy; in so doing, they established a platform from which to launch their drive to global brand dominance.

REGAINING COST COMPETITIVENESS

Philips tried to compete on cost but had more difficulties than RCA and Zenith. First, the European TV industry was more fragmented than that of the United States. When the Japanese entered Europe, twice as many European as American TV makers fought for positions in national markets that were smaller than those in the United States.

Second, European governments frustrated the attempts of companies to use offshore sources or to rationalize production through plant closings, layoffs, and capacity reassignments. European TV makers turned to political solutions to solve competitive difficulties. In theory, the resulting protectionism gave them breathing space as they sought to redress the cost imbalance with Japanese producers. Because they were still confined to marginal, plant-level improvements, however, their cost and quality gap continued to widen. Protectionism reduced the incentive to invest in cost competitiveness; at the same time, the Japanese producers were merging with Europe's smaller manufacturers.

With nearly 3 million units of total European production in 1976, Philips was the only European manufacturer whose volume could fund the automation of manufacturing and the rationalization of product lines and components. Even though its volume was sufficient, however, Philips's tube manufacturing was spread across seven European countries. So it had to demonstrate (country by country, minister by minister, union by union) that the only alternative to protectionism was to support the development of a Pan-European competitor. Philips also had to wrestle with independent subsidiaries not eager to surrender their autonomy over manufacturing, product development, and capital investment. By 1982, it was the world's largest color TV maker and had almost closed the cost gap with Japanese producers. Even so—after ten years—rationalization plans are still incomplete.

Philips remains vulnerable to global competition because of the difficulties inherent in weaving disparate national subsidiaries into a coherent global competitive team. Low-cost manufacturing and international distribution give Philips two of the critical elements needed for global competition. Still needed is the coordination of national business strategies.

Philips's country managers are jealous of their autonomy in marketing and strategy. With their horizon of competition often limited to a single market, country managers are poorly placed to assess their global vulnerability. They can neither understand nor adequately analyze the strategic intentions and market entry tactics of global competitors. Nor can they estimate the total resources available to foreign competitors for local market share battles.

Under such management pressure, companies like Philips risk responding on a local basis to global competition. The Japanese can "cherry pick" attractive national markets with little fear that their multinational rival will retaliate.

The Strategic Imperative

International companies like General Motors and Philips prospered in the fragmented and politicized European market by adopting the "local face" of a good multinational citizen. Today Philips and other MNCs need a global strategic perspective and a corresponding shift in the locus of strategic responsibility away from country organizations. That need conflicts with escalating demands by host governments for national responsiveness. The resulting organizational problems are complex.

Nevertheless, companies must move beyond simplistic organizational views that polarize alternatives between world-product divisions and country-based structures. Headquarters will have to take strategic responsibility in some decision areas; subsidiaries must dominate in others. Managers cannot resolve organizational ambiguity simply by rearranging lines and boxes on the organization chart. They must adopt fundamentally new roles.

National subsidiaries can provide headquarters with more competitive intelligence and learn about world competitors from the experiences of other subsidiaries. They must fight retaliatory battles on behalf of a larger strategy and develop information systems, decision protocols, and performance measurement systems to weave global and local perspectives into tactical decisions. Rather than surrender control over manufacturing, national subsidiaries must interact with the organization in new and complex ways.

Such a realignment of strategic responsibility takes three steps:

Analyze precisely the danger of national fragmentation.

Create systems to track global competitive developments and to support effective responses.

Educate national and headquarters executives in the results of analysis and chosen organization design.

This reorientation may take as long as five years. Managing it is the hardest challenge in the drive to compete successfully.

A NEW ANALYSIS

Managers must cultivate a mind-set based on concepts and tools different from those normally used to assess competitors and competitive advantage.

For example, the television industry case makes clear that the competitive advantage from global distribution is distinct from that due to lower manufacturing costs. Even when they don't have a cost advantage, competitors with a global reach may have the means and motivation for an attack on nationally focused companies. If the global competitor enjoys a high price level at home and suffers no cost disadvantage, it has the means to cross-subsidize the battle for global market share.

Price level differences can exist because of explicit or implicit collusion that limits competitive rivalry, government restrictions barring the entry of new companies to the industry, or differences in the price sensitivity of customers.

The cash flow available to a global competitor is a function of both total costs and realized prices. Cost advantages alone do not indicate whether a company can sustain a global fight. Price level differences, for example, may provide not only the means but also the motivation for cross-subsidization.

If a global competitor sees a more favorable industry growth rate in a foreign market populated by contented and lazy competitors, who are unable or unwilling to fight back, and with customers that are less price sensitive than those at home, it will target that market on its global road. Domestic competitors will be caught unaware.

The implications for these strictly domestic companies are clear. First, they must fight for access to their competitors' market. If such access is unavailable, a fundamental asymmetry results. If no one challenges a global competitor in its home market, the competitor faces a reduced level of rivalry, its profitability rises, and the day when it can attack the home markets of its rivals is hastened. That IBM shares this view is evident from its pitched battle with Fujitsu and Hitachi in Japan.

Global competitors are not battling simply for world volume but also for the cash flow to support new product development, investment in core technologies, and world distribution. Companies that nestle safely in their home beds will be at an increasing resource (if not at a cost) disadvantage. They will be unable to marshal the forces required for a defense of the home market.

Not surprisingly, Japanese MNCs have invested massively in newly industrializing countries (NICs). Only there can European and American companies challenge Japanese rivals on a fairly equal footing without sacrificing domestic profitability or facing market entry restrictions. The failure of Western organizations to compete in the NICs will give the Japanese another uncontested profit source, leaving U.S. and European companies more vulnerable at home.

New Concepts

Usually, a company's decision whether to compete for a market depends on the potential profitability of a particular level of market share in that country. But the new global competition requires novel ways of valuing market share; for example:

Worldwide cost competitiveness, which refers to the minimum world market share a company must capture to underwrite the appropriate manufacturing-scale and product-development effort.

Retaliation, which refers to the minimum market share the company needs in a particular country to be able to influence the behavior of key global competitors. For example, with only a 2% or 3% share of the foreign market, a company may be too weak to influence the pricing behavior of its foreign rival.

Home country vulnerability, which refers to the competitive risks of national market share leadership if not accompanied by international distribution. Market leadership at home can create a false sense of security. Instead of granting invincibility, high market share may have the opposite effect. To the extent that a company uses its market power to support high price levels, foreign competitors—confident that the local company has little freedom for retaliation—may be encouraged to come in under the price umbrella and compete away the organization's profitability.

CRITICAL NATIONAL MARKETS

Most MNCs look at foreign markets as strategically important only when they can yield profits in their own right. Yet different markets may offer very different competitive opportunities. As part of its global strategy, an organization must distinguish between objectives of (1) low-cost sourcing, (2) minimum scale, (3) a national profit base, (4) retaliation against a global competitor, and (5) benchmarking products and technology in a state-of-the-art market. At the same time, the company will need to vary the ways in which it measures subsidiary performance, rewards managers, and makes capital appropriations.

PRODUCT FAMILIES

Global competition requires a broader corporate concept of a product line. In redefining a relevant product family—one that is contiguous in distribution channels and shares a global brand franchise—an organization can, for example, scrutinize all products moving through distribution channels in which its products are sold.

In a corollary effort, all competitors in the channels can be mapped against their product offerings. This effort would include a calculation of the extent of a competitor's investment in the distribution channel, including investment in brand awareness, to understand its motivation to move across segments. Such an analysis would reveal the potential for segment expansion by competitors presently outside the company's strategic horizon.

SCOPE OF OPERATIONS

Where extranational-scale economies exist, the risks in establishing world-scale manufacturing will be very different for the company that sells abroad only under license or through private labels, compared with the company that controls its own worldwide distribution network. Cost advantages are less durable than brand and distribution advantages. An investment in world-scale manufacturing, when not linked to an investment in global distribution, presents untenable risks.

In turn, investments in worldwide distribution and global brand franchises are often economical only if the company has a wide range of products that can benefit from the same distribution and brand investment. Only a company that develops a continuous stream of new products can justify the distribution investment.

A company also needs a broad product portfolio to support investments in key technologies that cut across products and businesses. Competitors with global distribution coverage and wide product lines are best able to justify investments in new core technologies. Witness Honda's leadership in engine technology, a capability it exploits in automobiles, motorcycles, power tillers, snowmobiles, lawnmowers, power generators, and so forth.

Power over distribution channels may depend on a full line. In some cases, even access to a channel (other than on a private-label basis) depends on having a "complete" line of products. A full line may also allow the company to cross-subsidize products in order to displace competitors who are weak in some segments.

Investments in world-scale production and distribution, product-line width, new product development, and core technologies are interrelated. A company's ability to fully exploit an investment made in one area may require support of investments in others.

RESOURCE ALLOCATION

Perhaps the most difficult problem a company faces in global competition is how to allocate resources. Typically, large companies allocate capital to strategic business units (SBUs). In that view, an SBU is a self-contained entity encompassing product development, manufacturing, marketing, and technology. Companies as diverse as General Electric, 3M, and Hewlett-Packard embrace the concept. They point to clear channels of management accountability, visibility of business results, and innovation as the main benefits of SBU management. But an SBU does not provide an appropriate frame of reference to deal with the new competitive milieu.

In pursuing complex global strategies, a company will find different ways to evaluate the geographic scope of individual business subsystems—manufacturing, distribution, marketing, and so on. The authority for resource allocation, then, needs to reside at particular points in the organization for different subsystems, applying different criteria and time horizons to investments in those subsystems.

Global competition may threaten the integrity of the SBU organization for several reasons. A strong SBU-type organization may not facilitate investments in international distribution. To justify such investments, especially in country markets new to the company, it may have to gain the commitment of several businesses who may not share the same set of international priorities.

Even if individual SBUs have developed their own foreign distribution capability, the strategic independence of the various businesses at the country level may make it difficult to cross-subsidize business segments or undertake joint promotion. The company loses some of the benefits of a shared brand franchise.

Companies may have to separate manufacturing and marketing subsystems to rationalize manufacturing on a local-for-global or local-for-regional basis. Economic and political factors will determine which subsidiaries produce which components for the system. In such a case, a company may coordinate manufacturing globally even though marketing may still be based locally.

Companies might also separate the responsibility for global competitive strategy from that for local marketing strategy. While national organizations may be charged with developing some aspects of the marketing mix, headquarters will take the lead role in determining the strategic mission for the local operation, the timing of new product launches, the targeted level of market share, and the appropriate level of investment or expected cash flow.

GEOGRAPHY-BASED ORGANIZATIONS

For the company organized on a national subsidiary basis, there is a corollary problem. It may be difficult to gain commitment to global business initiatives when resource allocation authority lies with the local subsidiary. In this case, the company must ensure that it makes national investments in support of global competitive positions despite spending limits, strategic myopia, or the veto of individual subsidiaries.

Finally, the time limit for investments in global distribution and brand awareness may be quite different from that required for manufacturing-cost take-out investments. Distribution investments usually reflect a long-term commitment and are not susceptible to the same analysis used to justify "brick and mortar" investments.

New Strategic Thought

Global competitors must have the capacity to think and act in complex ways. In other words, they may slice the company in one way for distribution investments, in another for technology, and in still another for manufacturing. In addition, global competitors will develop varied criteria and analytical tools to justify these investments.

In our experience, few companies have distinguished between the intermediate tactics and long-run strategic intentions of global competitors. In a world of forward-thinking competitors that change the rules of the game in support of ultimate strategic goals, historical patterns of competition provide little guidance. Executives must anticipate competitive moves by starting from new strategic intentions rather than from precooked generic strategies.

It is more difficult to respond to the new global competition than we often assume. A company must be sensitive to the potential of global competitive interaction even when its manufacturing is not on a global scale. Executives need to understand the way in which competitors use cross-subsidization to undermine seemingly strong domestic market share positions. To build organizations capable of conceiving and executing complex global strategies, top managers must develop the new analytic approaches and organizational arrangements on which our competitive future rests.

Notes

1. See Thomas Hout, Michael E. Porter, and Eileen Rudden, "How Global Companies Win Out," *Harvard Business Review* September–October 1982, p. 98.

2. See Theodore Levitt, "The Globalization of Markets," *Harvard Business Review* May–June 1983, p. 92.

3. See Craig M. Watson, "Counter-Competition Abroad to Protect Home Markets," *Harvard Business Review* January–February 1982, p. 40.

4. See John J. Nevin, "Can U.S. Business Survive Our Japanese Trade Policy?" *Harvard Business Review* September–October 1978, p. 165.

4
Managing in a Borderless World

Kenichi Ohmae

Most managers are nearsighted. Even though today's competitive landscape often stretches to a global horizon, they see best what they know best: the customers geographically closest to home. These managers may have factories or laboratories in a dozen countries. They may have joint ventures in a dozen more. They may source materials and sell in markets all over the world. But when push comes to shove, their field of vision is dominated by home-country customers and the organizational units that serve them. Everyone—and everything—else is simply part of "the rest of the world."

This nearsightedness is not intentional. No responsible manager purposefully devises or implements an astigmatic strategy. But by the same token, too few managers consciously try to set plans and build organizations as if they saw all key customers equidistant from the corporate center. Whatever the trade figures show, home markets are usually in focus; overseas markets are not.

Effective global operations require a genuine equidistance of perspective. But even with the best will in the world, managers find that kind of vision hard to develop—and harder to maintain. Not long ago, the CEO of a major Japanese capital-goods producer canceled several important meetings to attend the funeral of one of his company's local dealers. When I asked him if he would have done the same for a Belgian dealer, one who did a larger volume of business each year than his late counterpart in Japan, the unequivocal answer was no. Perhaps headquarters would have had the relevant European manager send a letter of condolence. No more than that. In Japan, however, tradition dictated the CEO's presence. But Japanese tradition isn't everything, I reminded him. After all, he was the head of a global, not just a Japanese organization. By violating the principle of equidistance, his attendance underscored distinctions among dealers. He was sending the wrong signals and reinforcing the wrong values. Poor vision has consequences.

It may be unfamiliar and awkward, but the primary rule of equidistance is to see—and to think—global first. Honda, for example, has manufacturing divisions in Japan, North America, and Europe—all three legs of the Triad—but its managers do not think or act as if the company were divided between Japanese and overseas operations. Indeed, the very word "overseas" has no place in Honda's vocabulary because the corporation sees itself as equidistant from all its key customers. At Casio, the top managers gather information directly from each of their primary markets and then sit down together once a month to lay out revised plans for global product development.

There is no single best way to avoid or overcome nearsightedness. An equidistant perspective can take many forms. However managers do it, however they get there, building a value system that emphasizes seeing and thinking globally is the bottom-line price of admission to today's borderless economy.

A Geography Without Borders

On a political map, the boundaries between countries are as clear as ever. But on a competitive map, a map showing the real flows of financial and industrial activity, those boundaries have largely disappeared. What has eaten them away is the persistent, ever speedier flow of information—information that governments previously monopolized, cooking it up as they saw fit and redistributing in forms of their own devising. Their monopoly of knowledge about things happening around the world enabled them to fool, mislead, or control the people because only the governments possessed real facts in anything like real time.

Today, of course, people everywhere are more and more able to get the information they want directly from all corners of the world. They can see for themselves what the tastes and preferences are in other countries, the styles of clothing now in fashion, the sports, the lifestyles. In Japan, for example, our leaders can no longer keep the people in substandard housing because we now know—directly—how people elsewhere live. We now travel abroad. In fact, ten million

Japanese travel abroad annually these days. Or we can sit in our living rooms at home, watch CNN, and know instantaneously what is happening in the United States. During 1988, nearly 90% of all Japanese honeymooners went abroad. This kind of fact is hard to ignore. The government now seriously recognizes that it has built plants and offices but has failed to meet the needs of its young people for relaxation and recreation. So, for the first time in 2,000 years, our people are revolting against their government and telling it what it must do for them. This would have been unthinkable when only a small, official elite controlled access to all information.

In the past, there were gross inefficiencies—some purposeful, some not—in the flow of information around the world. New technologies are eliminating those inefficiencies, and, with them, the opportunity for a kind of top-down information arbitrage—that is, the ability of a government to benefit itself or powerful special interests at the expense of its people by following policies that would never win their support if they had unfettered access to all relevant information. A government could, for example, protect weak industries for fear of provoking social unrest over unemployment. That is less easy to do now, for more of its people have become cosmopolitan and have their own sources of information. They know what such a policy would cost them.

In Korea, students demonstrate in front of the American embassy because the government allows the United States to export cigarettes to Korea and thus threaten local farmers. That's what happens when per capita GNP runs in the neighborhood of $5,000 a year and governments can still control the flow of information and mislead their people. When GNP gets up to around $10,000 a year, religion becomes a declining industry. So does government.

At $26,000 a year, where Japan is now, things are really different. People want to buy the best and the cheapest products—no matter where in the world they are produced. People become genuinely global consumers. We import beef and oranges from the United States, and everyone thinks it's great. Ten years ago, however, our students would have been the ones throwing stones at the American embassy. Our leaders used to tell us American and Australian beef was too lean and too tough to chew. But we've been there and tasted it and know for ourselves that it is cheap and good.

Through this flow of information, we've become global citizens, and so must the companies that want to sell us things. Black-and-white television sets extensively penetrated households in the United States nearly a dozen years before they reached comparable numbers of viewers in Europe and Japan. With color television, the time lag fell to about five or six years for Japan and a few more for Europe. With videocassette recorders, the difference was only three or four years—but this time, Europe and Japan led the way; the United States, with its focus on cable TV, followed. With the compact disc, household penetration rates evened up after only one year. Now, with MTV available by satellite across Europe, there is no lag at all. New music, styles, and fashion reach all European youngsters almost at the same time they are reaching their counterparts in America. We all share the same information.

More than that, we are all coming to share it in a common language. Ten years ago when I would speak in English to students at Bocconi, an Italian university, most of them would listen to me through a translator. Last year, they listened to me directly in English and asked me questions in English. (They even laughed when they should at what I said, although my jokes have not improved.) This is a momentous change. The preparation for 1992 has taken place in language much sooner than it has in politics. We can all talk to each other now, understand each other, and governments cannot stop us. "Global citizenship" is no longer just a nice phrase in the lexicon of rosy futurologists. It is every bit as real and concrete as measurable changes in GNP or trade flows. It is actually coming to pass.

The same is true for corporations. In the pharmaceutical industry, for example, the critical activities of drug discovery, screening, and testing are now virtually the same among the best companies everywhere in the world. Scientists can move from one laboratory to another and start working the next day with few hesitations or problems. They will find equipment with which they are familiar, equipment they have used before, equipment that comes from the same manufacturers.

The drug companies are not alone in this. Most people, for example, believed that it would be a very long time before Korean companies could produce state-of-the-art semiconductor chips—things like 256K NMOS DRAMs. Not so. They caught up with the rest of the Triad in only a few short years. In Japan, not that long ago, a common joke among the chip-making fraternity had to do with the "Friday Express." The Japanese engineers working for different companies on Kyūshū, Japan's southwestern "Silicon Island" only 100 km or so away from Korea, would catch a late flight to Korea on Friday evenings. During the weekend, they would work privately for Korean semiconductor companies. This was illegal, of course, and violated the engineers' employment agreements in Japan. Nonetheless, so many took the flight that they had a tacit gentleman's agreement not to greet or openly recognize each other on the plane. Their trip would have made no sense, however, if semiconductor-related machines, methods, software, and workstations had not already become quite similar throughout the developed world.

Walk into a capital-goods factory anywhere in the developed world, and you will find the same welding machines, the same robots, the same machine tools. When information flows with relative freedom, the old geographic barriers become irrelevant. Global needs lead to global products. For managers, this universal flow of information puts a high premium on learning how to build the strategies and the organizations capable of meeting the requirements of a borderless world.

What Is a Universal Product?

Imagine that you are the CEO of a major automobile company reviewing your product plans for the years ahead. Your market data tell you that you will have to develop four dozen different models if you want to design separate cars for each distinct segment of the Triad market. But you don't have enough world-class engineers to design so many models. You don't have enough managerial talent or enough money. No one does. Worse, there is no single "global" car that will solve your problems for you. America, Europe, and Japan are quite different markets with quite different mixes of needs and preferences. Worse still, as head of a worldwide company, you cannot write off any of these Triad markets. You simply have to be in each of them—and with first-rate successful products. What do you do?

If you are the CEO of Nissan, you first look at the Triad region by region and identify each market's dominant requirements. In the United Kingdom, for example, tax policies make it essential that you develop a car suitable for corporate fleet sales. In the United States, you need a sporty "Z" model as well as a four-wheel drive family vehicle. Each of these categories is what Nissan's president, Yutaka Kume, calls a "lead country" model—a product carefully tailored to the dominant and distinct needs of individual national markets. Once you have your short list of "lead-country" models in hand, you can ask your top managers in other parts of the Triad whether minor changes can make any of them suitable for local sales. But you start with the lead-country models.

"With this kind of thinking," says Mr. Kume, "we have been able to halve the number of basic models needed to cover the global markets and, at the same time, to cover 80% of our sales with cars designed for specific national markets. Not to miss the remaining 20%, however, we also provided each country manager with a range of additional model types that could be adapted to the needs of local segments. This approach," Mr. Kume reports, "allowed us to focus our resources on each of our largest core markets and, at the same time, provide a pool of supplemental designs that could be adapted to local preferences. We told our engineers to 'be American,' 'be European,' or 'be Japanese.' If the Japanese happened to like something we tailored for the American market, so much the better. Low-cost, incremental sales never hurt. Our main challenge, however, was to avoid the trap of pleasing no one well by trying to please everyone halfway."

Imagine, instead, if Nissan had taken its core team of engineers and designers in Japan and asked them to design only global cars, cars that would sell all over the world. Their only possible response would have been to add up all the various national preferences and divide by the number of countries. They would have had to optimize across markets by a kind of rough averaging. But when it comes to questions of taste and, especially, aesthetic preference, consumers do not like averages. They like what they like, not some mathematical compromise. Kume is emphatic about this particular point. "Our success in the U.S. with Maxima, 240 SX, and Pathfinder—all designed for the American market—shows our approach to be right."

In high school physics, I remember learning about a phenomenon called diminishing primaries. If you mix together the primary colors of red, blue, and yellow, what you get is black. If Europe says its consumers want a product in green, let them have it. If Japan says red, let them have red. No one wants the average. No one wants the colors all mixed together. Of course it makes sense to take advantage of, say, any technological commonalities in creating the paint. But local managers close to local customers have to be able to pick the color.

When it comes to product strategy, managing in a borderless world doesn't mean managing by averages. It doesn't mean that all tastes run together into one amorphous mass of universal appeal. And it doesn't mean that the appeal of operating globally removes the obligation to localize products. The lure of a universal product is a false allure. The truth is a bit more subtle.

Although the needs and tastes of the Triad markets vary considerably, there may well be market segments of different sizes in each part of the Triad that share many of the same preferences. In the hair-care market, for instance, Japanese companies know a lot more about certain kinds of black hair, which is hard and thick, than about blond or brown hair, which is often soft and thin. As a result, they have been able to capture a few segments of the U.S. market in, say, shampoos. That makes a nice addition to their sales, of course. But it does not position them to make inroads into the mainstream segments of that market.

Back to the automobile example: there is a small but identifiable group of Japanese consumers who want a "Z" model car like the one much in demand in the United States. Fair enough. During the peak season, Nissan sells about 5,000 "Z" cars a month in the United States and only 500 in Japan. Those 500 cars make a nice addition, of course, generating additional revenue and expanding the perceived richness of a local dealer's portfolio. But they are not—and cannot be—the mainstay of such portfolios.

There is no universal "montage" car—a rear axle from Japan, a braking system from Italy, a drive train from the United States—that will quicken pulses on all continents. Remember the way the tabloids used to cover major beauty contests? They would create a composite picture using the best features from all of the most beautiful entrants—this one's nose, that one's mouth, the other one's forehead. Ironically, the portrait that emerged was never very appealing. It always seemed odd, a bit off, lacking in distinctive character. But there will always be beauty judges—and car buyers—in, say, Europe, who, though more used to continental standards, find a special attractiveness in the features of a Japanese or a Latin American. Again, so much the better.

For some kinds of products, however, the kind of globalization that Ted Levitt talks about makes excellent sense. One of the most obvious is, oddly enough, battery-powered products like cameras, watches, and pocket calculators. These are all part of the "Japan game"—that is, they come from industries dominated by Japanese electronics companies. What makes these products successful across the Triad? Popular prices, for one thing, based on aggressive cost reduction and global economies of scale. Also important, however, is the fact that many general design choices reflect an in-depth understanding of the preferences of leading consumer segments in key markets throughout the Triad. Rigid model changes during the past decade have helped educate consumers about the "fashion" aspects of these products and have led them to base their buying decisions in large measure on such fashion-related criteria.

With other products, the same electronics companies use quite different approaches. Those that make stereophonic equipment, for example, offer products based on aesthetics and product concepts that vary by region. Europeans tend to want physically small, high-performance equipment that can be hidden in a closet; Americans prefer large speakers that rise from the floor of living rooms and dens like the structural columns of ancient temples. Companies that have been globally successful in white goods like kitchen appliances focus on close interaction with individual users; those that have prospered with equipment that requires installation (air conditioners, say, or elevators) focus on interactions with designers, engineers, and trade unions. To repeat: approaches to global products vary.

Another important cluster of these global products is made up of fashion-oriented, premium-priced branded goods. Gucci bags are sold around the world, unchanged from one place to another. They are marketed in virtually the same way. They appeal to an upper bracket market segment that shares a consistent set of tastes and preferences. By definition, not everyone in the United States or Europe or Japan belongs to that segment. But for those who do, the growing commonality of their tastes qualifies them as members of a genuinely cross-Triad, global segment. There is even such a segment for top-of-the-line automobiles like the Rolls-Royce and the Mercedes-Benz. You can—in fact, should—design such cars for select buyers around the globe. But you cannot do that with Nissans or Toyotas or Hondas. Truly universal products are few and far between.

Insiderization

Some may argue that my definition of universal products is unnecessarily narrow, that many such products exist that do not fit neatly into top-bracket segments: Coca-Cola, Levi's, things like that. On closer examination, however, these turn out to be very different sorts of things. Think about Coca-Cola for a moment. Before it got established in each of its markets, the company had to build up a fairly complete local infrastructure and do the groundwork to establish local demand.

Access to markets was by no means assured from day one; consumer preference was not assured from day one. In Japan, the long-established preference was for carbonated lemon drinks known as saida. Unlike Gucci bags, consumer demand did not "pull" Coke into these markets; the company had to establish the infrastructure to "push" it. Today, because the company has done its homework and done it well, Coke is a universally desired brand. But it got there by a different route: local replication of an entire business system in every important market over a long period of time.

For Gucci-like products, the ready flow of information around the world stimulates consistent primary demand in top-bracket segments. For relatively undifferentiated, commodity-like products, demand expands only when corporate muscle pushes hard. If Coke is to establish a preference, it has to build it, piece by piece.

Perhaps the best way to distinguish these two kinds of global products is to think of yourself browsing in a duty-free shop. Here you are in something of an oasis. National barriers to entry do not apply. Products from all over the world lie available to you on the shelves. What do you reach for? Do you think about climbing on board your jetliner with a newly purchased six-pack of Coke? Hardly. But what about a Gucci bag? Yes, of course. In a sense, duty-free shops are the precursor to what life will be like in a genuinely borderless environment. Customer pull, shaped by images and information from around the world, determine your product choices. You want the designer handbag or the sneakers by Reebok, which are made in Korea and sold at three times the price of equivalent no-brand sneakers. And there are others like you in every corner of the Triad.

At bottom, the choice to buy Gucci or Reebok is a choice about fashion. And the information that shapes fashion-driven choices is different in kind from the information that shapes choices about commodity products. When you walk into the 7-Elevens of the world and look for a bottle of cola, the one you pick depends on its location on the shelf, its price, or perhaps the special in-store promotion going on at the moment. In other words, your preference is shaped by the effects of the cola company's complete business system in that country.

Now, to be sure, the quality of that business system will depend to some extent on the company's ability to leverage skills developed elsewhere or to exploit synergies with other parts of its operations— marketing competence, for example, or economies of scale in the production of concentrates. Even so, your choice as a consumer rests on the power with which all such functional strengths have been brought to bear in your particular local market—that is, on the company's ability to become a full-fledged insider in that local market.

With fashion-based items, where the price is relatively high and the purchase frequency low, insiderization does not matter all that much. With commodity items, however, where the price is low and the frequency of purchase high, the insiderization of functional skills is all-important. There is simply no way to be successful around the world with this latter category of products without replicating your business system in each key market.

Coke has 70% of the Japanese market for soft drinks. The reason is that Coke took the time and made the investments to build up a full range of local functional strengths, particularly in its route sales force and franchised vending machines. It is, after all, the Coke van or truck that replaces empty bottles with new ones, not the trucks of independent wholesalers or distributors. When Coke first moved into Japan, it did not understand the complex, many-layered distribution system for such products. So it used the capital of local bottlers to re-create the kind of sales force it has used so well in the United States. This represented a heavy, front-end, fixed investment, but it has paid off handsomely. Coke redefined the domestic game in Japan—and it did so, not from a distance, but with a deliberate "insiderization" of functional strengths. Once this sales force is in place, for example, once the company has become a full-fledged insider, it can move not only soft drinks but also fruit juice, sport drinks, vitamin drinks, and canned coffee through the same sales network. It can sell pretty much whatever it wants to. For Coke's competitors, foreign and domestic, the millions of dollars they are spending on advertising are like little droplets of water sprinkled over a desert. Nothing is going to bloom— at least, not if that is all they do. Not if they fail to build up their own distinctive "insider" strengths.

When global success rests on market-by-market functional strength, you have to play a series of domestic games against well-defined competitors. If the market requires a first-class sales force, you simply have to have one. If competition turns on dealer support programs, that's where you have to excel. Some occasions *do* exist when doing more better is the right, the necessary, course to follow. Still, there are usually opportunities to redefine these domestic games to your own advantage. Companies that fail to establish a strong insider position tend to mix up the strategies followed by the Cokes and the Guccis. The managers of many leading branded-goods companies are often loud in their complaints about how the Japanese market is closed to their products. Or, more mysteriously, about the inexplicable refusal of Japanese consumers to buy their products when they are obviously better than those of any competitor anywhere in the world. Instead of making the effort to understand Japanese distribution and Japanese consumers, they assume that something is wrong with the Japanese market. Instead of spending time in their plants and offices or on the ground in Japan, they spend time in Washington.

Not everyone, of course. There are plenty of branded-goods companies that *are* very well represented on the Japanese retailing scene— Coke, to be sure, but also Nestlé, Schick, Wella, Vicks, Scott, Del Monte, Kraft, Campbell, Unilever (its Timotei shampoo is number one in Japan), Twinings, Kellogg, Borden, Ragu', Oscar Mayer, Hershey, and a host of others. These have all become household names in Japan. They have all become insiders.

For industrial products companies, becoming an insider often poses a different set of challenges. Because these products are chosen largely on the basis of their performance characteristics, if they cut costs or boost productivity, they stand a fair chance of being accepted anywhere in the world. Even so, however, these machines do not operate in a vacuum. Their success may have to wait until the companies that make them have developed a full range of insider functions—engineering, sales, installation, finance, service, and so on. So, as these factors become more critical, it often makes sense for the companies to link up with local operations that already have these functions in place.

Financial services have their own special characteristics. Product globalization already takes place at the institutional investor level but much less so at the retail level. Still, many retail products now originate overseas, and the money collected from them is often invested across national borders. Indeed, foreign exchange, stock markets, and other trading facilities have already made money a legitimately global product.

In all these categories, then, as distinct from premium fashion-driven products like Gucci bags, insiderization in key markets is the route to global success. Yes, some top-of-the-line tastes and preferences have become common across the Triad. In many other cases, however, creating a global product means building the capability to understand and respond to customer needs and business system requirements in each critical market.

The Headquarters Mentality

By all reasonable measures, Coke's experience in Japan has been a happy one. More often than not, however, the path it took to insiderization—replicating a home-country business system in a new national market—creates many more problems than it solves. Managers back at headquarters, who have had experience with only one way to succeed, are commonly inclined to force that model on each new opportunity that arises. Of course, sometimes it will work. Sometimes it will be exactly the right answer. But chances are that the home-country reflex, the impulse to generalize globally from a sample of one, will lead efforts astray.

In the pharmaceutical industry, for example, Coke's approach would not work. Foreign entrants simply have to find ways to adapt to the Japanese distribution system. Local doctors will not accept or respond favorably to an American-style sales force. When the doctor asks a local detail man to take a moment and photocopy some articles for him, he has to be willing to run the errands. No ifs, ands, or buts.

One common problem with insiderization, then, is a misplaced home-country reflex. Another, perhaps more subtle, problem is what happens back at headquarters after initial operations in another market really start paying off. When this happens, in most companies everyone at home starts to pay close attention. Without really understanding why things have turned out as well as they have, managers at headquarters take an increasing interest in what is going on in Japan or wherever it happens to be.

Functionaries of all stripes itch to intervene. Corporate heavyweights decide they had better get into the act, monitor key decisions, ask for timely reports, take extensive tours of local activities. Every power-that-be wants a say in what has become a critical portion of the overall company's operations. When minor difficulties arise, no one is willing to let local managers continue to handle things themselves. Corporate jets fill the skies with impatient satraps eager to set things right.

We know perfectly well where all this is likely to lead. A cosmetics company, with a once enviable position in Japan, went through a series of management shake-ups at home. As a result, the Japanese operation, which had grown progressively more important, was no longer able to enjoy the rough autonomy that made its success possible. Several times, eager U.S. hands reached in to change the head of activities in Japan, and crisp memos and phone calls kept up a steady barrage of challenges to the unlucky soul who happened to be in the hot seat at the moment. Relations became antagonistic, profits fell, the intervention grew worse, and the whole thing just fell apart. Overeager and overanxious managers back at headquarters did not have the patience to learn what really worked in the Japanese market. By trying to supervise things in the regular "corporate" fashion, they destroyed a very profitable business.

This is an all-too-familiar pattern. With dizzying regularity, the local top manager changes from a Japanese national to a foreigner, to a Japanese, to a foreigner. Impatient, headquarters keeps fitfully searching for a never-never ideal "person on the spot." Persistence and perseverance are the keys to long-term survival and success. Everyone knows it. But headquarters is just not able to wait for a few years until local managers—of whatever nationality—build up the needed rapport with vendors, employees, distributors, and customers. And if, by a miracle, they do, then headquarters is likely to see them as having become too "Japanized" to represent their interests abroad. They are no longer "one of us." If they do not, then obviously they have failed to win local acceptance.

This headquarters mentality is not just a problem of bad attitude or misguided enthusiasm. Too bad, because these would be relatively easy to fix. Instead, it rests on—and is reinforced by—a company's entrenched systems, structures, and behaviors. Dividend payout ratios, for example, vary from country to country. But most global companies find it hard to accept low or no payout from investment in Japan, medium returns from Germany, and larger returns from the United States. The usual wish is to get comparable levels of return from all activities, and internal benchmarks of performance reflect that wish. This is trouble waiting to happen. Looking for 15% ROI a year from new commitments in Japan is going to sour a company on Japan very quickly. The companies that have done the best there—the Coca-Colas and the IBMs—were willing to adjust their conventional expectations and settle in for the long term.

Or, for example, when top managers rely heavily on financial statements, they can easily lose sight of the value of operating globally— because these statements usually mask the performance of activities outside the home country. Accounting and reporting systems that are parent-company dominated—and remember, genuinely consolidated statements are still the exception, not the rule—merely confirm the lukewarm commitment of many managers to global competition. They may talk a lot about doing business globally, but it is just lip service. It sounds nice, and it may convince the business press to write glowing stories, but when things get tough, most of the talk turns out to be only talk.

Take a closer look at what actually happens. If a divisionalized Japanese company like Matsushita or Toshiba wants to build a plant to make widgets in Tennessee, the home-country division manager responsible for widgets often finds himself in a tough position. No doubt, the CEO will tell him to get that Tennessee facility up and running as soon as possible. But the division manager knows that, when the plant does come on-stream, his own operations are going to look worse on paper. At a minimum, his division is not going to get credit for American sales that he used to make by export from Japan. Those are now going to come out of Tennessee. The CEO tells him to collaborate, to help out, but he is afraid that the better the job he does, the worse it will be for him—and with good reason!

This is crazy. Why not change company systems? Have the Tennessee plant report directly to him, and consolidate all widget-making activities at the divisional level. Easier said than done. Most companies use accounting systems that consolidate at the corporate, not the divisional, level. That's traditional corporate practice. And every staff person since the time of Homer comes fully equipped with a thousand reasons not to make exceptions to time-honored institutional procedures. As a result, the division manager is going to drag his feet. The moment Tennessee comes on-line, he sees his numbers go down, he has to lay off people, and he has to worry about excess capacity. Who is going to remember his fine efforts in getting Tennessee started up? More to the point, who is going to care—when his Japanese numbers look so bad?

If you want to operate globally, you have to think and act globally, and that means challenging entrenched systems that work against collaborative efforts. Say our widget maker has a change of heart and goes to a division-level consolidation of accounts. This helps, but the problems are just beginning. The American managers of a sister division that uses these widgets look at the Tennessee plant as just another vendor, perhaps even a troublesome one because it is new and not entirely reliable. Their inclination is to treat the new plant as a problem, ignore it if possible, and to continue to buy from Japan where quality is high and delivery guaranteed. They are not going to do anything to help the new plant come on-stream or to plan for long-term capital investment. They are not going to supply technical assistance or design help or anything. All it represents is fairly unattractive marginal capacity.

If we solve this problem by having the plant head report to the division manager, then we are back where we started. If we do nothing, then this new plant is just going to struggle along. Clearly, what we need is to move toward a system of double counting of credits—so that both the American manager *and* the division head in Japan have strong reasons to make the new facility work. But this runs afoul of our entrenched systems, and they are very hard to change. If our commitment to acting globally is not terribly strong, we are not going to be inclined to make the painful efforts needed to make it work.

Under normal circumstances, these kinds of entrepreneurial decisions are hard enough to reach anyway. It is no surprise that many of the most globally successful Japanese companies—Honda, Sony, Matsushita, Canon, and the like—have been led by a strong owner-founder for at least a decade. They can override bureaucratic inertia; they can tear down institutional barriers. In practice, the managerial decision to tackle wrenching organizational and systems changes is made even more difficult by the way in which problems become visible. Usually, a global systems problem first comes into view in the form of explicitly local symptoms. Rarely do global problems show up where the real underlying causes are.

Troubled CEOs may say that their Japanese operations are not doing well, that the money being spent on advertising is just not paying off as expected. They will not say that their problems are really back at headquarters with its superficial understanding of what it takes to market effectively in Japan. They will not say that it lies in the design of their financial reporting systems. They will not say that it is part and parcel of their own reluctance to make long-term, front-end capital investments in new markets. They will not say that it lies in their failure to do well the central job of any headquarters operation: the development of good people at the local level. Or at least they are not likely to. They will diagnose the problems as local problems and try to fix them.

Thinking Global

Top managers are always slow to point the finger of responsibility at headquarters or at themselves. When global faults have local symptoms, they will be slower still. When taking corrective action means a full, zero-based review of all systems, skills, and structures, their speed will decrease even further. And when their commitment to acting globally is itself far from complete, it is a wonder there is any motion at all. Headquarters mentality is the prime expression of managerial nearsightedness, the sworn enemy of a genuinely equidistant perspective on global markets.

In the early days of global business, experts like Raymond Vernon of the Harvard Business School proposed, in effect, a United Nations model of globalization. Companies with aspirations to diversify and expand throughout the Triad were to do so by cloning the parent company in each new country of operation. If successful, they would create a mini-U.N. of clonelike subsidiaries repatriating profits to the parent company, which remained the dominant force at the center. We know that successful companies enter fewer countries but penetrate each of them more deeply. That is why this model gave way by the early 1980s to a competitor-focused approach to globalization. By this logic, if we were a European producer of medical electronics equipment, we had to take on General Electric in the United States so that it would not come over here and attack us on our home ground. Today, however, the pressure for globalization is driven not so much by diversification or competition as by the needs and preferences of customers. Their needs have globalized, and the fixed costs of meeting them have soared. That is why we must globalize.

Managing effectively in this new borderless environment does not mean building pyramids of cash flow by focusing on the discovery of new places to invest. Nor does it mean tracking your competitors to their lair and preemptively undercutting them in their own home market. Nor does it mean blindly trying to replicate home-country business systems in new colonial territories. Instead, it means paying central attention to delivering value to customers—and to developing an equidistant view of who they are and what they want. Before everything else comes the need to see your customers clearly. They— and only they—can provide legitimate reasons for thinking global.

About the Contributors

David D. Hale is the chief economist for Kemper Financial Companies. Since 1990, he has also consulted to the U.S. Department of Defense on how changes in the global economy are affecting U.S. security relationships. Hale writes on a broad range of economic subjects, with articles appearing in such publications as the *Wall Street Journal*, the *New York Times*, the *Financial Times of London*, and the *Far Eastern Economic Review*. He was the 1990 recipient of the William F. Butler Award, presented annually by the National Association of Business Economists.

Gary Hamel is a visiting professor of strategic and international management at the London Business School and president of Hamel, Inc. His current research focuses on the challenge of competing in global industries, the problems of managing international strategic alliances, and the value-added of top management. Professor Hamel has worked extensively at the board level in many of the world's most successful multinationals, and his groundbreaking concepts have been applied in hundreds of companies worldwide. He is the co-author, with C.K. Prahalad, of *Competing for the Future* (Harvard Business School Press, 1994) and is featured, with Prahalad, in the Harvard Business School Management Productions video (1995) of the same title.

Charles Hampden-Turner is a permanent visitor at the Cambridge University Judge Institute of Management Studies and a professor on extended leave from the Wright Institute in Berkeley, California. He worked for Group Planning in the Shell International Petroleum Company from 1981 to 1985 and was Shell Senior Research Fellow at the London Business School from 1985 to 1990. Professor Hampden-Turner is the author of eleven books, including his best-selling *Maps of the Mind* and, most recently, *Seven Cultures of Capitalism.*

T George Harris is an editor-in-residence of the UCSD-CONNECT Entrepreneurs Program. He is also the American editor for *Psychologie Heute*, a Frankfurt-based social science magazine, a consulting editor for *Modern Maturity*, and a consultant to several media and food companies. A specialist in health issues, with a long career in journalism, Harris was a founding editor of *American Health* magazine, the originator and on-camera commentator of PBS's *Bodywatch*, former editor in chief of *Psychology Today*, and a former editor of the *Harvard Business Review*. Harris has worked closely with Peter F. Drucker since 1969.

Herbert A. Henzler is the chairman of McKinsey & Company, Inc., Germany. He is also a lecturer in international management and an honorary professor of strategy and organizational consulting at the University of Munich. He has published extensively on the strategic management and organization of international corporations, economics, and socio-political issues.

Jay Jaikumar is the Daewoo Professor of Business Administration at the Harvard Business School, where he has taught manufacturing, technology, and operations management in the MBA and Executive Education programs. His research focuses on computer-integrated manufacturing, with an emphasis on building more intelligence into manufacturing control systems. Professor Jaikumar serves on several committees of the National Research Council, and has been an advisor to the Congressional Office of Technology Assessment and the U.S. Senate Subcommittee on Science and Technology.

John Kao is a senior lecturer in general management at the Harvard Business School, where he specializes in the areas of business innovation and new venture start-ups. He is the author of numerous books and articles on these subjects, including the recently published series *Managing Creativity, The Entrepreneur*, and *The Entrepreneurial Organization*. Professor Kao is also the founder of several start-up companies, including BioSurface Technology, K.O. Technology, Pacific Artists, and Electric Space and is regularly involved in consulting and research projects with companies in such fields as biotechnology, entertainment, computer software, and financial services.

Paul Krugman is a professor of economics at Stanford University, where his current research focuses on the application of ideas from complexity theory and the concept of self-organizing systems to economics. Actively involved in economic and trade policy debates, Professor Krugman is one of the founders of the "new trade theory," a major rethinking of the theory of international trade, for which he received the 1991 John Bates Clark medal from the American Economic Association. He is the author or editor of 12 books and more than 100 papers in professional journals and edited volumes.

Ira C. Magaziner is a senior advisor to the President for policy development, and has managed the development of President Clinton's health care reform initiative. Prior to his White House appointment, Magaziner was a prominent corporate strategist, building two consulting firms and directing policy analysis for major corporations. During the past two decades, he has conducted hundreds of corporate strategy studies for companies competing in the global economy and has led a wide variety of public service initiatives. Magaziner is the author of three books, most recently *The Silent War: Inside the Global Business Battles Shaping America's Future*, co-authored with Mark Patinkin.

Kazuo Nukazawa was the director of the International Economic Affairs Department of the Keidanren (the Japan Federation of Economic Organizations) at the time of his article's original publication. Nukazawa has spent several years in the United States, first as economic research consultant at the U.S.-Japan Trade Council in Washington, D.C., and later as a visiting research fellow at the Rockefeller Foundation in New York.

Kenichi Ohmae is the founder and chairman of Heisei Ishin no Kai, a citizen's political movement striving for fundamental reform of Japan's political and administrative systems, and is founder and managing director of the Heisei Research Institute. He was formerly a partner of McKinsey & Company's Tokyo office for 23 years, where he was a co-founder of the company's strategic management practice. Ohmae is the author of more than 50 books, including *Triad Power, Beyond National Borders, The Mind of the Strategist*, and *The Borderless World*, and has contributed numerous articles to major business and political reform publications.

Mark Patinkin has spent the last 15 years writing a syndicated column for the *Providence Journal-Bulletin*. He also hosts a weekly interview show on the Rhode Island NBC television affiliate. In 1987, Patinkin was a Pulitzer Prize finalist for dispatches on religious violence in Northern Ireland, India, and Beirut. He published *An African Journey*, a chronicle of famine, in 1985 and received a Presidential End Hunger Award in 1991.

Tom Peters is founder of The Tom Peters Group, three training and communication companies headquartered in Palo Alto, California. He also writes a bimonthly column for *Forbes ASAP* and a syndicated column for Tribune Media Services that appears in over 100 U.S. and foreign newspapers. Peters is the author of several books, including the best-selling *In Search of Excellence* and *Liberation Management*, and numerous articles that have appeared in such publications as *Business Week*, the *Financial Times*, the *New York Times*, and *The Economist*. Peters has created and been featured in a number of popular corporate training videos and presents management seminars around the world.

Michael E. Porter is the C. Roland Christensen Professor of Business Administration at the Harvard Business School and a leading authority on competitive strategy. He has served as a counselor on competitive strategy to many leading U.S. and international companies and speaks widely on issues of international competitiveness to business and government audiences throughout the world. Professor Porter is the author of 14 books, including *Competitive Advantage: Creating and Sustaining Superior Performance*, which won the Academy of Management's 1985 George R. Terry Book Award, and *The Competitive Advantage of Nations*. Actively involved in economic policy initiatives, his most recent work focuses on the development of America's inner cities.

C.K. Prahalad is the Harvey C. Fruehauf Professor of Corporate Strategy and International Business Administration at the University of Michigan's Graduate School of Business Administration. His research focuses on the role and value-added of top management in large, diversified, multinational corporations and he has consulted with the top management of numerous firms worldwide. Professor Prahalad is the author with Yves Doz of *The Multinational Mission: Balancing Local Demands and Global Vision* and, most recently, the co-author with Gary Hamel of *Competing for the Future* (Harvard Business School Press, 1994); he is also featured, with Hamel, in the Harvard Business School Management Productions video, *Competing for the Future* (1995).

Robert B. Reich is the United States Secretary of Labor. Under his leadership, the Labor Department has worked on several initiatives to build the skills of American workers, including signing the School-to-

Work Opportunities Act and introducing the Reemployment Act. Reich has also implemented the Family and Medical Leave Act and established the Office of the American Workplace to encourage greater collaboration between workers and managers. Before coming to the Labor Department, Reich served on the faculty of Harvard University's John F. Kennedy School of Government. He has written seven books and more than 200 articles on the global economy and the U.S. work force.

Klaus Schwab is founder and president of the World Economic Forum, which, since its establishment in 1971, has evolved into the foremost global institution integrating leaders from business, government, and the sciences to identify issues on the global agenda. Since 1972, he has also been professor of business policy at the University of Geneva. Schwab is active on company boards, in academic affairs, and in advisory functions to governments and international organizations. He is a member of both the High-Level Advisory Board to the United Nations Secretary-General and the Earth Council.

Rajendra S. Sisodia is an associate professor of marketing at George Mason University. His research, teaching, and consulting expertise span the areas of marketing productivity, strategic uses of information technology in business, and the reengineering of marketing and other business processes. Professor Sisodia has consulted with numerous organizations and companies in the information technology, telecommunications, real estate, health care, and financial services industries. He is associate editor of both the *Journal of Asia Pacific Business* and the International Engineering Consortium's *Annual Review of Communications*. He has published over 40 articles in conference proceedings and numerous journals and is the co-author with John T. Mentzer of *Marketing Decision Systems: Transformation Through Information Technology*.

Claude Smadja is the director of News & Current Affairs at the Swiss Broadcasting Corporation in Geneva and is a senior adviser at the World Economic Forum. A lecturer on macroeconomic and political issues for international corporations, he also provides analytical briefs on economic and political issues at various World Economic Forum events around the world. Smadja regularly visits most East Asian countries and has developed an extensive knowledge of the region's fast-moving economic and political realities. He also focuses on Europe's economic and political evolution, especially the process of European integration and the consequences of the collapse of the Soviet empire.

INDEX